SLOW ANTI-AMERICANISM

SLOW ANTI-AMERICANISM

SOCIAL MOVEMENTS AND
SYMBOLIC POLITICS IN CENTRAL ASIA

EDWARD SCHATZ

STANFORD UNIVERSITY PRESS ▪ STANFORD, CALIFORNIA

Stanford University Press
Stanford, California

© 2021 by the Board of Trustees of the Leland Stanford Junior University. All rights reserved.

No part of this book may be reproduced or transmitted in any form or by any means, electronic or mechanical, including photocopying and recording, or in any information storage or retrieval system without the prior written permission of Stanford University Press.

Printed in the United States of America on acid-free, archival-quality paper

Library of Congress Cataloging-in-Publication Data
Names: Schatz, Edward, author.
Title: Slow anti-Americanism : social movements and symbolic politics in Central Asia / Edward Schatz.
Description: Stanford, California: Stanford University Press, 2021. | Includes bibliographical references and index.
Identifiers: LCCN 2020020359 (print) | LCCN 2020020360 (ebook) | ISBN 9781503613690 (cloth) | ISBN 9781503614321 (paperback) | ISBN 9781503614338 (epub)
Subjects: LCSH: Anti-Americanism—Asia, Central. | Public opinion—Political aspects—United States. | Social movements—Asia, Central. | Symbolism in politics—Asia, Central. | Asia, Central—Foreign relations—United States. | United States—Foreign relations—Asia, Central. | Asia, Central—Politics and government—1991-
Classification: LCC DK857.75.U6 S33 2021 (print) | LCC DK857.75.U6 (ebook) | DDC 303.48/258073—dc23
LC record available at https://lccn.loc.gov/2020020359
LC ebook record available at https://lccn.loc.gov/2020020360

Cover design: Rob Ehle

Typeset by Motto Publishing Services in 10/14 Minion Pro

CONTENTS

	Preface	vii
	Introduction: Slow Anti-Americanism	1
1	America's Changing Image	19
2	Islamist Trajectories	40
3	Human Rights Trajectories	66
4	Labor, Disorganized	88
	Conclusion: Shaping the Slow Politics of Anti-Americanism	112
	Appendix: Reflections on Methods and Methodology	125
	Notes	137
	Bibliography	179
	Index	211

PREFACE

In December 2006, ten years before Donald Trump's election as US president sent shockwaves across the globe, Central Asia seemed to face a test of anti-Americanism. Zachary Hatfield, a member of the 376th Air Expeditionary Wing of the United States Air Force, had shot and killed Aleksandr Ivanov, a local truck driver, outside the US Manas Air Base in Kyrgyzstan. Although Hatfield was legally immune from prosecution, loud voices in Kyrgyzstani civil society called for him to stand trial locally. When Hatfield departed Kyrgyzstan in March 2007, still-louder voices demanded his extradition. The niceties of bilateral relations for the moment prevailed, and the popular outcry gradually subsided.

Things seemed to change when early in 2009 Kyrgyzstan's president Kurmanbek Bakiev announced at a press conference in Moscow his decision to close Manas. Bakiev cited inadequate compensation for the base, and, as Radio Free Europe / Radio Liberty reported it, "'negative feelings' among the population, who 'justifiably' question[ed] the rationale for the U.S. presence."[1] The decision left the Obama administration scrambling to find substitute refueling and resupply arrangements for NATO coalition forces in Afghanistan.

What happened in Kyrgyzstan? On the surface, the decision to close the base seemed buoyed by a rising tide of popular anti-American sentiment. Likewise, a 2005 decision to shutter the Karshi-Khanabad base in neighboring Uzbekistan seemed the product of similar societal forces. Yet, closer inspection reveals that anti-Americanism's causal role was unclear, and subsequent events would call it further into question. Whatever "negative feelings" had troubled the population of Kyrgyzstan, they soon lost political steam. On 25 June 2009, the Kyrgyzstani parliament rubber-stamped a bilateral deal to keep Manas open. It seemed a startling reversal, with pro-American sentiments apparently winning the day.

What should we make of the zigzagging politics of the Manas case? Did the base remain open because of popular opinion or in spite of it? The reality is that anti-American popular opinion—especially in an authoritarian context with enormous incentives for strategic cooperation with the US—often has little direct, short-term impact on bilateral relations. Yet popular sentiment is not irrelevant. As this book demonstrates, social movements can use images of the United States to political effect, altering the shape of domestic politics and in turn affecting the global position of the United States.

In this book, I argue that our usual ways of thinking about anti-Americanism are flawed. Instead, I propose an analytic framework that captures the essential dynamics of what scholars have termed "anti-Americanism" but takes better stock of its trajectories. It is true that popular anti-Americanism did not determine the fate of the Manas Air Base,[2] but only a flawed approach would have expected it to do so.[3] The framework I advance is based not on "high politics" or "geopolitics," but on what might be termed the "slow politics" of anti-Americanism.

The idea for this research first emerged in 1998 when I was in the midst of dissertation fieldwork in Central Asia. Although I had spent much time in former Soviet space since doing a student exchange in 1989, I had not previously encountered ambivalence about the United States. To the contrary, in earlier conversations ex-Soviet citizens had tended to embrace America as worthy of emulation. Now, the change was palpable; ordinary people described mixed feelings about the social, economic, and political tumult they were experiencing—a tumult that they associated with the adoption of an American model.

Yet Central Asians' ambivalence did not mean that they were indifferent. Quite the contrary: they harbored a range of complex and sometimes contradictory feelings about the United States, but "America" as a symbol remained salient. This struck me as strange. The United States was hegemonic, but it was quite a distant hegemon. Some military-to-military cooperation, some humanitarian aid, and some economic interests brought government, NGO, and business actors to Central Asia, but in the 1990s the American footprint in the region was relatively light. In the meantime, the salience of the United States as symbol easily outpaced its salience as a policy actor on the ground. I had trouble making sense of how the US could be simultaneously remote and relevant, both abstract and germane.

Then, terrorist attacks on US territory launched a broad—and deeply polarized—public discussion about anti-Americanism. At one pole, some argued that the potential for virulent anti-Americanism was inherent in particular political cultures or in specific civilizational blocks.[4] Appearing to capture an essential ideological standoff between the United States (or the West, more generally) and the "Muslim world," such approaches were seductive. But I also found them frustrating since they mistook description of a particular world-historical moment for explanation. I was not trained as a historian, but even I could see what was missing; any minimal attention to change over time should undermine simplistic depictions of static cultures based on supposedly immutable anti-Western principles.[5]

At the other pole, we were told that anti-Americanism was just the opposite. It was a reasonable, well considered, and therefore fundamentally justified response of global publics to US military, economic, and cultural dominance; it was a rejection of the "American model."[6] The populations depicted as blinded by irrational anti-Western principles were now recast as deeply sensible. Yet, what do we gain by replacing the madness of the crowd with the rationality of the crowd? The normative question (has US foreign policy had deplorable downstream consequences?) is different from the empirical question (do publics in fact deplore the consequences of US foreign policy?). While US foreign policy moves can shift the attitudes of global publics, most US policy affects attitudes only indirectly and gradually. In sum, when global publics leveled criticism of the US, were they offering well-considered, rational reactions to the United States or were they using the US as a symbol in their own struggles?

Policy debates were no more satisfying. Some argued that the United States should ignore anti-American sentiment as just so much inconsequential "noise." If sentiment emerges from realms beyond the rational—from deep and unchanging cultures, from essentially static and backward religious dogma, or from fundamental emotions—then devising policy to win the "hearts and minds" of those who are different, intransigent, unreasonable, and emotional is a task that is both too tall and too expensive.[7] With equal vehemence, the other side lamented that anti-Americanism has real consequences. As Joseph Nye famously offered, the United States suffers from diminished "soft power," the power to attract. The consequence was not just moral; it was practical, since declining soft power undermines the US's ability to exercise power in its harder forms. Its social model, political freedoms, and economic power less attractive than ever, America ceased to be the country with which foreign publics wanted to associate.[8] This raised the costs for cooperation and undermined US foreign policy objectives.

Yet, all of this was too polarizing for my tastes. A debate that asked me to choose between an anti-Americanism that was inevitable and therefore insignificant and an anti-Americanism that was avoidable and therefore critical to counteract was a debate that seemed to lead nowhere. The goal of this book is to use fresh material from the Central Asian cases to move beyond the polarities. Doing so will require refocusing our gaze away from high politics and toward the slower-moving, partially occluded, and socially embedded processes that ground how "America" becomes political in Central Asia.[9]

My thinking about anti-Americanism and Central Asia did not emerge in a vacuum. A haole raised by Canadian parents in the fiftieth of the United States, a Hawaii-raised student studying Soviet and then Central Asian politics and society in Connecticut, Wisconsin, and then Illinois, and an American making his professional and family life in Canada, I found little unusual about residing in liminal space. Maybe this insider-outsider status doomed me to regard the US with a mix of admiration and frustration. All of that is hard to know. What I do know is that an amazing array of friends, family members, colleagues, and students helped to refine, challenge, and advance my thinking. Over a long gestation period, this book benefited from so much constructive input that I am hard-pressed to call it solely my own.

Research began with a generous grant from the National Council for Eurasian and East European Research. Writing two NCEEER working papers allowed me to develop some key ideas. Moreover, the grant supported exceptional research assistance. Anna Gregg and Mark Mills thoughtfully and productively coded data from Radio Free Europe / Radio Liberty. Chiara Fabrizio conducted several important interviews in Kyrgyzstan for the project. Later, Dillon Byrd, Olga Kesarchuk, Darmen Koktov, and Olga Klymenko provided expert help with aspects of the manuscript. Ben McVicker supplied crucial insights on how to think about the impact of the Soviet-Afghan War. With NCEEER support, a team of Central Asian scholars and friends contributed enormously to this research, though they are in no way responsible for my interpretations. They include Fatima Ahmedova, Gulnara Dadabaeva, Asel Doolotkeldieva, Umeda Gafurova, Armon Jonboboev, Sunatullo Jonboboev, Abdurahim Juraev, Toqjan Kizatova, Alla Kuvatova, Yasmin Lodi, Abdusattor Nuraliev, Nurbek Omuraliev, Irina Shubina, Pavel Shumkin, Abylay Stambayev, and Joomart Sulaimanov.

During many stays in Central Asia, I benefited from the wise counsel, good cheer, exceptional patience, and unsurpassed hospitality of dozens of people. Nurbulat Masanov was a top scholar, productive critic, and extraordinary human being; he is dearly missed. Joomart Sulaimanov challenged all my ideas, while keeping terrific company and buoying my mood. Toqjan Kizatova continually reminded me that passion and commitment are rather universal human traits. Countless others from Central Asia—some of whom I cannot name and others whose names I never knew—provided guidance and shared their worldviews.

I was privileged to be a faculty member at Southern Illinois University Carbondale. At SIUC, Uday Desai was unfailingly supportive of this project. Scott McClurg and Tobin Grant provided expertise on how to conduct a survey experiment and present the resulting data. The relationships developed in Carbondale will last a lifetime. At the University of Toronto, where this book came to fruition, I am deeply grateful to Ronnie Beiner, Randall Hansen, Jeff Kopstein, and Graham White for their ongoing support. The intellectual environment at U of T is nothing short of extraordinary. Robert Austin broadened my geographic and disciplinary horizons, all the while fostering a sense of intellectual humility and unsurpassed comradeship. Jacques Bertrand exemplified analytic clarity and unfailing good sense. Lucan Way has been my co-traveler since before this book was conceived, and my work always benefits by having him in the audience. Additional critical (in both senses of the word) feedback came from Diana Fu, Lilach Gilady, Seva Gunitsky, Phil Triadafilopoulos, and Linda White. Kristin Cavoukian, Sude Beltan, and Lama Mourad all wrote terrific PhD dissertations that shaped my thinking.

Outside U of T, an array of scholars supplied insightful critiques from across the continent and beyond. These include Jane Desmond, Jorge Domínguez, Virginia Domínguez, Payam Foroughi, Roger Haydon, Pauline Jones, Larry Markowitz, Eric McGlinchey, Ellen Lust-Okar, Scott Radnitz, Bryn Rosenfeld, John Schoeberlein, Quintan Wiktorowicz, and Saulesh Yessenova.

Thanks to *International Studies Quarterly* for permission to publish material that originally appeared as Edward Schatz and Renan Levine, "Framing, Public Diplomacy, and Anti-Americanism in Central Asia," *International Studies Quarterly* 54, vol. 3 (September 2010): 855–69. Renan Levine did not just run the statistical analysis and help to interpret the results; his creative intellect was crucial to our undertaking. Thanks also to the University of Illinois Press for permission to publish material that originally appeared as Edward Schatz, "Understanding Anti-Americanism in Central Asia," in *Global Perspectives on the United States: Pro-Americanism,*

Anti-Americanism, and the Discourses Between, ed. Virginia R. Domínguez and Jane C. Desmond (Champaign: University of Illinois Press, 2017), 131–51.

Finally, thanks go to the superb team at Stanford University Press. Jessica Ling and Caroline McKusick were an absolute pleasure to work with. Barbara Armentrout provided truly exceptional copyediting that strengthened my voice. None of this would have been possible without Alan Harvey's incisive and unfailingly good judgment. To him, as well as to the anonymous reviewers who provided the kind of thoroughgoing critiques that a scholar can only hope for, I am deeply thankful.

When I was a child and then an adolescent, the dinnertime debates about politics that Irwin Schatz mischievously fostered and Barbara Schatz heroically tolerated were always rooted in a healthy skepticism about received wisdom that I share with my three brothers. That tradition has continued with my own family. I dedicate this book to Julian, Micah, and Noah—each exceptional and each critical-minded—and especially to my life-partner, Lara, who always nurtures independence of mind and critical inquiry, even as she supports the sometimes-crazy choices that a scholarly life entails. For that and everything else she does, I am forever and lovingly grateful.

SLOW ANTI-AMERICANISM

INTRODUCTION

Slow Anti-Americanism

CONSIDER THE USUAL METAPHORS. For some, anti-Americanism is a rising tide that inundates entire societies. For others, anti-Americanism is a conflagration that engulfs political actors. For still others, anti-Americanism is a crushing force that compels hostility to US initiatives. Emphasizing the immediate and direct power of sentiment poised against the United States, these metaphors have a certain appeal. After all, the US remains the globe's most powerful actor. If anti-Americanism is to stand a chance against the power of the US itself—indeed, if it is to deserve our attention—it might seem to require metaphors that describe how it inundates, engulfs, or compels those in high politics.

Yet, tempting as it is to unleash such tropes, political impact comes in many forms. As the following chapters show, anti-Americanism often proceeds slowly and sometimes ambiguously. Like symbols more generally, "America" often resides quietly in the mundane before linking up with powerful social movements that amplify its importance and change the political landscape. A focus on high politics can blind us to the essential dynamics of anti-Americanism.

In this chapter, I contest approaches that privilege high politics and foreign policies. Instead, I detail what I mean by *slow anti-Americanism*, previewing how the Central Asian cases provide new analytic traction on a complex problem.

High Politics, Foreign Policy, and Anti-Americanism

Let us begin with a few exceptions. Sometimes, anti-Americanism does indeed seem overpowering. In the Iranian Revolution of 1979, "the Islamic Republic raised anti-Americanism to a near religion. The burning of American flags, the inflammatory rhetoric of Iran's leaders, the mass demonstrations against the U.S., and the Hostage Crisis attest to this."[1] Venezuela's Hugo Chávez infamously called President George W. Bush the devil at the United Nations in 2006 and on other occasions referred to him as drunk, a terrorist, genocidal, and a donkey.[2] Revolutionary Iran and Bolivarian Venezuela are sites of vibrant politics where anti-Americanism plays a crucial, if not determinative, role. This role is easy to spot: it makes for high-drama TV that commands our attention.

Less dramatic but also exceptional are cases like Mexico. In an opinion poll conducted before the 2006 presidential elections, the single best predictor of a Mexican voter's preference was how he or she evaluated Cuba's Fidel Castro, on the one hand, and George W. Bush, on the other. Thus, it is no exaggeration to say that views of the United States centrally structured the field of political relations in Mexico.[3] This was not terribly surprising. Given the long US border, the complex history of close (and by no means always friendly) relations with the US, and Mexico's then-emerging democratic institutions, Mexicans seemed likely to train their political gaze on the United States.

These instances have the virtue of being recognizable and familiar, but if we consider a broader range of cases, from Europe to Latin America to Asia, rarely do views about the United States have an immediately discernable impact on political outcomes.[4] Indeed, when one examines ordinary cases, it can appear that anti-Americanism packs no political punch. As Peter Katzenstein and Robert Keohane conclude:

> In view of the attention that anti-Americanism has received in the media and by politicians, it is surprising how little hard evidence can be found ... that anti-American opinion has had serious direct and immediate consequences for the United States on issues affecting broad US policy objectives.[5]

Theirs is a high standard. One would be hard-pressed to find *any* societal phenomenon that generates consequences that are "serious," "direct," and "immediate" for "broad US policy objectives." But if we focus less on their standard and more on their logic, do they have a point?

At root, Katzenstein and Keohane's idea is that popular anti-Americanism influences policy when two conditions are met: (1) a regime is willing to endure the costs of alienating in the United States, and (2) anti-American opinion flows unimpeded into the policy process. They consider evidence from quasi-democratic Turkey and democratic Germany and Canada, where, according to their logic, the impact of anti-Americanism on high politics should be most pronounced. Finding no definitive proof of anti-Americanism's independent and systematic impact, Katzenstein and Keohane therefore conclude that the "burden of proof" shifts "toward those who believe that anti-Americanism is having major effects."[6]

In two senses, their logic is persuasive. First, it is a fact that few states embrace the costs of alienating the United States. For every Hugo Chávez of Venezuela or Mahmoud Ahmadinejad of Iran who in the 2000s verbally attacked the United States in no uncertain terms, there are hundreds of other world leaders who—whatever their innermost preferences might be—are more risk averse. The hesitation of the leaders of Canada, France, and Germany to push back against the anti-NATO rhetoric of President Trump in 2018 was a visible manifestation of a common reluctance to anger the United States. More typically, such hesitation is not televised.

Second, anti-American public opinion may raise the cost of cooperating with the US, but by how much? Rising (or falling) anti-US sentiment is probably more like other dimensions of public opinion: its impact on policy is highly mediated and indirect. In democracies, publics historically tend to defer to their elected representatives on matters of foreign affairs, even while they demand regular input into matters of domestic policy.[7] Publics in nondemocratic contexts have even less influence. Indeed, in places as diverse as Canada, France, and Saudi Arabia the impact of public opinion depends upon the specific social institutions and communication channels available for influencing policymakers. Even in Latin America, where anti-American popular sentiment has at times percolated into palpable policy change, its influence faded. As Alan McPherson writes, "By the late 1960s . . . [elites] had virtually ceased trying to make anti-U.S. speeches or devise anti-U.S. policies, lest they alienate Washington, their only supporter in the hemisphere."[8]

How far does a high-politics approach get us? First, it is worth underscoring that the "costs" of alienating the United States are ever-changing. If the global shift to multiple centers of economic activity means anything, it means a multiplication of possible economic and political relationships. Alternatives to the United States exist. Even if in some places and times the US remains the most attractive option, America is far from being "the indispensable nation."[9] It remains costly to turn against the United States, but doing so becomes thinkable.[10]

Second, the double-barreled assumption that under democracy, opinion flows unimpeded into the policy process, and under authoritarianism, such opinion is blocked from doing so may not be sustainable. As increasingly sophisticated work on authoritarianism makes clear,[11] nondemocratic regimes may be influenced by societal pressure, even if this pressure is indirect or not particularly welcome; any political system that fails to heed the interests of key stakeholders relies increasingly on coercion and fear—itself a costly proposition. The rapidity of political change that emerged with the Arab uprisings reminds us that a vibrant politics occurs behind the scenes of regimes that only *seem* to be unchanging.[12] Moreover, the widespread use of social media allows for forms of coordination and communication with the public that provide for unusual policymaking opportunities, whether political institutions are democratic or authoritarian.

In short, just because anti-Americanism does not have an easily discernible and immediate effect on high politics does not mean that it is toothless. Katzenstein and Keohane admit as much: "The fact that accurate predictions about the long-term, indirect effects of anti-Americanism are difficult in no way undermines their substantive importance for U.S. foreign policy and world politics."[13] It is precisely this longer-term and indirect path that the following chapters address. As the Central Asian examples demonstrate, any understanding of the phenomenon requires a long time-horizon and close attention to ground-level processes.

The Power of Symbolic Politics

If anti-Americanism is not a rising tide, a conflagration, or an overwhelming force, what is it? Below I will argue that "America" is a *symbol*, and that anti-Americanism is a pronounced tendency to deploy negative evaluations of symbolic America in social and political life. Let me first clear some conceptual brush by briefly considering two related perspectives.

Perhaps anti-Americanism is a matter of the mind, a "psychological tendency to hold negative views of the United States and of American society in general."[14] Such an approach can usefully move us away from high politics, but ultimately, pinning our hopes on psychology creates problems. In this approach, "the further one moves from pro to anti, the more one works on the register of affect rather than reason. That is, systematic bias takes over from distrust or simple opinion."[15] Pro-Americanism is assumed to be natural and reasonable, while anti-Americanism is painted to be the product of psychological predispositions.[16] In such an approach, those who systematically oppose the United States cannot be in their right mind.

To oppose a state categorically is indeed to take an extreme position, and it is hard to sympathize with those who see zero value in anything that the United States does. But if it is true that no right-minded person would systematically *oppose* the United States, should it not also be true that no right-minded person would systematically *favor* the United States? When anti-Americanism springs from emotion and pro-Americanism emerges from rational thought, have we deployed an adequate vocabulary? And, if that were not enough, "anti-Americanism" is both a category of analysis and a category of practice; its use by practitioners deeply complicates its use by analysts.[17] Perhaps an overdrawn distinction between rationality and irrationality lies at the root of the problem; human behavior in fact involves complex motivations, contextual factors, and a variety of heuristic shortcuts linked to symbols. It becomes hard to view such complexity when we are faced with the binaries of "anti" and "pro."[18]

Maybe anti-Americanism (or its invisible cousin pro-Americanism) is simply one dimension of "public opinion." The term indexes a venerated tradition in the social sciences that has spawned a widely recognized industry of globe-trotting opinion measurers. And it is hard to deny that opposition to or support for the US is a matter of opinion, however well informed. If so, we might use survey methodologies to design questions that would measure what people think on a battery of topics, including those related to the United States. Bringing in the broader public would also be a welcome move away from high politics.

Yet, such research takes us only so far. Public opinion scholarship tends to assume that an identifiable *public* has already-formed *opinions* that are waiting to be discovered (rather than constantly changing in the course of social interaction), that can be *counted* via survey methods (rather than by other approaches), and that are *heeded* by elected representatives (rather than formed by political leaders). Such assumptions are problematic, even in democracies where they should rest on reasonably solid ground. In reality, opinions are often half-formed and changeable, elites often shape opinions as much as they represent them, and surveys have inherent and nontrivial limitations.[19] True for democratic contexts, this is even truer for authoritarian ones.

We need a new vocabulary that generates analytic possibilities that the old vocabulary forecloses. That vocabulary should attend to the fact that individuals use both logic and emotion,[20] consider both goals and process, and are affected by a striking array of inputs as they process information and make decisions in real-world situations.[21] And it needs to be as much sociological as psychological.

A focus on symbols is particularly promising. It helps us to lay bare how changing public attitudes shift social relations in politically significant ways. Instead of seeking evidence of popular opinion's direct impact on policymaking,[22] this approach considers how changing symbolic depictions of the United States recombine the raw material available for social mobilizers. The result is that the changing stock of images about the United States empowers some societal actors and disempowers others. The story of anti-Americanism thus is rarely about a rising tide that swamps or a conflagration that overwhelms; more typically, it is about a gradual sedimentation of social meanings that changes the political landscape.

Symbols and Symbolic America

How does "America," the symbol, become political? In some research traditions, symbolic politics are about how individuals develop lasting political predispositions through primary socialization.[23] That is, symbols are like schemata that individuals use to simplify a complex world and to imagine alternatives against the backdrop of accumulating experience.[24] Durable, these constructs can last a lifetime, quietly reinforcing political attitudes by doing emotional work.[25] In theory, discussion could end here, with the simple observation that individuals' personal worldviews change slowly, if they change at all.[26] We could simply conclude that what "America" symbolizes is fairly well "baked in" by the time an individual becomes an adult.

But we do not live atomistic lives. Vibrant social ties continually shift, challenge, unsettle, and redefine the content and contours of relevant symbols.[27]

As Trevor Purvis and Alan Hunt, following Saussure, explain, "The openness of the connection between signified and signifier has the consequence that language is always more than denotative (as in pointing a finger at a physical entity and saying 'cat'). As a consequence 'meaning' is never fully referential and is always contestable."[28] One need only think of the highly emotive, polyvalent, changeable symbol of the American flag; the referent remains the same, but what political work it does depends on how it is used, who is doing the using, and who is viewing the process.

Continuing a tradition that runs from Durkheim to Geertz to Edelman and beyond, I treat symbols as collective representations.[29] Though in flux, their meanings are intersubjective; they are shared. As Serge Moscovici writes:

> Social representations concern the contents of everyday thinking and the stock of ideas that gives coherence to our religious beliefs, political ideas and the connections we create as spontaneously as we breathe. They make it possible for us to classify persons and objects, to compare and explain behaviors and to objectify them as parts of our social setting. While social representations are often located in the minds of men and women, they can just as often be found in the society as a whole and, as such, can be examined separately.[30]

This approach to symbols departs from how the term is used in ordinary conversation, where something is considered "symbolic" if it lacks import. To the contrary, symbols are powerful because human beings reside in *meaningful* communities. To make sense of human behavior, we require attention to symbols, since "intersubjective meanings ... [render certain actions] plausible or implausible, acceptable or unacceptable, conceivable or inconceivable, respectable or disreputable, etc."[31] Symbols thus pack political punch, though their impact may be diffuse and long-term.

So, what is "America" as a symbol? If in general a *symbol* is "something that stands for, represents, or denotes something else (not by exact resemblance, but by vague suggestion, or by some accidental or conventional relation),"[32] then *symbolic America* is a shorthand for a multidimensional and polysemous cluster of resonant representations about the United States. Let me take each aspect in turn.

Symbolic America is multidimensional. What it represents to a given community on, for example, the economic dimension may differ from what it represents on a cultural, military, or political dimension. Each meaning is worth considering separately. A community may associate the American economy with vitality and technological progress while viewing American culture as superficial and morally degenerate. Or a community could view the American economy as representing class inequality while admiring American cultural products such as jazz, hip-hop, and Hollywood.

Symbolic America is also polysemous. If all symbols contain multiple meanings, symbolic America is no different. Naturally, there are common narratives about the United States, and we can describe how one or another narrative resonates in a given time and place, but individuals within any given community are exposed to novel stimuli that can shift in nontrivial ways what "America" comes to stand for. Any study of symbolic America that ignores the creativity of actors on the ground will be blind to the processes by which change occurs.

Finally, symbolic America is resonant. As Ignazio Silone once evocatively remarked, "America is everywhere . . . It is in Karachi and Paris, in Jakarta and Brussels. An idea of it, a fantasy of it, hovers over distant lands."[33] Looming over global politics, symbolic America provides ample raw material for social and political actors to use as they pursue their local agendas. Symbolic America does not *cause* local actors to make the choices they make, but it does provide a resonant language that enables certain behaviors and inhibits others. This is immensely important and powerfully political.

Multidimensional, polysemous, and resonant, symbolic America matters for politics in Central Asia and beyond. To see how, let us put it in motion.

Putting Symbols into Motion

In the chapters that follow, I first deploy geologic vocabulary meant to capture how symbolic America changes over time. Second, I turn to an approach that considers how social and political actors frame their movements, using symbolic America to further their aims. Together, these processes constitute what I mean by *slow Anti-Americanism*.

Geologic Metaphors

Just as sediment travels in waterways before settling in a new location, the raw material that constitutes the United States as a symbol is in fluid motion. Thus, views of the United States can flow both vertically into the state apparatus and horizontally into various segments of society. Consider Egypt, which "combines extremely close relations with the U.S. government with among the highest levels of expressed anti-Americanism."[34] On its face, it would appear to be a state determinedly ignoring popular sentiment. But the situation has never been simple. The Mubarak regime persistently criticized US policy, and even pro-democracy groups like Kefaya, which actively opposed Mubarak in 2004–5, offered vocal indictments of US policies.[35] Thus, anti-American symbols and argumentation were a staple in Egyptian politics. The re-emergence of an explicitly pro-American regime under General Sisi after a coup in 2013 changed bilateral relations but did little to undermine these essential dynamics.

Views of the United States may also traverse political boundaries. In the 1980s, more than twelve thousand Saudi men went to fight jihad in Afghanistan. As Gwenn Okruhlik describes, these individuals were primed for political dissent. Moreover, the stationing of US troops in Saudi Arabia during the first Gulf War generated a "fever pitch" of opposition to the United States.[36] In Yemen, views of the United States were deeply affected by labor migrants who found themselves working in Saudi oil fields starting in the 1970s.[37] The possibilities for such cross-border flows are many, as long as mobility remains part of the human condition.

Just as sediment that travels in waterways can settle and gradually become part of the layered bedrock in its new location, shifts in attitude about the United States have the potential to become part of fundamental social meanings. Such meanings can be quarried by future generations for political benefit. Discussing the rapid rise of anti-Americanism in Latin America in the 1950s, Alan McPherson observes that Venezuelan protesters in 1958 "had accumulated a vast repertoire of anti-U.S. imagery over decades—the predatory eagle, the omnipresent octopus, greedy Wall Street tycoons, the impersonal boots of U.S. Marines, and so on."[38] Such sedimentation is not sufficient to generate anti-American mobilization or to drive policy change, but it does represent necessary raw material for such possibilities. This raw material becomes socially and politically potent via the framing processes described below.

By using geologic metaphors, I seek to emphasize that the process of change, while slow and hard to predict, can become powerful. Of course, I do not mean that change literally occurs in geologic time. My purview is not millennia, but years and decades. If that seems a long span, this tells us much about the time-horizons normally used in analyses of politics.

Framing Processes

Scholars of social movements consider the processes by which mobilizers *frame* their efforts. A frame is a schema that enables people "to locate, perceive, identify, and label" their experience and their understanding of the world.[39] In the context of social movements, frames link grievances to meaningful social and political action.[40] Thus, collective action frames are "action-oriented sets of beliefs and meanings that inspire and legitimate the activities and campaigns of a social movement organization (SMO)."[41]

By considering framing processes, we further put symbols into motion. Consider important questions that frames help us to address: (1) Why do some people behave in ways that contravene their narrowly construed material self-interest? (2) Why do some people tolerate deplorable material conditions while others mobilize for change? (3) Why do mobilizers exert such effort and expend such resources to build a rhetoric that persuasively links local concerns to extra-local ones? (4) Why do certain framing efforts fall on deaf ears while others resonate broadly? A framing approach reminds us that symbols are powerful not only "when conventional material resources are lacking."[42] Nor do symbols merely provide the "grounds or warrants for the political activity [already] engaged in."[43] Rather, symbols are a staple of contentious politics and give meaning and direction to political trajectories.

As the empirical chapters that follow will make clear, framing choices necessarily entail a fair degree of strategic action. This should not surprise. Framers seek to gain new recruits, secure the sympathy of broader publics, broker coalitions, mobilize their members to action, and tap into broadly resonant identities and discourses.[44] All the while, framers can fairly be assumed interested in preserving or enhancing their own personal status and privilege. Thus, when we think about framing, we ought to be mindful of framers' strategic calculations.

Yet strategy and outcome have a complex relationship; one does not reliably predict the other. In some cases, mobilizers may make framing choices that are rational in the short term but hamper mobilization over the medium- and longer-term. Lawrence Markowitz gives an example from Central Asia, in which mobilizers in Tajikistan and Uzbekistan relied heavily on anti-imperialist nationalist frames—something that made short-term sense but ultimately led them into the political wilderness.[45] In other cases, mobilizers avoid particular frames because they cannot predict the effects such frames will have. Thus, while Fidel Castro would ultimately take full advantage of negative popular images of the United States, he "eschewed anti-Americanist themes prior to revolutionary victory."[46]

Any understanding of framing choices must therefore attend to the concrete social and political contexts that define the horizons of the thinkable.[47] These contexts are complex, in motion, and ask much of mobilizers. For one, mobilizers have no monopoly on framing processes; framing occurs throughout social life. Framers must contend with other frames and with other framers.[48] For example, in 2020 in the United States, mobilizers used the powerful Black Lives Matter frame but also had to contend with counterframing from those who proclaimed that "All Lives Matter." Moreover, framing choices must relate to larger symbolic universes.[49] Framers who ignore such universes risk contradicting long-standing cultural frameworks, thereby undermining their own efforts to achieve popular resonance.

In short, framing is a widely used practice in the top-down management of ideas and images, but it is not a frictionless exercise in strategic manipulation. Recognizing this, our task is to take an analytic step backward, acknowledging that framing occurs in specific contexts rich with preexisting symbols. These contexts do not determine outcomes, but they necessarily create constraints on choice. Put differently, we should take stock of established raw material, how it flows, and what happens when it becomes sedimented again. These processes may be slow, but they are ongoing and dynamic. Moreover, they contain the potential for major social and political change.

Social Movements under Authoritarianism

While we tend to associate social movements with democratic and democratizing contexts, important forms of contention can occur under authoritarian rule. In fact, as social movement theorists demonstrate, regime type is only the roughest of maps to the dynamics of contention.[50] Some political institutions under democracy can constrain mobilization, while some political institutions under authoritarianism can enable mobilization.[51] Of course, autocracies generally have less "oxygen" for meaningful contention than do democracies, but they still can have a surprisingly lively and dynamic politics along many dimensions.[52]

Like social movements everywhere, those under authoritarianism are located primarily in society, rather than in the state, regime, or high politics.

Unlike political parties, the military, lobbies, or informal pressures groups, social movements aim not to institutionalize their influence over those in power. They do aim for social and political change, but the point of origin for their activities remains societal. Because of this location, changes in popular views of the US have an impact on social movements before any impact is felt in high politics.

At the same time, social movements under authoritarianism have distinctive qualities. Where high politics is closely managed by the regime, social movements are unusual for enjoying comparative autonomy. The regime continually exerts its influence, but this influence rarely extends as effectively to the far reaches of society as it does to those contesting for political power.[53] Such movements do have political agendas based on a critique of the status quo. Whether their calls are for an Islamic caliphate, for a stop to authoritarian abuses of human rights, or for improvements to labor and environmental protections, they mobilize to change the existing order. Their activities may be trivialized (or exaggerated, as the case may be), but they contain the seeds of potent political change.[54]

An authoritarian context matters in at least one additional way. Pressure and enticements from the regime (as well as an important degree of self-censorship) truncate social movement activities. Even when a movement is tolerated by officialdom, it is tolerated *by degree*, and the size of mobilization may be limited by the preferences of regime actors. Thus, political opportunity to mobilize has an impact on the type of movement that can function under authoritarianism.

Given these constraints, movements have different framing techniques depending on the degree to which the authoritarian regime tolerates them. *Broad-cast movements* enjoy adequate political opportunity to reach a wide public with their message. They seek to project an image of grassroots public support and to compel the regime to take their agenda seriously. Looking for wide resonance, they develop framing strategies that link movement grievances and goals to the predicaments their recruits might face. If they can produce a message that transcends the particulars of local circumstance, their recruits might imagine themselves as a part of a larger, translocal community.[55]

Not all movements, however, seek to broaden their membership base and to project their message as widely as possible. Especially under authoritarian circumstances, keeping numbers low and activities sheltered from state scrutiny can ensure that those involved are committed and loyal. Thus, *narrow-cast movements* are not failed broad-cast movements; instead, they have adapted to prevailing authoritarian conditions by developing small, nimble, perhaps even conspiratorial, forms of organization.

Broad- and narrow-cast movements approach framing in different ways. The former are typically involved in what the literature refers to as "frame bridging"—that is, an effort to link collective action frames to each other.[56] In this tactic, the framer appeals differently to different audiences that have different symbolic frames of reference. Such acts of framing require creativity to connect publics that otherwise do not imagine themselves as bonded together in a common cause. Shifting symbolic America engenders new possibilities for frame bridging, as the case of Hizb ut-Tahrir illustrates in chapter 2.

By contrast, narrow-cast movements are more typically involved in "frame amplification." In this process, framers call attention to the salient aspects of their movement to invigorate the core values of their small group of supporters. The Islamic Movement of Uzbekistan, covered in chapter 2, is an exemplar. As the following chapters detail, it matters much whether a movement is broad- or narrow-cast and therefore whether it relies on frame bridging or frame amplification.

Contention in Central Asia

If social movements under authoritarianism deserve our attention, why focus specifically on Central Asia? US relations with Iran, Central Asian energy resources, a complex occupation of and reconstruction effort in Afghanistan, and the evolving strategic interactions with Russia and China make Central Asia *central* to any calculus of US global interests.[57] Central Asian publics are typically ambivalent about the United States, harboring neither the largely anti-American sentiments of parts of the Middle East nor the predominantly pro-American sentiments of parts of Bosnia, Albania, and Kosovo.[58] Which way these publics go matters for US policymakers, very much as it matters for their Chinese, Russian, and other counterparts.

In this sense, it is no exaggeration to suggest that Central Asia is a pivot[59] that can shift the balance of geopolitical forces. While these states are not on the brink of failure, state weakness (especially in Tajikistan and Kyrgyzstan) exacerbates transboundary problems of terrorism and narcotics trafficking.[60] While Central Asian states are unlikely to be overwhelmed by Islamic militancy,[61] the activities of various underground groups that weak states are incapable of appeasing, co-opting, or coercing can have political "reverberation effects" far out of proportion with their material influence.[62] While Central Asian states are unlikely to undergo democratic transformations in the near term, the ongoing activities and support of the European Union contain the potential for the long-term democratization of the region.[63] State failure, Islamic revolution, and democratic development of course are all extreme outcomes. Chances are greater that Central Asia's political development will be a hybrid for the medium term. The crucial question is what sort of hybrid Central Asia will become; which way Central Asia goes matters enormously.

The Central Asian examples speak to other world regions as well. First, although religious practices in the region are distinctive, the globalization of Islamic discourse ensures that the same questions are asked in every Muslim-majority context, although the answers to those questions differ dramatically. Thus, even enormously secular Albania and Bosnia face newly devout publics that ask penetrating questions about the relationships between politics and faith; the same is doubly true in less thoroughly secular contexts.[64] Given such essentially political debates, the United States becomes a potent symbolic touchstone.

Second, Central Asia presents an analytic opportunity to view the impact of symbols. The United States as an *actor* was largely absent from the region in the 1990s. Nonetheless, its impact as a *symbol* was palpable, significant, and variable during that period. This distant hegemon loomed large in the Central Asian imagination well before the United States stepped up its military presence in the region in late 2001. Through the Central Asian cases we therefore gain analytic purchase on the general dynamic through which symbols—as analytically separable from action—affect politics. As we will see, nonmaterial factors have an enormous impact.

Finally, Central Asia reminds us that the political influence of the US image becomes noticeable over the long term. When symbols become lodged in everyday social imaginaries, institutionalized informally in a society's political structures, and routinized and normalized in a society's political culture, they may be particularly difficult to address. If we are interested in what happens before path dependency sets in or before a habitus develops, we should seek to view the process at its earliest stage.

Central Asia's social movements broadly follow patterns visible across Eurasia. For the most part sparsely populated,[65] hampered by poverty, and long dominated by autocrats both foreign and indigenous, Central Asia has had a modest history of social mobilization. At the same time, while Central Asian societies are not the "movement societies" depicted in literatures on social movements, pre-Soviet and Soviet-era mobilization achieved notable scope and political significance.[66]

After the waves of street protests that contributed to the dissolution of the Soviet state receded, societies across the ex-USSR generally demobilized in the 1990s.[67] This demobilization was understandable, given the challenges ordinary people faced. Socioeconomic decline, accompanied by a pervasive language of "transitions" that stressed the rightness of the new political order,[68] preoccupied broad swathes of the population. Initially, lacking resources and political opportunity, would-be mobilizers faced an inauspicious environment in which to pursue their goals.

By the middle of the 1990s, this had begun to change. On the resource side, civil society activists, groups, and movements that promoted an economically and politically liberal agenda were able to tap into foreign assistance from the West, principally the United States. To a lesser extent, they began to avail themselves of domestic resources for their efforts. Others, promoting an agenda to revive Islamic piety, began to enjoy largely in-kind help (mosque construction, publication of religious literature), principally from sources in other Muslim-majority states. As for political opportunities, they varied widely. Plentiful in the relatively open (though still authoritarian) Kyrgyzstan, they were more limited in the constrained environments of Tajikistan and Kazakhstan, and nearly nonexistent in hard-authoritarian Uzbekistan and sultanistic Turkmenistan.

Resources and political opportunities are part of the story, but a full account of social mobilization in an inauspicious environment needs to consider frames and framing. As the following chapters detail, the environment for framing changed markedly beginning in the mid-1990s. Symbolic America shifted from animating a politics that undergirded hegemonic notions of political and economic liberalization to informing various ways of calling into question the emerging order. This shift had a tremendous effect on movement trajectories.

The Argument: Slow Anti-Americanism in Central Asia

Let me pause to recap. First, symbols have major political influence, in part because they pervade social and political life. Second, frames draw upon

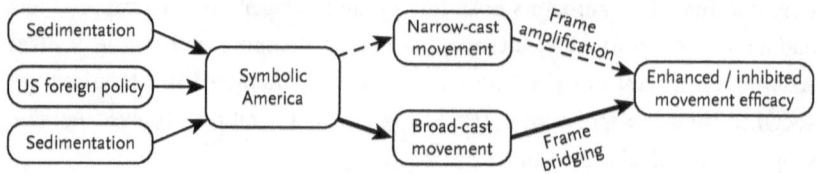

FIGURE 1. How symbolic America affects social movements.

resonant symbols whose resonance is the product of, inter alia, what I call sedimentation. Third, frames matter under authoritarianism, and their significance depends upon how broadly cast or narrowly cast a given movement is. Finally, such forms of contention in Central Asia deserve our attention. Figure 1 offers a stylized version of the argument that the following chapters cover in detail.

The process begins with the United States itself, whose policy moves may trigger a chain of consequences. These moves may be dramatic and controversial, such as the 2003 decision to invade Iraq; more typically, they are quiet and initially unremarkable. Such changed configurations become locally meaningful only as they are mediated by and interpreted through local circumstances, especially political ones. The NATO-led bombings in Kosovo in 1999, for example, were interpreted in wildly different ways in Moscow and in Tirana. Any given fact of foreign relations is refracted through the prism of local concerns; such refractions, in turn, have the potential to shift popular sentiment.

Yet, what the United States does is not the only influence on the stock of available symbols. First, sediment begins to flow. Ideological currents bring novel ways of thinking about the United States. Migrants, business travelers, tourists, exchange students, and a series of other border-crossers bring with them new experiences and influences. Violent conflict may cross political frontiers. Moreover, sediment may include spillover from one issue area to another. For example, a novel assessment of American cultural products can influence evaluations of American foreign policy.

Second, sedimentation occurs. Some of these novel influences may become part of the bedrock interpretations of the United States that come to prevail in any given context. What was previously considered alien and marked as such might become unmarked, assimilated as a constituent part of local imaginings. This is the process by which interpretations become indigenized. For example, normative theories of liberal democracy initially coded as American came to be viewed as essential to European political history in spite of, or perhaps because of, Europe's violent wars of the first half of the twentieth century.[69]

Once shifts to American policy combine with sedimentation processes, the symbolic raw material available for social and political mobilizers also changes. This changing stock of available images has an impact.[70] Of course, any impact is not automatic; symbols are by definition multidimensional and polysemous, lending themselves to a range of possible uses. Actual social actors and political entrepreneurs must exercise their creative agency effectively if this impact is to materialize.

What happens next varies by political regime, but in authoritarian Central Asia, symbolic America becomes available to social mobilizers who pursue particular agendas. Some kinds of mobilization (broad-cast movements) rely heavily on image-making in their efforts; such movements find their efficacy especially challenged by changes to symbolic America. (In figure 1, this impact is represented by solid arrows.) Other kinds of mobilization (narrow-cast movements) rely less on image-making efforts; their efficacy may change to a lesser extent. (In figure 1, this weaker relationship is represented by dotted arrows.)

Figure 1 guides us through the empirical chapters that follow. In chapter 1, I trace how symbolic America shifted from the moment of the Soviet collapse into the 2000s. While these shifts were particularly notable in response to key moments in US foreign policy, there were powerful, slower-moving, and often-overlooked changes as well. This chapter covers the sedimentation processes that precede framing choices made by social mobilizers.

In chapter 2, I consider three very different Islamist movements in Central Asia: Hizb ut-Tahrir (HT), the Islamic Renaissance Party of Tajikistan (IRPT), and the Islamic Movement of Uzbekistan (IMU). In addition to highlighting how the rise of Islamism follows changes to symbolic America (rather than preceding such changes, as is widely assumed to occur), the chapter elaborates the key difference between narrow- and broad-cast movements.

In chapter 3, I examine human rights activism in Central Asia. The activities of dedicated individuals were generally challenged by the changing stock of images about the United States, but human rights activism also came in broad-cast varieties and narrow-cast ones. The latter were less hampered by the shift to symbolic America than were the former. Even the broad-cast movements, which relied heavily on street protests for their efforts, remained buoyed by an ongoing hegemony of liberal political arrangements.

In chapter 4, I consider labor activism. In the language of social science research design, labor represents a "negative case."[71] What this means is that we learn as much from cases where a given outcome fails to materialize (in this instance, changes to movement efficacy), as from cases where such outcomes do in fact occur.[72] Specifically, we are reminded that frames do not spring forth automatically from circumstances; it takes a concerted effort of movement activists to deploy frames that will resonate.

In the Conclusion, I show how these social movement trajectories in turn have an impact. Their impact may not be "serious, direct, and immediate,"[73] but it is no less dramatic, fundamentally altering domestic politics in Central Asian states and thereby creating novel challenges to US foreign policy interests. Finally, I ask, "What is to be done?" Marshaling original evidence from survey experiments conducted in the region, I consider how US policy might itself incorporate framing efforts in the region and beyond.

Some readers may wonder whether it makes sense to treat Islamism, human rights mobilization, and labor activism within the same framework. Are these not so many apples, oranges, and pears? As I hope the following chapters will make clear, it is precisely by putting them into a single analytic framework that we gain purchase on the complex dynamics of anti-Americanism.

1

AMERICA'S CHANGING IMAGE

> The images are invented ones of supernatural and sinister control of events, of devilish manipulation of everyone's lives. They lead to farfetched expectations that the United States should manipulate all events to everyone's satisfaction regardless of who they are and where they live. They lead to disappointment.[1]
>
> Barry Sanders

WHEN SANDERS WROTE OF "farfetched expectations" and "disappointment," he was advancing a general claim, but he easily could have been describing the post-Soviet era. After a decade of hoping that state socialism's retreat would bring broad-based prosperity in its wake, publics were frustrated and linked their frustrations to symbolic America. To understand how this occurred, we need to pay attention to the specifics of time and place. After all, we cannot make sense of symbols if we ignore the contexts in which they emerge.[2] Ultimately, the aim is to produce insights that will be portable to other times and places, but we first must get to know Central Asia well. Of course, politics is the "art of the possible,"[3] but contexts are thick with norms and regularized practices that ultimately limit what can be done; not all outcomes are equally possible.

In this chapter, I trace how images of the United States changed in the Central Asian region. Setting the stage for the discussion of social movements that follows, I make three crucial points. First, Central Asia's initial imaginings of the United States were the product of the Soviet period, and symbolic

America for Central Asians was similar to what it was for other Soviet citizens: an ambiguous cluster of polyvalent but resonant images. Second, after an initial post-Soviet period of being overwhelmed by positive images of the United States, Central Asian opinions of the US declined in the aggregate. This downward trend occurred less because of concrete changes to US policy in the region than because of the slow-moving processes of sedimentation. Third, while the decline on aggregate is clear, more important for social mobilizers was the fact that images of the United States multiplied and diversified during this period; a wider range of images had become available for social mobilizers. They would be the symbolic raw material for Central Asia's social movements to use in the 2000s and beyond.

Limited Contact, Significant Imagining

Central Asia is a vast, diverse region with distinctive and proud traditions. Largely on the receiving end of the transformations triggered by the Bolsheviks' 1917 coup in remote Petrograd, Central Asians experienced the Soviet state in particular ways.[4] Over the course of seventy years, these transformations left a deep imprint on Central Asia.

Whatever their distinctiveness, in one key respect Central Asians came to be like other Soviet citizens: their views about the external world were heavily conditioned by the USSR's construction of symbolic America. *Pace* Western depictions that painted all Muslim-majority countries with the same brush, Soviet citizens did not harbor the distinctly negative views of the US that would become common among populations of the Arab Middle East.[5] Nor were Central Asian and American citizens entwined in a complex history of dense and varied contact at the level of ordinary people, unlike what long has been the case between Latin America and the United States.[6] Like most Soviet citizens, Central Asians felt a fundamental ambivalence about symbolic America. The difference was that Central Asians felt this ambivalence more remotely than did the populations of the European parts of the USSR.

The Soviet state's construction of symbolic America was more complex than we tend to imagine. On the one hand, propaganda famously vilified the United States. The prevailing Soviet view of US foreign policy

> . . . emphasizes the aggressiveness of the United States and our proclivity to use force. It does not disparage American capabilities or willpower. At

the same time it constantly reiterates the growing limits to American control and the historical inevitability of imperialism's downfall. In this picture the United States remains strong but the forces in opposition have grown and now with resolution and unity can contain American designs.[7]

This was an enduring Soviet "enemy image" of the US that was largely impervious to change. Had the US altered its foreign policy, the enemy image would have remained.[8]

In the view of Soviet propaganda, American foreign policy was a natural extension of the "bourgeois" values that characterized its domestic scene. As Vladimir Shlapentokh describes, "Since the mid-1970s, the average American has been portrayed as a person absorbed with material interests, indifferent to others, and far from real cultural values."[9] This depiction enabled the Soviet state "to rationalize the growing economic and technological gap between the two countries."[10] American imperialism overseas and a poverty of "real" values domestically were portrayed as inextricably linked.

State propaganda about the United States thus offered a clear and scathing denunciation of American political values, geopolitical ambitions, and crass materialism. Yet, propaganda was never the whole story. Alongside these messages that saturated public space was an opportunity for Soviet citizens to develop their own private awareness of the United States and selectively appropriate aspects of Americanism. This began in the early Soviet period and found full flourish in the 1970s and 1980s.

Consider business and financial ties. Propaganda routinely depicted American private capital and government assistance as driven by the implacable logic of exploitative capitalism and therefore inherently dangerous, but such messaging belied a more complex reality. Soviet links to both capital and foreign aid flows were nontrivial. American businesspeople traveled to and even invested in Soviet commercial enterprises in the 1920s. The US provided aid to the USSR through its generous lend-lease program during World War II. Khrushchev famously was infatuated with American agribusiness. Brezhnev admired and selectively adopted aspects of American technology. Gorbachev pursued major social and political openings that showed admiration for aspects of the American model. Throughout the Soviet period, such contacts brought the Soviet public some exposure to a complex symbolic America.

Exposure to symbolic America was not limited to high-level interactions. The party-state curated information about the Western bloc, but such information became increasingly available to the broader public as technologies changed and Soviet rule matured. After Stalin's death, the state promoted shortwave radios to foster in the public an appreciation of the great achievements taking place across the vast expanses of Soviet territory, not to mention the "internationalist" successes of socialist governance in the developing world.[11] Citizens simply could not grasp the extent of Soviet triumphs without such devices. Radio in turn brought a wider range of programming about the West in general and the United States in particular.

The public thus apprehended the United States in ways that were heavily influenced, but not determined outright, by the Soviet state. Much of the information reaching the public was consistent with state-propagated values—for example, when American soldiers in Vietnam committed atrocities—but far from all of it. In music and literature, for example, America loomed large. Alexei Yurchak writes, "Between the 1940s and 1970s jazz was continuously praised for its roots in the creative genius of the slaves and the working people and condemned as bourgeois pseudo-art that lost any connection to the realism of people's culture."[12]

Not exclusively panned nor simply praised, America as ambiguous symbol became inescapable fact, an "other" against which Soviet life was consistently compared and contrasted. Official ideology vilifying the United States did not disappear until the very late Soviet period; nor did most ordinary citizens dismiss the tenets of Soviet ideology as wrongheaded or, pejoratively speaking, "propaganda." This public vilification was accompanied by a quiet and increasingly tolerated glorification of the American experience.

Rarely was it a political act to engage with symbolic America. American political values were important for dissidents in particular, but the majority of those exposed to symbolic America were not motivated by political conviction. To the contrary, in the late Soviet period, one could perform pro-Soviet political roles and simultaneously admire aspects of American life. How was this possible? Consider by analogy Nazi Germany, where doctors working in concentration and labor camps underwent an experience of "doubling," in which they psychologically divided themselves "into two functioning wholes, so that a part-self acts as an entire self."[13] Thus bifurcated, a doctor could make good on essentially contradictory obligations—those to patients as prescribed by the Hippocratic oath and those to the fascist regime as prescribed by Nazi ideology.

Ordinary Soviet citizens faced choices far less likely to demand such extreme psychological gymnastics. Nonetheless, their context required a similar kind of "doubling." Following in the tradition of J. L. Austin, Yurchak distinguishes the *constative* (i.e., speech acts designed to describe reality) and the *performative* (i.e., speech acts whose impact lies in what they do rather than in how descriptively accurate they are.) While the two can be in tension, this does not necessarily produce cognitive dissonance. The distinction helps us to understand life under late state socialism. Yurchak provides an illuminating example of voting among members of Komsomol, the youth organization of the Communist Party. Since the (positive) outcome of a vote was foreordained, the exercise would appear pointless, but it was not. When asked to vote on a resolution,

> they collectively responded not to the constative meaning of this question ("Do you support the resolution?") but to its performative meaning ("Are you the kind of people who understand that the norms and rules of the current ritual need to be performatively reproduced, that constative meanings do not necessarily have to be attended to, who act accordingly, and who, therefore, can be engaged in other meanings?").[14]

This kind of bifurcation matters for thinking about symbolic America during the Soviet period. One could simultaneously be critical of bourgeois American values in a performative sense, while admiring (some) American values in a constative sense. Thus, it is not that the Soviet state forced its citizens to be anti-American in public while they were pro-American in private. Nor is it that Soviet citizens were engaging in resistance by falsifying their public preferences and patiently waiting for a safe moment to reveal their actual preferences.[15] Rather, ordinary people carried ambivalent attitudes about the United States to the very end of Soviet power.[16]

Central Asia in the Soviet Context

Did Central Asians under Soviet rule view the US differently than did other Soviet citizens? Much distinguished Central Asia from other parts of the Soviet Union, but it is worth considering whether their major distinguishing traits matter specifically for the politics of symbolic America.

First consider Islam. Although the Middle Volga, North Caucasus, and South Caucasus regions also have long-established Muslim populations,

Central Asia has far greater numbers over a much vaster territory. The region also occupies a central place in the history of Islam and Islamic thought. Without a doubt, Islam has "left a deep and indelible impression" on the region.[17]

There is little evidence, however, that Islam per se structured distinctive views of the West. Perhaps this should not surprise. As the Introduction discussed, strained relations with the West are best understood as the product of particular historical moments (rather than as the product of Islam as a belief system). Middle Eastern Muslim publics in the 2000s strongly embraced views critical of the United States, but Muslim communities that came under Russian influence lived in entirely different cultural and political milieux.[18] Central Asian Islam has been notably unconcerned with relations with the West.[19]

The distinctiveness of Central Asian Islam must be understood in the context of Soviet-era transformations. The party-state brutally removed religion from the public sphere, radically scaling back its role as a comprehensive theology and social system and largely reducing it to a marker of ethnonational identity. In its modernizing and secularizing zeal, the Soviet state initially resembled but ultimately exceeded its Turkish republican counterpart.[20] At the moment of the USSR's collapse, Islam loosely informed lifestyle rites and spiritual practices of various kinds[21] and was widely understood to be a defining trait of Central Asia's ethnonational communities, but it did not imply views, one way or another, about the United States.

Some analysts seeking to uncover to the roots of Islam's post-Soviet revival describe the 1970s as ushering in a period of tremendous ferment in "underground" or "parallel" Islam. In their view, this ferment represented an incipient challenge to Soviet governance.[22] The argument is that because the USSR in the 1970s and 1980s could not turn a blind eye to a global Islamic revival, Leonid Brezhnev started a concerted, if highly selective, effort to connect Central Asians to the broader Muslim world.[23]

This religious revival was real and significant, but we should keep it in perspective. Some of the figures schooled in Islamic thought during the Soviet period would later become prominent actors in post-Soviet society,[24] but at the time underground Islam was politically quietest and limited in scope.[25] Whatever happened among budding theologians, scholars, and pilgrims in the 1970s and early 1980s should not be confused with the nearly perfect isolation that ordinary Central Asians felt from the non-Soviet Muslim world.

Moreover, even if a given Central Asian were exposed to those undergoing an Islamic revival, there is little reason to expect that this would structure his or her view of the United States.

Tajikistan, Turkmenistan, and Uzbekistan all share a border with Afghanistan, so the Soviet-Afghan War (1979–89) had the potential to affect the region in distinctive ways. Did Central Asians in fact experience the war differently from their counterparts from other Soviet republics? Early scholarship contended that Central Asian soldiers defected in exceptionally high numbers and that Moscow withdrew troops of Central Asian origin from the war theater precisely to prevent fraternization with the anti-Soviet mujahideen.[26] In a story that would later become an urban legend, one of the leaders of the Islamic Movement of Uzbekistan (IMU) was so moved by contact with coreligionists that during his military service he radicalized. Not only is there no evidence that this occurred, but there is strong evidence that his service in Afghanistan would in fact become a source of embarrassment for the IMU.[27]

Historians with fuller access to archives and to participants' testimony have revisited this question. As it turns out, defection rates were similar across groups.[28] Non-Slavs were in fact underrepresented in the officer corps;[29] given what we know about hazing and deteriorating conditions in the armed forces, this might have disproportionately affected non-Slavs and theoretically could have created greater resentment of the Soviet army as an institution. In general, the war would become fodder for domestic criticism of foreign policymaking, just as Vietnam had been for the United States[30]—criticism that could imply sympathy for an alternative, pro-American perspective. Yet, we cannot conclude that Central Asian soldiers and civilians questioned the morality of the Soviet invasion of Afghanistan any more than did other Soviet soldiers and civilians.[31] Even less should we conclude that any such sentiment produced particular feelings about the United States.

Hypothetically, transboundary patterns of settlement could have mattered. Communities of Uzbeks and Tajiks living in Afghanistan—many descended from those who fled Soviet power in the 1920s and 1930s—represented potential for common cause. One might imagine that, motivated by this historical memory, Uzbeks and Tajiks still living within the Soviet state might resent and oppose Soviet policy in Afghanistan. If true, perhaps this sense of common cause could have been even stronger if Uzbeks or Tajiks, as minority groups in Afghanistan, were dissatisfied with the status quo under a Pashtun-dominated, Soviet-backed government. One might further imagine that this could produce an overrepresentation of Uzbeks and Tajiks among the anti-Soviet mujahideen and a distinctive anti-Soviet spirit among Soviet citizens of Uzbek and Tajik background.

It is true that the pro-Soviet regime in Kabul, first under Karmal and then under Najibullah, was strongly ethnic Pashtun. By contrast, the mujahideen were a series of loosely coordinated antiregime elements who themselves tended to divide by ethnicity.[32] Perhaps a local Tajik or Uzbek would be more likely to resist the Soviet-backed regime than would a local Pashtun, but many ethnic Uzbeks selected "exit" instead of resistance, fleeing from Afghanistan as refugees.[33] In high politics, the most powerful Uzbek leader, Abdul Rashid Dostum, and the most powerful Tajik one, Burhanuddin Rabbani, fought on different sides before Rabbani's 1992 volte-face changed the nature of the civil war.[34] If ethnicity was a weak predictor of views of the United States in Afghanistan proper, there is every reason to expect that any relationship would be even weaker among co-ethnics living under Soviet rule.

One final possibility deserves mention. Soviet soldiers serving in Afghanistan were exposed to symbolic America via the material goods that they encountered. One soldier recounted:

> We looted enemy boots, clothes and food. Our flak-jackets were so heavy you could hardly lift them. The American ones were preferred—they didn't have a single metal part. They were made from some kind of bullet-proof material which a Makarov pistol couldn't penetrate at point-blank range, and a tommy-gun only from a hundred metres at most. American sleeping-bags we captured were 1949 models, but as light as a feather. Our padded jackets weigh at least seven kilograms.[35]

American quality impressed, yet there is no reason to conclude that Central Asian soldiers were more taken by lightweight American sleeping bags than were the other underequipped soldiers of the Soviet army.

If the evidence does not suggest that Central Asians harbored particular sympathies or antipathies toward the United States, Central Asia was distinctive in a crucial way. Geographic distance made a remote symbol even more remote. Not only were they far from the United States, but titular Central Asian populations disproportionately lived in rural areas, at an even greater distance from the cities where late-socialist citizens quietly traded in Western culture and symbolism. This remoteness meant that symbolic America traveled in weakened ways to the region.

But the pattern, while weaker, was similar to that across the vast Soviet state. Indeed, in historical perspective, it was normal. Central Asians had long experienced the West—its intellectual currents, its political ideologies, and its cultural products—via Russians as intermediaries. During the tsarist period, great works of Western philosophy and literature were first admired in Russia, then translated into Russian, and eventually brought to the region by Russophone Central Asians. Medical advances followed similar paths, brought by tsarist administrators to be imposed, sometimes forcibly, on local populations.[36] To this day, Slavs and the behaviors associated with them (such as liberal views on gender relations) are often coded in public discourse as "European" (the extreme value of which is "American"). Symbolic America may have been more remote, but it operated in similar ways across post-Soviet space.

The American Tide: Hegemony from a Distance

When the Soviet state collapsed and its ideology as a belief system failed, many assumed its liberal opposite to be self-evidently true. Overnight, the long-standing ambivalence about the United States disappeared from obvious sight. This was not a metaphorical "vacuum," in which the nearest existing ideology quickly moved to fill the void. Rather, it was a rising tide. Inundated by liberal ideology, post-Soviet space saw alternatives vanish. Eventually the tide would ebb, and key elements of the preceding order would resurface, if in altered form.[37]

For most ex-Soviet states in the 1990s, liberalism was not ideology at all, but rather a "natural" state of affairs to which any "normal" state aspired.[38] Seventy years of Soviet rule were assumed a detour on an otherwise well defined, inexorable, and indeed teleological—if sometimes slow—march toward normality. Academics, policymakers, and broader publics at least outwardly accepted the inevitability of economic and political "transition"; this language idealized and reified the Western, and especially the American, experience. Enormous public and private financing promoted the cause. Liberalism was hegemonic.[39] Given this liberal order and the US's position as sole surviving superpower, Central Asian publics widely viewed the US as the paragon of virtue and the defining model for social, political, and economic relations. Just as landing a book in the Library of Congress was viewed as an achievement,[40] American expertise was assumed the ideal source of inspiration for reform;[41] American multiculturalism was viewed as uniquely enlightened;[42] highest honors went to US diplomats;[43] American technology was considered to be unsurpassed;[44] American military discipline was the standard-bearer;[45] and American democratic institutions were viewed as superlative.[46] For its own part, the US did little to undermine the impression that it was (1) the epitome of a market economy and a democratic society, (2) morally bound to encourage free markets and democratic societies outside its borders, and (3) capable of doing so.[47]

The region's newspapers illustrate the centrality of symbolic America. In the early 1990s, articles appeared in the local press that embedded positive assumptions about the United States, about American life or products, and about the US role in international affairs. For example, one 1991 article from the Kyrgyzstani newspaper *Delo Nomer* lauded American-style economic liberalism as a model for the agricultural sector, saying:

> The only defense that the American farmer has from economic fluctuations [*ot ekonomicheskikh vetrov*] is knowledge. If you know how to produce a good harvest but keep poor finances and do not know how best to sell your produce, do not count on being successful. The freedom that we here talk so much about and lack is a freedom of choice: to act. No more and no less than the well-being of the family depends on this choice.[48]

An article from a 1992 issue of *Kazakhstanskaia pravda* attempted to trace Americans' economic success to their childhood, arguing:

> Child psychologists consider that the basis of the American psyche [*osnovy amerikanskogo kharaktera*]—and of its characteristics such as industry, freedom of thought, an ability to take on reasonable risk—emerges in the cradle. This occurs because no shackles are placed on the child's hands or feet, and thus virtuous activities at such a tender age are not prohibited.[49]

These passages may or may not be descriptively accurate, but they do capture the period's general infatuation with America.

This was hegemony, but it was from a distance.[50] What was notable about actual US policy toward Central Asia during the 1990s was how limited it was.[51] Aside from the important work done via the Cooperative Threat Reduction program to remove Kazakhstan's nuclear weapons arsenal, the US government was mostly absent, limited to establishing low-level contacts with Central Asian militaries[52] and funding economic and political reform initiatives at similarly low levels. There was some attention to Islamic revivalism, to pipeline politics, and to Russia's role in its "near abroad" that played itself out in Western newspapers.[53] But in general for Washington, Central Asia was an afterthought, subsumed by the US's larger strategy toward Russia.[54] The United States and Central Asia were just about as far from each other as one could imagine.[55] This would change.

The terrorist attacks of September 11, 2001, and the ensuing war in Afghanistan transformed the region into a central concern for Washington within the span of a few weeks. Official government assistance to the region in the two years after the attacks approximated what the US had given in the entire decade of the 1990s.[56] US government contracts generated ample opportunity for Central Asia's privileged elites to enrich and empower themselves.[57] US bases in both Kyrgyzstan and Uzbekistan, as well as stepped-up military-to-military relations in the other states, provided a massive influx of income to previously stagnant service sectors. US government trainers now worked with civil society actors, border guards, police units, universities, and so on; there were few aspects of Central Asian states and societies entirely untouched by the US presence and its focus on security. Once a distant hegemon, the US was now a local actor whose presence had become palpable virtually overnight.

The Return of Ambivalence

The power of symbolic America is not a simple function of the United States' presence or absence in a given region.[58] Popular attitudes about US foreign policy may shift with relatively little concrete US involvement. Thus, at least in parts of Central Asia, the US and its preoccupation with security had already become visible. After the Islamic Movement of Uzbekistan (IMU) staged two violent incursions into Kyrgyzstan in 1999 and 2000, the US stepped up assistance to local governments, focusing on Special Forces training and putting the IMU on its list of terrorist organizations.[59] Second and more generally, popular unease about the US's paramount role in the post–Cold War world had long been rising, particularly with NATO's 1999 intervention in Kosovo, which the Russian-language press treated as illegitimate. Less than two months earlier, bombing runs on terrorist camps in Afghanistan (and Sudan) seemed to confirm the US's willingness to use force whether or not local populations wanted it to.[60] That the Russian press viewed NATO action through the prism of its own massive economic recession in 1998 and a re-emerging pan-Slavism[61]—both of which were largely irrelevant to Central Asians—did nothing to stop Central Asians from receiving their news from Russia. The pattern by which the West arrived in Central Asia largely via Russia was alive and well.

Reactions to the 9/11 attacks betrayed popular ambivalence.[62] Across the globe, sympathy for the victims mingled with unsparing critiques of US foreign policy.[63] Central Asia was similar. Ordinary people in Kazakhstan offered condolences but conveyed a feeling that the US had "set itself up for the tragedy"[64] and that "Americans should get a sense what bombings feel like, since America has too often bombed other countries."[65] In Tashkent, at a small anti-American rally that was quickly halted by the police, a woman reversed the rhetoric of terrorism, criticizing President Bush and Uzbek president Islam Karimov: "Bush is the No. 1 terrorist in the world. . . . Karimov is terrorist No. 2."[66] In northern Tajikistan, one journalist reported that "the majority of Leninabad residents believe that Washington itself provoked the acts of terrorism by its own anti-Islamic policy. People are afraid that if the United States begins revenge action in reality it will not be a battle with terrorists, but the murder of Muslims."[67] Likewise, after an immediate outpouring of sympathy, the Russian press quickly changed its tune.[68]

Much of this reaction tapped into widely available conspiracy theories. For example, a wild hypothesis spread: that Israel was behind the terrorism.[69] In June 2002, news reports filtered into Central Asia that the FBI and perhaps even President Bush himself had possessed critical information that might have prevented the attacks. This led conspiracy-mongers to conclude that Bush was the mastermind. Their reasoning was impeccable (even if their evidence was not): because the terrorist attacks apparently allowed the US to pursue its foreign policy interests without obstacle, Bush simply must have engineered them in the first place.[70] It was not just fringe groups that called the attacks a source of "moral satisfaction" for "millions."[71] It was part of ordinary discourse to view the United States as having somehow "deserved" the violence. While it is impossible to know the extent of such perspectives, at a minimum ambivalence had once again become normal.

US foreign policy choices clearly mattered, but key sources of symbolic America's trajectory lay in Central Asia itself. By the middle of the 1990s, promises of prosperity had failed to produce desired outcomes. Economic contraction was painful for all but the truly well connected among Central

Asians.[72] Unevenly but clearly, the region's citizens began to question the West's model of economic and political development, casting a wary eye toward the local regimes apparently beholden to Western capital and geopolitical interests. Those Central Asians working in the oil and gas sectors, which benefited from a rapid influx of Western capital, and a small middle class connected to international organizations, continued to esteem the US, but others began to express grievances, their high expectations quickly run aground against disappointing social, political, and economic realities. Given that the United States was all-powerful, it must have been conspiracy of malice that inevitably produced disappointment. The epigraph about "farfetched expectations" and "disappointment" that opens this chapter applies well to Central Asia.

The sources of distress were many and should not be reduced to rapacious local elites or ill conceived (if well meaning) international schemes. For many, the experience was much more banal. American cultural products had quickly taken hold in a Central Asian marketplace that for more than seventy years had been starved of desired consumer goods. The particular products that reached the Central Asia were impressive, but not for the right reasons. Third-rate (and typically pirated) films glamorized guns, materialism, and substance abuse. Alcohol and tobacco, normal features of Soviet life, now were aggressively marketed and universally available. Liberal sexual mores—also part of a Soviet legacy but one that had remained private—now were actively, publicly, and forcefully promoted by those peddling the beauty, fashion, and lifestyle of the West. The West's cultural products made the West manifest.

A 1994 article from the Kazakhstani newspaper *Panorama* reported the position of the Kazakhstani Ecology Minister, who asserted that American specialists who had come to the Semipalatinsk former nuclear test site were "actively collecting information on the use of plutonium, and not environmental activities" and were conducting "espionage."[73] Less conspiratorial in tone but no less notable was criticism of largely American oil company Tengizchevroil for its excessive environmental pollution of Kazakhstani territory.[74]

This rising ambivalence assumed a variety of nascent political forms.[75] Those inclined to economic nationalism noted the irony that, in spite of the Soviet collapse, Lenin had been correct: foreign economic interests indeed promoted an imperialism that looked like the "highest stage of capitalism."[76]

The United States did not create a Marshall Plan for Central Asia to rescue it from the Soviet detritus; rather, America dispatched its capitalists in search of profit. A variety of sources began to report popular concern about contracts won by foreign—and principally American—companies operating in Kazakhstan's energy-rich regions.[77] The metaphors used to refer to America shifted to the decidedly less complimentary.[78]

Those inclined to social conservatism trotted out what they considered ample evidence of America's hyper-materialism and deep interest in promoting moral decay. So, for example, the parliamentary newspaper of Uzbekistan in January 1998 wrote that, "Americans spend much money on restaurants and little on reading. This is apparently explained by the habit of Americans to learn the main news from the radio during their commute [*vo vremia avtomobil'nykh poezdok*]."[79] The same newspaper, citing an unnamed work of "international sociological research," reported that Americans apparently "lead the world" in adulterous behavior.[80]

Even committed liberal democrats, the United States' natural ideological supporters, began to wonder whether the US was more interested in economic domination than in supporting democratic initiatives. An article from the liberal Kyrgyzstani newspaper *Respublika* in 1999 argued:

> One cannot fail to notice that western [financial] assistance was governed by good intentions, the assistance was given in the guise of democracy support [*pod demokratiiu*], and the result achieved was exactly the opposite. In all the countries of the CIS, including Russia, authoritarian regimes were consolidated. So, it turns out that the continuation of assistance strengthens the economic and political strength of the established regime, feeding corruption. As a result, this assistance and the role of international financial institutions in the reform process [*v prodvizhenii reform*] once and for all discredit themselves.

One Kyrgyzstani human rights activist characterized the mood in late 2002, writing, "As many experts say, America with its much-vaunted democraticness [*khvalenaia demokratichnost'*], agreed to a deal with Akaev and now closes its eyes at his actions."[81]

This was part of a much broader post-Soviet trend with various local manifestations. In an ethnography of Altai neocommunists, Oushakine captures the tragedy experienced by a region marginalized in the 1990s. In addition to material deprivation,

[I]t was the theme of deception that channeled the motivation for political engagement ... As [Nikolai, an interlocutor] put it, apart from his personal experience, there was "another important thing" that influenced the formation of his political view during the Yeltsin era: "It was the impression that 'They' constantly lie on TV. That is to say, there was a huge discrepancy between official propaganda and the reality that surrounded us."[82]

In such a context, America and American values were no longer unambiguously virtuous. Critical voices coalesced in discourses that ran counter to the prevailing hegemonic one. One survey indicates that frustration with claims to democracy was already afoot by 1993, as "half of all respondents in Uzbekistan and almost two-thirds of Kazakhstani respondents supported 'any [political] system, as long as there is order.'"[83] By 1997, Central Asians were increasingly willing to express ambivalence or (less commonly) outright hostility toward to the US.[84] At the elite level, many Western scholars and policy advisors by the latter part of the decade spoke of "expert fatigue." Whereas in the past, they had been welcomed warmly, now there was on-the-ground resistance to their work.

To be clear: Central Asia was not suddenly engulfed by anti-Americanism. Opinion polls continued to show generally positive orientations toward the US. But by the middle of the 1990s,[85] the situation had become more complex; space had now opened for actors to benefit from a changed US image as they pursued their particular goals. A newly pluralized symbolic America presented new political possibilities.

Trending Downward

How might we capture this pattern more systematically? Because polling data directly on Central Asia are too spotty to be used in longitudinal fashion,[86] I instead use news coverage of the region to reconstruct local discourse about and local behaviors concerning the United States.

To record discourse and behavior regarding the United States, I coded every news item from each Thursday's Radio Free Europe / Radio Liberty (RFE/RL) *Newsline* from 1991 through 2001. About 7 percent of the more than 17,000 items coded describe an event in which a societal or governmental actor expresses an attitude about the United States. Thus, public statements, protest demonstrations, legislation pending or enacted in local parliaments,

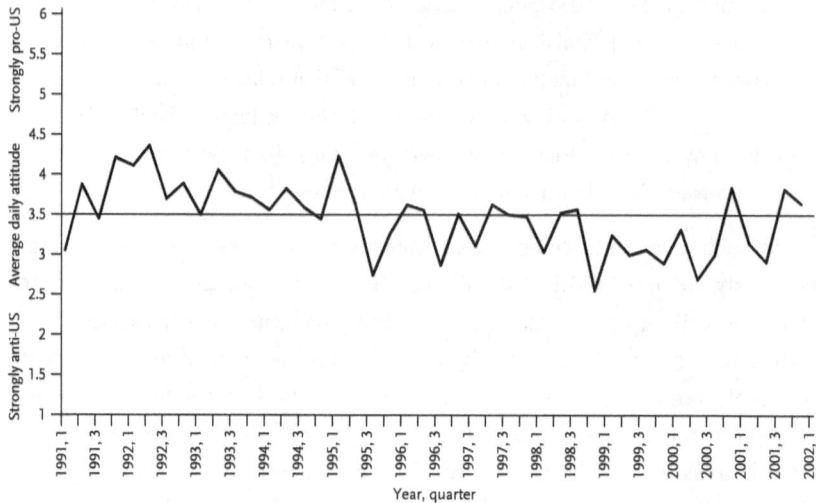

FIGURE 2. Behaviorally expressed attitudes about the United States, 1991–2002, ex-USSR. Source: Radio Free Europe / Radio Liberty *Newsline* daily reports.

news conferences, leafleting efforts, diplomatic negotiations, and a whole series of other reported events all contain information about how actors feel about the United States. I judged each relevant news item on a six-point scale; a 6 was strongly pro-US, 1 strongly anti-US. The daily scores were averaged and then aggregated into quarters. I coded not only news items on Central Asia but those on the entire ex-USSR.[87]

Three broad patterns emerge. First, the mid-1990s witnessed a general deterioration in attitudes about the United States; this was true both for societal and governmental actors. Second, while governments generally expressed more positive views of the United States, publics were more ambivalent. Third, this decline in attitudes about the United States occurred in the middle of the decade, preceding many of the factors usually assumed to cause changes in attitude. (I elaborate on this point below.)

Figure 2 covers all of post-Soviet space. Given the bluntness of the instrument, we should not read too much into specific changes, but the fact that attitudes about the United States experienced a decline in the middle of 1995 deserves note. From that point onward, the mean attitude scarcely rises above 3.5 (the neutral point) until 2000. There are reasons to believe that this was a significant change. As I detail below, most news reports cover governmental actors who usually prefer not to alienate the hegemon. Over the decade, the mean attitude expressed by governmental actors was 3.5 (versus a mean of 2.8 by societal actors). Any change that lasts (as in that from 1995 to 2000) likely underestimates the magnitude of attitude change experienced among broader swathes of the population.

Figure 3 compares the post-Soviet trend to that of Russia, on one hand, and the Central Asian states, on the other. Russia comes consistently lower than the post-Soviet region as a whole, while Central Asia comes higher. On the surface, it would seem that Russia was more anti-American and Central Asia more pro-American.[88] Table 1 helps us to make sense of the patterns.

Table 1, which arrays countries from the least to the most positive attitudes, shows that the RFE/RL dramatically underrepresented societal actors in its coverage. There were two main reasons for this. First, RFE/RL's Russia coverage was simply better. Russia was a still powerful former superpower that screamed out for press attention; moreover, its correspondents were better connected in Russia than they were outside Russia.

Second, especially before the rise of social media, government actors and the news they made were much easier to cover than the sometimes quiet

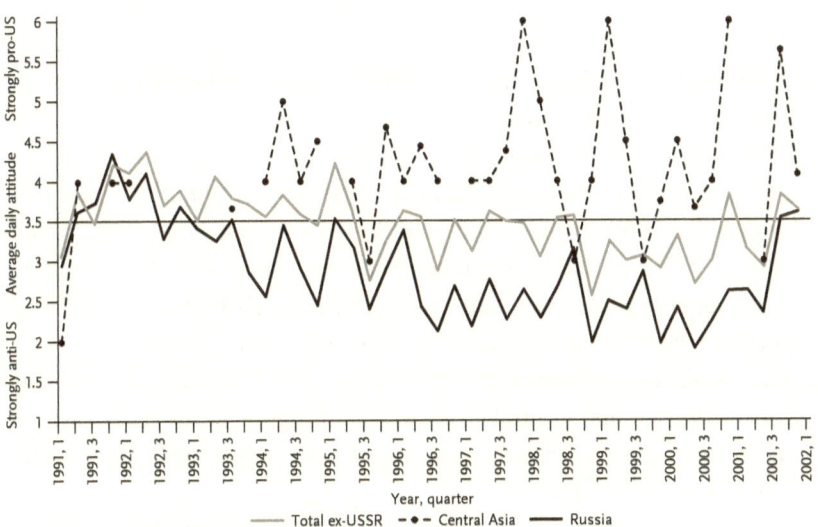

FIGURE 3. Behaviorally expressed attitudes about the United States, 1991–2002, comparisons. Source: Radio Free Europe / Radio Liberty *Newsline* daily reports.

TABLE 1. RFE/RL coverage, by country, with average attitude, 1991–2001

Country	Number of relevant cases[a]	Percent societal actors[b]	Average daily attitude
Belarus	45	20.00	2.36
Russia	707	15.13	2.84
Ukraine	90	13.33	3.87
Turkmenistan	13	0.00	4.00
Kazakhstan	38	13.16	4.20
Georgia	22	13.64	4.20
Armenia	30	3.33	4.28
Kyrgyzstan	12	16.67	4.33
Moldova	39	10.26	4.35
Uzbekistan	17	0.00	4.44
Azerbaijan	33	9.09	4.45
Tajikistan	10	0.00	4.60
Lithuania	68	5.88	4.63
Latvia	40	12.50	4.68
Estonia	49	4.08	5.04

[a] Of the more than 17,000 news items that were coded, 1,213 items contained a reference to the United States and an indication of a reaction to the US on the part of a local actor or actors.
[b] Societal actors include businesspeople, religious figures, intellectuals, NGO workers, and others without obvious ties to government.

developments occurring in broader societies. Thus, the better the coverage, the more likely societal voices were covered.

This underrepresentation of societal actors in reports on Central Asia underscores the nature of Central Asian political regimes. All of them were authoritarian, varying from the softer version in Kyrgyzstan to the sultanistic regime in Turkmenistan.[89] Social actors in these states were less mobilized and less likely to make news than were their counterparts in Russia. This was especially true in the 1990s, when Russia enjoyed greater political liberalism, and it remained true through the end of 2001 (the last year coded). When we compare Russian and Central Asian attitudes (figure 3), we are comparing Central Asian governmental attitudes with a more mixed bag of Russian governmental and societal attitudes.

Thus, the data on Russia are better than those on Central Asia, and we can use them as a proxy for Central Asian patterns, as long as we limit ourselves to changes over time within a given region. Based on the Russian data, two broad patterns become clear. First, we observe a decline in attitude about the United States that began in 1995 and continued through the end of the decade. The upsurge in pro-American attitudes in late 2001 coincides with an outpouring of sympathy after the September 11, 2001, attacks.[90] Subsequent analysis suggests that this was temporary.[91] Second, the timing also suggests that America's deteriorating image had little to do with US foreign policy, which was decidedly anemic in the region throughout the 1990s.

This is where many analyses end—with a firm if premature conclusion that because perceptions of the US are not simple and direct reactions to what the US does, they must not matter. In fact, ambivalence in the aggregate presents novel possibilities for social mobilization in concrete instances, as subsequent chapters detail.

Sedimentation

To appreciate more fully how this change to symbolic America occurred, let us return to our geologic metaphor of sedimentation. More than other post-Soviet contexts, Central Asia experienced Russian influence without serious interruption after the USSR's collapse. Central Asia had been catapulted to independence; the nationalist movements that pushed for sovereign statehood and decolonization in other contexts were much weaker in Central Asia, producing no great rift between Soviet-era practices and post-Soviet ones. What Mark Beissinger refers to as a post-socialist habitus is thus particularly apt for Central Asia under post-socialism.[92] Moreover, to the extent that Central Asian societies did drift from the Russian orbit, the alternatives were either distant (the United States, Western Europe, Japan, and South Korea) or lacking in resonance (China, South Asia, Iran, the Arab Middle East). In short, Central Asians in general continued to be influenced monumentally more by Russia than by any single other state.

Though consistent, Russian influence was also a source of change, especially because Central Asians continued to receive the lion's share of their information about global events from Russian media. As long as Russian interpretations deviated little from those produced in other world regions, this had little discernible impact. However, the Russian press began to change its coverage of American influence, beginning with the NATO bombings of Serb positions in Kosovo in 1999, which just preceded NATO's celebration of its fiftieth anniversary. The Russian media in 2000 projected additional, profound humiliation in 1999 when the parliaments of Azerbaijan and Georgia ratified the Baku-Ceyhan pipeline, a project that would bypass Russian oil export routes.[93]

While every Central Asian state pushed for more indigenous programming, especially in titular (i.e., non-Russian) languages,[94] the reality is that Russian television and radio, as well as selective Russian rebroadcasts of European and American programs, never exited Central Asia's information space. We lack good data on what media Central Asians were consuming in the 1990s, but the generally low quality of indigenous programming did little to attract viewers and listeners. By contrast, Russian programming was generally of better quality and considerably more popular.[95]

Of the Central Asian states, Kazakhstan was in the best position to forge its own media direction. Yet, in spite of Kazakhstan's relative affluence abetted by petrodollars, Russia's influence showed no signs of abating as late as the 2010s. Among other challenges, weak terrestrial signals often forced Kazakhstanis to seek satellite alternatives (which brought Russian programming).[96] Even a strong push to develop an alternative for news, which resulted in the First Channel Eurasia, ended up being 20 percent owned by the Russian government and included many rebroadcasts from Russian state TV (especially its First Channel).[97] Social media services thrived in the Russian market before Kazakhstani firms could develop their own versions; Russian firms came to dominate Kazakhstan's market. In August 2012 the top three sites used by Kazakhstanis were *Moi Mir* (mail.ru), *Odnoklassniki*, and *Vkontakte*—all hosting in the Russian language and based in the *.ru* domain.[98] While we cannot trace the specific content of information that travels via these media pathways, it is clear that they represented an important influence on how Central Asians imagined the United States. What is true for Kazakhstan, with its relatively stronger potential for engineering a break from Russian media influence, was doubly true for the other Central Asian states.

Shifts to symbolic America seeped into Central Asia not only via broadcast and online media. They also were the product of more mundane interactions that animated a conservative backlash. Many socially prominent figures began to discuss the moral decline they perceived as accompanying the much-changed political and social order of the 1990s. As V. N. Ushakov notes, "The West in the eyes of many devout Muslims is associated with debauchery [*razvrat*] and permissiveness [*vsedozvolennost'*]."[99] Among them were foreign coreligionists who brought printed literature about Islamic norms and proper codes of conduct.[100] Protestant missionaries also found fertile ground for their proselytizing in part because of the rapid decline in public morality.[101] Interestingly, as Mathijs Pelkmans describes, missionaries could distance themselves from other Western actors, including humanitarian workers, because citizens in Kyrgyzstan widely assumed that Westerners came to Central Asia with ulterior motives.[102] Nationalists intent on protecting their national culture against the onslaught of globalizing influences offered similar protestations about creeping cultural Americanization.[103]

All of this amounted to a complex process of sedimentation, in which some influences washed away while others were assimilated by their new environments. Some continued to be marked as foreign and abnormal, while others became assimilated as native and normal.

The process of sedimentation thus shifts symbolic America, altering the raw material available to social mobilizers. The change to any given context may occur slowly, complexly, and in hard-to-predict ways. But this fact does not make such a change any less sociologically or politically important. Symbolic America may not be set aflame, as some depictions of anti-Americanism would have it, but its influence remains palpable, observable, and crucial to consider.

2

ISLAMIST TRAJECTORIES

THE SLOW-MOVING CHANGES to Central Asia that occurred in the 1990s provided raw material for social mobilizers in the decades that followed. This is the first of three empirical chapters that trace the arcs of Central Asia's social movements, considering how activists used (or failed to use) changing material from symbolic America.[1] It addresses Islamist trajectories, which I deliberately use in the plural to emphasize their diversity and to call into question received wisdom about Islamism and anti-Americanism.

In Central Asia, publics generally considered themselves Muslim, but this rarely contained a political dimension. Before political Islam as a mode of engagement and an ideology was available, self-professed Muslims strongly tended to political quietism. In the meantime, public attitudes about the US began to decline. As I will detail, this sequencing matters. Whereas received wisdom holds that rising Islamism precedes and in fact causes anti-Americanism, the Central Asian examples speak to the opposite possibility: increasing ambivalence about symbolic America empowers certain kinds of Islamist actors.

The chapter proceeds in three steps. First, I introduce a plural understanding of Islamism, recognizing that whatever theological consensus the pious might imagine, real-world contexts witness a striking variety of ways that religion and politics intersect. Second, I consider the growth of Islamic piety in the region since the Soviet collapse, arguing against a simplistic notion that greater piety necessarily produces a politics inflected by religion. Finally, I examine three Islamist movements—Hizb ut-Tahrir (HT), the Islamic Renaissance Party of Tajikistan (IRPT), and the Islamic Movement of Uzbekistan (IMU)—which use the changing American image in a striking range of ways. The examples help to underscore that, while America's image matters in Central Asia, how precisely its significance becomes *political* depends on image-making efforts at play in each movement.

Islam and Islamisms

If we begin with theology, we might assume that the Islam's emphasis on unity (*tahwid*) or five pillars (*arkan al-Islam*) or God's revelation in the holy Quran would make all Islamic movements genetically similar. In fact, the opposite occurs. When truth resides in perfect sacred texts, when basic behavioral benchmarks define piety, and when a faith is declared indivisible, there is no need for a privileged class of intermediaries between God and the faithful. Nearly any Muslim can claim religious knowledge and may even issue religious judgments (fatwa), including those with political implications. This produces a plethora of competing views about what a good Muslim should do in political life and the ever-present potential for an effervescent discourse about religion and politics in majority-Muslim contexts. Posited theological unity ends up with real-world diversity.

Some observers nonetheless insist that this theorized theological unity matters more than institutional diversity; at root, Islamists—the claim goes—all share the goal of creating an Islamic order. For Mehdi Mozaffari, Islamism "is a religious ideology with a holistic interpretation of Islam whose final aim is the conquest of the world by all means."[2] In this view, the telos is shared; Islamists differ only in their tactics. For Igor Dobaev, "radicals" act differently only because they face different practical possibilities for "penetrating political structures, and especially of the regime and the law enforcement structures."[3] An Islamist who seems pragmatic is in fact being deceitful. A sheep is supposedly never just a sheep. In a world with wolves, sheep simply cannot exist.

Such a perspective obscures more than it reveals. First, from their earliest incarnations in real-world contexts, Muslim communities constructed a wide range of relationships between politics and religion. Ira Lapidus describes how the rise of Hanbalism in the ninth century forged a separation between power and piety: "The umma itself was now an independent and differentiated entity shaped by religious beliefs—a social body whose continued existence was no longer bound up with its nominal chief." In short, "Islam had . . . passed beyond the age of [its] primal unity."[4]

Second, Islamists differ—even vehemently so—over what an Islamic order would entail. They disagree over what kinds of links with non-Islamic orders and principles are to be countenanced. Like those harboring secular end-goals, some Islamists feel great urgency and prescribe swift action, while others seek steady and incremental change. The possibility for incrementalism was embedded in early Islamic thought. As Charles Butterworth writes, the "goal [in such thought] is not to urge radical change or to cajole actual rulers to act better by offering advice about how to rule, but to show what goals are to be pursued by a good ruler and what conduces to the achievement of those goals."[5] Moral injunctions logically presuppose absolute ends, but if we are interested in actual politics, we should consider how such injunctions are—or are not—acted upon.

Third, decisions initially taken for tactical reasons can change movements. One need only consider the shift to more moderate politics of Turkish Islamist parties and the Egyptian Muslim Brotherhood and Wasat Party to appreciate that pragmatism can develop a profound momentum.[6] Abstract theological pronouncements rarely fade to black, but their practical application leaves much room for a contingent politics.[7]

I consider Islamists to be *movements or groups that promote Islam and view political action as necessary to their efforts*. Islamism is therefore *a political ideology that views Islam as a guide for a just polity*.[8] Islamists vary in their views of appropriate political action, as well as in their specific interpretations of Islam. Within Central Asia, Hizb ut-Tahrir was a self-described nonviolent movement that sought to create in the region an Islamic caliphate largely through explicitly political propaganda work. The Islamic Movement of Uzbekistan was a network of individuals determined to oust the Karimov regime in Uzbekistan by using violence. The Islamic Renaissance Party of Tajikistan sought to reinsert Islamic piety and protect freedom of conscience for Muslims (and other religious individuals) via liberal democratic political institutions.

As elsewhere, Islam in Central Asia might be one but Islamisms are many.[9]

Islamic Revival and Political Islam

In a trivial sense, the emergence of Islamism in Central Asia after the Soviet collapse was inevitable. Given the official atheism of a state that had aspired to total control, piety was bound to increase. Moreover, given the difficulty of any kind of overt political contestation in the Soviet period, levels of political activism of all sorts were also likely to rise.[10]

While few deny that Central Asia witnessed rising public expressions of religiosity, evaluating its magnitude is more complicated.[11] Mosque construction, changes in dress, and positive answers about religion given to pollsters are all fraught indicators of religiosity; they tell us that religion was an increasingly normal marker of cultural background and social life, but whether this meant actual piety is a different matter.[12] Moreover, self-reported piety did not necessarily predict political viewpoints in early surveys of Central Asia.[13] Any visit to Central Asia involving a range of conversations with secular individuals would reveal the fear: strange dress, unusual religious customs, and overt demonstrations of piety were assumed to be clarion calls to radical politics. Alarmist analyses made the allure of radicalism seem irresistible.[14] And the paranoid imagination of the region's authoritarian presidents fed the beast: Salafis and Wahhabis lurked in every inscrutable corner of post-Soviet society.[15]

In fact, while political Islam grew in importance in the 1990s in Central Asia, the extent of its influence should not be overstated. First, the region's Hanafi tradition historically emphasized accommodation to the existing political order rather than confrontation with it. Political quiescence was the longstanding norm, and seventy years of Soviet rule had largely reinforced it.[16]

Second, the region had been deeply transformed by the Soviet experience (in spite of occasional claims to the contrary),[17] resulting in an overwhelmingly secular—even proudly atheist—normal worldview.[18] Some scholars emphasize how much this secular worldview had descended from its Stalin-era high-water mark by the 1970s and 1980s.[19] They correctly cite the fact that post-Stalin Central Asia experienced greater de facto freedom to discuss and practice pre-Soviet traditions, including religious ones. Moreover, this relative liberalization occurred at a particular world-historical moment when a global revival of Islamic piety was underway. Thus, the region started to be exposed—if in modest ways—to religious currents novel for Central Asia.

Martha Brill Olcott and Bakhtiar Babajanov discuss crucial Soviet-era Islamic figures whose thinking would much later affect the later theological and political trajectories of the post-Soviet period.[20] Vitalii Naumkin views this Soviet-era underground Islamic piety in the form of *hujra* circles as the direct forerunner of radical movements that would come later.[21] He finds an irony: Soviet authorities saw an ally in Salafi puritanical Islam against an apparently greater evil: locally resonant traditional Hanafi Islam that was deemed "anti-Soviet" because it linked up with nationalist and pan-Turkic sentiment.[22]

It is true that a discursive space for religious scholarship had emerged, but we should not read incipient debates about the faith anachronistically. Official atheism was still dominant, resonant, and inescapable, and the partial resurgence of piety occurred amidst limited information. Figures who would much later become prominent theologians were not on an inexorable path to radicalism; it is unlikely that their religious or political sensibilities were fully developed and coherent. It is far more likely that their thinking was in flux and theologically inconsistent. Perhaps this is why debates about whether these figures were at root Hanafi, Wahhabi, or Salafi are so inconclusive.

Nevertheless, did theological discourse affect wider publics? It is again tempting to read history backwards: when the Soviet state later lost its legitimacy, and space opened for the freer practice of religion, Muslim Central Asians "naturally" expressed their true, legitimate politico-religious inner preferences. Yet, it is a peculiar syllogism to conclude that the "underground" is the site of everything authentic and resonant, while the "aboveground" is the site of everything artificial and hollow. Central Asians were like others who, in the context of state socialism, falsified their public preferences,[23] but the broad-based nostalgia for the Soviet period that would emerge by the late 1990s reminds us that people engage in multiple performances, public and private, in ways that belie simple dichotomies like authentic/artificial and resonant/hollow.[24] In short, while expressions of religious piety had become more common by the late Soviet period, this was the result of lesser degrees of state control rather than an "organic" manifestation of the "authentic" Central Asian self.

A similar misconception about the supposed naturalness of rising Islamic piety sometimes emerges from discussions of the Soviet-Afghan War. Ahmed Rashid writes:

> After the Red Army invaded Afghanistan in 1979, thousands of Central Asians were drafted into the Red Army to fight the Afghan mujahideen. Central

Asian Muslims were thus reintroduced to the *umma*, or Islamic world community, through a war against their co-religionists, and many were deeply affected by the dedication of their opponents. Hundreds of Uzbek and Tajik Muslims travelled secretly to Pakistan and Saudi Arabia to study in madrasahs or to train as guerrilla fighters against the Soviets in Afghanistan.[25]

This is logically plausible, but is it accurate? First, to assume that Central Asians felt a primordial affinity to a transnational *umma* is strange, given the profound secularization of the Soviet period. Second, Rashid leaves us grasping for evidence that "many" (how many?) were "deeply" affected (by what metric?), leading hundreds of secret travelers (to whom he had exclusive access) to fight the Soviets. The war's effect on ordinary Central Asians is a research topic that currently lacks clear answers, but the bottom line is clear: we do ourselves no analytic favors by conflating piety and political activism.[26]

Third, we should not mistake Islamists' visibility for popular support. Start with Tajikistan, in which self-proclaimed Islamists were a major party in a civil war (1992–96). As a fighting force, they were reasonably remarkable, buoyed by an inflow of transnational mercenaries and support from the Taliban in Afghanistan.[27] The degree of popular support, however, is harder to know. In Tajikistan, "Islam" was a catchall category used to voice opposition to the Soviet- and later Russian-backed regime of Imomali Rakhmonov. With a 1997 peace settlement in which the IRPT was allowed to participate in electoral politics, public support for political Islam was low. In parliamentary elections in 2000, the IRPT received 7.5 percent of the vote, which translated into two seats. As I discuss below, this poor performance was in part a function of repression by the Rakhmon regime, but not only.[28] Politically oriented Islam had limited resonance in the 1990s.

For its part, Uzbekistan was the site of a strongly secular and deeply repressive anti-Islam campaign from the moment Karimov assumed power in 1989. To be sure, the Karimov regime regularly referred to incidents that it took as evidence of extremist Islamist activism.[29] For example, the regime reported an attempt on the president's life in February 1999, laying blame with former members of the Uzbek branch of the Islamic Renaissance Party, Juma Namangani and Tahir Yoldash. Namangani and Yoldash would later create the Islamic Movement of Uzbekistan.[30] The IMU in summer 1999 seized four Japanese geologists and eight Kyrgyzstani soldiers as hostages, taking advantage of porous boundaries with Kyrgyzstan. In summer 2000, a similar incident occurred, with IMU fighters apparently setting up camps in neighboring Tajikistan.[31] Yet, the picture is deeply complicated because radicalization is as much the *result* of Karimov's indiscriminate attacks on the pious as it is their cause.[32]

In Kyrgyzstan, political Islam enjoyed limited appeal through the mid-2000s. It had some audience among ethnic Uzbeks residing in the Kyrgyzstani portion of the Ferghana Valley; these communities had experienced marginalization under the Askar Akaev regime in Kyrgyzstan and enjoyed no help from neighboring Uzbekistan.[33] Elsewhere in Kyrgyzstan, politically oriented Islam was extremely rare; as in Kazakhstan and much of Turkmenistan, the nomadic and seminomadic traditions meant that—in the 1990s at least—apolitical Islamic practices were considered authentic and legitimate, while political ones were considered foreign and illegitimate.[34]

Islamism had thus become visible as a force influencing political dynamics, but much of its impact emerged because the region's leaders routinely exaggerated its import, in a series of self-fulfilling prophesies.[35] Uzbekistan's Karimov in particular sought to legitimate his rule by citing an Islamic threat, jailing thousands of political prisoners in the course of events. Even in more remote Kazakhstan, President Nursultan Nazarbaev painted himself as a guarantor of stability in the face of transnational Islamism.[36] The fact that Kazakhstan would in the 2010s experience small-scale terrorist attacks does not change the fact that Islam in the 1990s was rarely political in Central Asia.

In short, Islamism's rise might have been inevitable in a trivial sense, but the more important question is why Islamism took the forms that it did. My argument is simple: we cannot account for the forms of Central Asian Islamism in the 1990s and 2000s without reference to the interplay between local concerns, regional framings, and the master frame of anti-Americanism (or its ideological cousins: anti-Westernism, anti-globalism, and anti-Semitism). "Master frames," write David Snow and Robert Benford, "are to movement-specific collective action frames as paradigms are to finely tuned theories. Master frames are generic; specific collective action frames are derivative."[37] Operating at a higher level of abstraction, such frames have the potential to link disparate "small" causes, grievances, and struggles into a "larger" set of causes, grievances, and struggles. This marriage allowed some movements to overcome their initial weakness to assume broader social and political significance.

The trajectories of each of Central Asia's three most significant political Islamic movements changed as a result of their relative reliance on mass support and their initial evaluation of the United States. When images of the United States in the public imagination shifted, this presented enormous opportunities for Hizb ut-Tahrir. The same image change produced moderate liabilities for the IRPT and weak opportunities for the IMU.

Hizb ut-Tahrir

During the Soviet period, Hizb ut-Tahrir (HT) had no presence in Central Asia. By the early 2000s, it was widely recognized as the single most powerful Islamist movement of the region. The story of its emergence in Central Asia has been told elsewhere.[38] Here, I emphasize three interrelated points: (1) HT was a mass-based organization with deep reliance on image-making efforts; (2) its approach was flexible, attempting to bridge to other frames, such as those that were Soviet legacies; and (3) HT benefited from the deteriorating image of the United States.

That HT was a mass-based movement might seem counterintuitive. The organization had a cell structure, in which each cell (usually comprised of five people) played clearly defined (and limited) roles and abided by clearly defined (and limited) parameters for behavior and communication. This structure minimized unnecessary interaction, reducing risk to the overall organization in the event that a cell was compromised. Thus, avoiding undue attention, its organizational form mimicked that of other conspiratorial groups, including terrorist ones.[39] Indeed, HT eschewed the kinds of mass demonstrations of public support—like street protests—that we typically associate with social movements.

If one looks beyond its organizational structure, a fuller picture develops. Individuals in cells were linked to the larger movement *solely* by HT ideology. In such a structure, the fullness of normal human relations was reduced to the single dimension of communicating, elaborating, developing, and deeply imbibing this common—if monumentally underspecified—ideology.[40] Artificially cutting members off from each other, HT's ideology replaced organic, face-to-face encounters with the propagation of images and ideas.

Such image-making efforts brought material benefits. With the region mired in poverty exacerbated by the industrial and infrastructural decline of the 1990s, would-be activists were smart to tap sources of foreign assistance. As HT required little actual knowledge of Islam (a point to which I return below), individuals could parade their deep commitment by adopting HT positions on global political issues. In short, although it would be a mistake to assume that activism is the simple result of financial inducements, presenting oneself as a politically active Muslim to a global audience did have benefits.[41]

HT claimed that its goal was to use nonviolent approaches to restore a just and truly Islamic government in the form of a caliphate. This would proceed in stages. First, Islam would be accepted broadly by the general public. Second, the public would propagate the faith and its requirements. Finally, this would result in a grassroots revolution that would restore the caliphate. Utopian, expressly committed to nonviolence, and disdainful of existing forms of politics, HT occupied a peculiar niche among Islamist groups.

HT also advanced a crystal-clear negative evaluation of the United States. Since HT had been born and raised in the 1950s in a Middle East experiencing profound Western influence simultaneously with a global discourse demanding decolonization, HT's ideology was deeply infused by a spirit of defiance against the West, a conspiratorial approach, and the promise of a better future.[42] As far as HT was concerned, America's support of Israel made it the inheritor of European colonial rule. Like its imperial forebearers, the US was bent on a strategy of divide and rule. Naturally, only cross-cultural Muslim unity could fend off such American encroachments. The way forward was clear: transcend cultural and sectarian divisions among Muslims and push back aggressively against the United States. A just form of government would result.

Radical ideologies are legion, so why did HT's gain traction in Central Asia? If HT's "frames become popular because they draw their legitimacy from the Quran and other Islamic sacred texts,"[43] this would not distinguish their frames from those of Islamic competitors. Similarly, it cannot be that "the notion of governance according to sharia is deep-rooted in the collective subconsciousness due to the region's long Islamic tradition,"[44] given the marginal place that sharia occupied in Soviet and post-Soviet Central Asia. Finally, while it *could* be that "people join Hizb ut-Tahrir because they believe in its ideology; for them it is a religious duty before God to join an Islamic group and thus gain salvation,"[45] this assumes that Central Asians have religious commitments that are already fully formed rather than in the process of *becoming*. In reality, the history of state-driven atheism had deeply changed individuals' relation to faith.

Any convincing explanation of HT's resonance must consider timing. Not only did HT have an attractive mass orientation and an increasingly resonant negative evaluation of the United States; it also arrived in Central Asia at a particular moment. Specifically, HT arrived when Central Asians were experimenting with forms of political and spiritual engagement, seeking to figure out their novel and deteriorating condition via categories and logics that were commonsensical for being familiar.

HT's frames provided the promise of salvation when political and economic circumstances seemed to have conspired against its members. In this sense, its proponents were like other postwar Islamists. Path-defining Islamist scholar-activists like al-Banna and Maududi had a broad fascination with communist-type parties, at least for their organization and tactics.[46] Sayyid Qutb, one of the early inspirations behind radical Islamist actors, offered words reminiscent of Lenin's vanguardism:

> It is therefore necessary that Islam's theoretical foundation-belief materialize in the form of an organized and active group from the very beginning. It is necessary that this group separate itself from the *jahili* [religiously ignorant] society, becoming independent and distinct from the active and organized *jahili* society whose aim is to block Islam. The center of this new group should be a new leadership, the leadership which first came in the person of the Prophet—peace be on him—himself, and after him was delegated to those who strove for bringing people back to God's sovereignty, His authority and His laws.[47]

Likewise, HT members were privileged to join a vanguard enlightened and empowered to effect radical change, while the rest of Central Asian society could at best follow as it sought a way out of limited economic opportunity and authoritarian rule.[48]

HT's frames were thus unabashedly utopian at a time when the exigencies of everyday life presented towering challenges.[49] They resonated with Soviet-era promises and logics.

> Its discourse about the liberation of (Muslim) masses, the establishment of a just society, and the misdeeds of Western powers has capitalized on decades of similar Marxist-Leninist phraseology. Furthermore, there are some

striking parallels between the universality of Soviet foreign policy goals (i.e., worldwide propagation of communism, establishment of a global communist society) and Hizb ut-Tahrir's goals (i.e., worldwide spread of Islam, restoration of [the] Caliphate).[50]

HT rarely delved into specifics, but when it did, it invoked the social safety net, full employment, and free healthcare.[51] Its emphasis on the cultural unity of Central Asians also echoed the transcendent identity of *homo Sovieticus*.[52] This utopianism, even millenarianism, made many in officialdom extremely nervous.[53]

HT frames expressed a firm commitment to nonviolence at a time when violence of various sorts had become commonplace in everyday life.[54] HT would combat violence with nonviolence, thus maintaining the moral (and religious) high ground.[55] Similarly, it would work to end non-Muslims' violent exploitation of Muslims, decolonizing social and political institutions, and indeed the very minds of Muslims themselves. This harkened back to Soviet ideology that promised to free oppressed peoples from the clutches of exploitative Western capitalism.

The effectiveness of HT frames stemmed in part from their familiar utopianism, but this was not enough. Also essential was HT's anti-American master frame. Central Asians were not struggling in isolation; all Muslims were linked via a global and peaceful struggle against an unjust American order. This frame did not subsume Central Asians' concerns in global ones, effacing their legitimacy and disrespecting the specifics of the Central Asian condition. Rather, it legitimated them by producing broader imaginings that empowered and scaled up Central Asians' grievances.[56] Further, it allowed Central Asians to be overtly political under authoritarianism. Where their ire might normally have been reserved for the local regime, the frame invited much of that anger to be expressed globally. There was safety in numbers, safety in abstractions, and safety in lodging blame with a distant hegemon.

It might be tempting to assume that HT's anti-American rhetoric began to resonate with the run-up to the globally unpopular Iraq war in 2003.[57] In fact, while 9/11 and the Iraq War gave HT's message greater palpability and therefore greater credence, HT's appeal had begun to increase well before 2001. As chapter 1 showed, ambivalence about the United States distinctly *preceded* the major US foreign policy changes of the 2000s. Local concerns in Central Asia emerged first, and the global message of HT gave resonant voice to them.[58]

Adeeb Khalid summarizes: "People see [HT's] global message through the prism of local concerns."⁵⁹

Let us have a closer look at HT's anti-American master frames, which clearly expressed defiance against the West, and especially against the United States and America's assumed proxy Israel, at a time when the United States' power was uncontested.⁶⁰ Igor Rotar' describes leaflets from the Ferghana Valley in 2000 that stated: "The crazy [beshenaia] attack of the Jewish infidel Islam Karimov and the organizations of his state against the party that calls for Islam, Hizb ut-Tahrir [protiv prizyvaiushchei k islamu partii] does not weaken. . . . Muslims, do not lose your spirit!"⁶¹ Emmanuel Karagiannis has assembled a wide array of materials:

- A leaflet from Uzbekistan in July 2000 calls the US "the greatest enemy of Islam and Muslims."
- A leaflet from Uzbekistan, December 2000 decries American propaganda, contending, "Millions of dollars have been invested to build, not tens, but hundreds of colleges and lecture halls, and to publish hundreds and thousands of books in order to spread the Western lifestyle and mentality."
- A leaflet from Uzbekistan from July 2002 states, "Only one thing can explain Karimov's shamelessness and hypocrisy, and that is not only that he is a Jew but that he is an insolent and evil Jew, who hates you and your Deen."
- A leaflet that appeared in the Uzbek language in October 2002 explains, "Who fills his pocket and which states' budget benefits from the profit of sales of gold, oil and gas that are excavated by American and European companies? These natural resources belong to Muslims, but the profit is not shared among them."
- A leaflet from Tajikistan, June 2003, claims that Westerners "establish ties with schools and higher education institutions, set up exchange programs, under which they send children of the Islamic Ummah to their countries, poisoning their minds with nationalism and patriotism."⁶²

Similarly, Igor Savin cites an HT leaflet from southern Kazakhstan: "Instead of a pliant leadership, people who support God's *sharia* will come, restore the religion of Islam and necessarily will spread it throughout the world. And instead of those who help the Jews, they will raise a unified *caliphate*."⁶³

This stance was unambiguous even before the major US foreign-policy shifts of the early 2000s, though the presence of US troops in Afghanistan (and at supply and transit bases in the region) gave it greater palpability. On 12 September 2001, leaflets glorifying the terrorist acts appeared in a university in Bishkek, Kyrgyzstan.[64] Emmanuel Karagiannis notes:

- A leaflet from Uzbekistan in December 2001 states, "The land of Uzbekistan, which served in the past as a military base for Russian troops, now has become a ground for American to attack Islam and Muslims."
- An audio compact disc probably from 2002 or 2003, entitled *A Cry of Imam from Uzbekistan*, produced by Hizb ut-Tahrir Britain, offers, "This is a struggle and clash that involves you automatically, even if you choose not to take part in this struggle . . . for it is apparent, more than ever, that there is a war against Islam and there now are two camps: America and Western nations stand in one and the entire Muslim ummah in the other."[65]

The point is simple: a movement with a negative evaluation of the United States that was fundamentally reliant on image-making in its activities was poised to gain strength. Because of this dynamic, by 2010 HT had become a crucial organization with the potential to alter domestic politics across the region.

If this makes sense on a macroscopic scale, what happened for individuals? Were they successfully recruited because they learned what the United States did and represented? Did hatred of the US deepen involvement with HT? Recruitment and participation in social movements are multidimensional processes that should not be reduced to one factor,[66] and the same goes for Islamist movements.[67] But did the fragmentation of opinion about the US facilitate these processes?

Available evidence suggests that it did.[68] Based on his interviews, Savin describes this recruitment moment: "The recognition that on the other side of the earth people are battling [srazhaiutsia] under similar slogans leads one to think that this struggle of a global—and therefore righteous [pravednyi]—nature."[69] At the same time, HT adherents "attuned their da'awa [proselytizing] to local 'folk' Islamic traditions,"[70] rather than being dismissive of widespread pre-Islamic practices, such as shrine worship. Similarly, HT adherents did not prohibit the mixing of sexes or handshakes as a form of greeting between the sexes, since to do so would be to dismiss Soviet-era behaviors.[71] Recruitment occurred through the most mundane channels: "Membership is usually expanded directly through a loose association of close friends, family members and relatives, mimicking traditional social networks. Indeed, meetings are often held under the guise of traditional weekly meetings of men, who share food, either at home or in a restaurant."[72]

My own interviews and conversations in southern Kyrgyzstan with HT members were consistent with these findings. One interviewee described his epiphany at realizing that he was "a part of something larger" (chast' chego-to bol'shego), and one recruiter, when asked if he mentioned the United States in his recruitment efforts, replied, "Well, we *do* tell them the truth" (Dovodim do nikh pravdu).[73] In the meantime, the recruiter emphasized (to his Canadian-American interlocutor) that he admired the United States for its religious freedom, only accusing it of hypocrisy in foreign affairs and objecting to the compact between Central Asia's authoritarian strongmen and American power. His concerns were essentially local, expressed in global terms.[74]

Islamic Renaissance Party of Tajikistan

The trajectory of the Islamic Renaissance Party of Tajikistan (IRPT) reminds us how varied political Islam can be.[75] Unlike HT and the IMU, the IRPT would emerge from the Tajik Civil War with a positive evaluation of the United States. Unlike HT, which overwhelmingly relied on image-making, and the IMU, which engaged in weak image-making efforts, the IRPT relied on image-making to a moderate degree. As we shall see, these two factors created a moderate liability for the IRPT to pursue its political agenda within Tajikistan. In October 2015, the IRPT, which had been a crucial actor forging the political settlement ending the Tajik Civil War in 1997, was declared a terrorist organization and banned by Tajik authorities. While symbolic America is not responsible for the increasing repression by the Tajikistani regime, shifts in images of the United States did hamper the party's ability to survive in a difficult political environment.

The Early IRPT

The IRPT began as an offshoot of the Soviet-era All-Union Islamic Renaissance Party, which had been founded in 1990 in Astrakhan, Russia. As the

Soviet Union's slow disintegration began to accelerate, politics shifted increasingly from Moscow to the republics. From its creation in October 1990, the Tajik branch was the most active of the branches and ultimately would become the only legal Islamic party in ex-Soviet space.

Before the civil war began in 1992, the IRPT was less a party than a movement whose leaders were "adhering to a rather broad religious agenda striving to reestablish their idea of a Sunni-Hanafi normativity among the Muslims in the Tajik SSR."[76] Its platform forwarded a socially conservative, broad, vague, and inclusive appeal to Islamic and Tajik values. Its leaders clearly disavowed any notion of an Islamic state or sharia law, instead proclaiming their commitment to electoral democracy.[77] Its main message was that the atheist Soviet order was anti-Islam and therefore ill suited to the flourishing of an authentic Tajik Muslim identity.[78] There was also a clear regional dimension. The IRPT stood against the northern Khujandi elites, who disproportionately ruled Soviet-era Tajikistan and its early post-Soviet incarnation.[79] Overlaying these other principles was a regular reference to liberal principles of rights and freedoms.[80] The party's charter laid out, among other things, the goal of fostering a "political awakening and the realization of the right of every Muslim to build his life on the basis of the Quran and Sunna."[81]

Aside from its orientation against Soviet power, the party had symbolic America partially in its sights, and its early ideology can best be described as ambivalent about the West. On the one hand, its leaders recognized that the West created the modern world and that Muslims must learn to adapt to Western values.[82] On the other hand, they expressed clear concern about the extent to which American universalism in fact promoted American political and economic dominance in this world order.[83] Having said this, for the most part the West was notable for its absence in this early period. Regarding the party newspaper *Najot*, Olivier Roy writes:

> Interestingly enough, there was also a small attack against the United States—articles complained that Islamist movements were misunderstood by the West, which had dubbed them "fundamentalist" and "extremist," and had used double standards as far as democracy was concerned. No articles appeared condemning the U.S. presence in the Gulf; strangely, the only article on the Gulf dealt with the idea that the participation of women in the armed forces is not against Islamic tradition. This article also noted the high number of American women serving as troops. One of the few articles mentioning

current conflicts where other Muslims have been oppressed—namely, Bosnia-Herzegovina, Palestine, and Lebanon—placed responsibility on the "communist system," which, although collapsed, was compared to a "scorpion with seven tails."[84]

Civil war has a way of shifting the political and discursive ground. The IRPT played a political and combat role, attracting individual Tajiks to the banner of the United Tajik Opposition (UTO) for a wide variety of reasons. For some, it was to join a regional, patronage-based movement pursuing the liberalization of politics against the ruling Khujandi elite. For others, it was an outlet for armed struggle at a moment of severe economic decline. For still others, it was about Islamic piety and religious freedom.

While all sides were implicated in civil war violence, narratives after the war about the supposedly destabilizing potential of Islamist actors gained traction, in part because of the Soviet-era depictions of the so-called Islamist threat.[85] In actual fact, the IRPT's 1999 charter made no mention of an Islamic state and was entirely consistent with the ideas it forwarded throughout the civil war, in spite of accounts that mistakenly claim that the party tactically hid its true intentions.[86] Nor would party members after the civil war have any necessary interest in forging ties with militants from Afghanistan, Pakistan, or Iran, simply because they once had found themselves in exile in these places.[87]

In spite of what some might assume about Islamist political parties, not only did the IRPT come to support democracy, but it proposed a strong separation of religion and state based largely on an American, rather than a European, model. Some date this to 1991, when leaders supported "a democratic state ruled by law, a government which the nation would trust and which would include representatives of different political forces,"[88] or what one observer called a "government of national trust."[89] The leading expert on the IRPT's evolution characterizes the party's post–civil war agenda as following the official line "in which political pluralism, democracy, 'peace,' and vague Islamic values are conjured but never explicitly defined."[90]

Part of the UTO, the IRPT was initially a major actor in the peace settlement. Being in government, even as a junior player allocated 30 percent of seats in the parliament, shifted the party toward pragmatic politics. If some citizens were nervous about religion-based political parties, the IRPT sought to reassure them with its platform mentioning Islam only once among party objectives: "The development of Islamic values, as well as national and human values, among the people of Tajikistan."[91] Although it remained unclear what the IRPT had in mind by "Islamic" as separate from "national" or "human," it was clear that this was no radical ideology. In fact, by the early 2000s the IRPT looked like an ordinary national parliamentary party.[92]

The IRPT's evaluation of the United States was positive for the latter's commitment to religious freedom. As one party member declared in a focus group in Khujand, he would allow his daughter to marry the national of any country "as long as it is a democratic country with free speech.... And it would be better if the religion there was Islamic." Another participant in the same focus group later added, "In addition to [its] freedom of conscience, I would give my daughter in marriage to [someone in] America, since the state there defends free speech."[93]

Yet, the party began to exhibit a creeping ambivalence about the United States. A series of articles from the party's newspaper *Najot* provides a glimpse. On the moral front, one article from June 2000 starkly contrasted Christian and Islamic ways of treating women, concluding with the superiority of the latter.[94] Another article from June 2000 proposed that market relations, along with Russian TV, were responsible for moral decline.[95] A piece published in January 2001 claimed that the West was in a spiritual crisis in spite of its material achievements.[96] Another, in December 2000, criticized "Western propaganda of the cult of force and sexual permissiveness" that reached Tajikistan through cinema. It called on the people "to oppose the Western cultural expansion by disseminating the Islamic cultural values and norms."[97] Still another, in May 2000, criticized "the propaganda of violence and pornography in Western films and videos has dealt a death blow at society," saying that "it is ruining public morals and negatively affects the rising generation."[98] An article from July 2000 opined:

> Today Tajik women and girls prefer the European style that is far removed from the Islamic culture and customs. This clothing leads to moral degradation.... Fascination with European fashions and Western values has reached the point where our Afghan and Iranian sisters prefer naked West for the sake of urban styles and clothes. I do not believe that they remember Allah.[99]

Beginning with the NATO campaign in Afghanistan in late 2001, the IRPT was thrust into an especially awkward position. On the one hand, it had expressed admiration for American values. On the other hand, embracing these values was insufficient to promote the interests of devout Muslims. Any willingness to suspend judgment about the effort to oust the Taliban faded quickly as the United States invaded Iraq in 2003. To add insult to injury, American rhetoric in 2005 began to heat up regarding a possible bombing of Iran.[100] Even though Tajiks are predominantly Sunni and Iranians are largely Shia, their linguistic closeness means that Tajiks can consume Iranian media. Devout Tajiks came to strongly oppose US foreign policy.[101]

In the meantime, the Rakhmon government was increasing its pressure on the IRPT; rather than confronting the regime, the IRPT largely ceded political ground and gained a reputation for lacking political will. In popular discourse, the IRPT leadership was more interested in pursuing its own interests than in representing the interests of broad Muslim publics.[102]

A Discursive Dilemma

The dilemma gradually came to a head. On the one hand, the regime's approach had moved from pressure and enticement to harassment and intimidation, making ongoing alliance with the regime an unattractive option. Naumkin reports that while fifty-three high-level IRPT members received high-level appointments at the civil war's end, only twelve remained in 2003.[103] Inexplicably, crimes committed against IRPT members proliferated. In 2003, deputy chairman Shamsuddin Shamsuddinov was arrested and sentenced to sixteen years in prison, before dying under suspicious circumstances in custody in 2008. This ushered in a period of intensifying harassment, defamation, and regime-sponsored repression that would eventually culminate with the outright legal banning of the party in 2015. The United States, with its all-consuming focus on security, did not exert meaningful pressure on Dushanbe to treat the IRPT and other opposition parties fairly.

On the other hand, the IRPT found it more difficult to present liberal democracy as the best protection for religion against autocratic encroachments. However laudable democracy was in theory, in Tajikistan so-called democracy brought rickety political institutions, economic stagnation, and moral decline. Yet, embracing a nondemocratic approach to defending Islam would have accelerated the party's demise, as it would have supplied the secular regime with justification for a crackdown. Moreover, it was unclear that its core supporters would have remained with the party had it taken a sudden nondemocratic turn.

As it happened, the IRPT changed in two ways. First, longtime party leader Said Abdullo Nuri died in 2006, having groomed a successor in Muhiddin Kabiri. Under Kabiri, the party gradually shifted its gaze away from the United States and toward Europe and Turkey. Unlike the United States, whose approach to domestic politics translated into a muscular foreign policy that generated controversy, European democracies were better at accommodating Muslims without starting major wars.[104] And in Europe, major Islamic thinkers provided ways to reconcile deep religious commitments with democratic institutions.[105] Similarly, Turkey served as a model of how a socially and fiscally conservative party could support both Islamic values and embrace democratic institutions.[106] In an interview with the author, Kabiri noted that he traveled frequently to Turkey to take stock of the example of the ruling Justice and Development Party, which in 2007 was spearheading a campaign to join the European Union.[107] Local activists in the Soghd region suggested that Russia, rather than the United States, was better at providing human rights protections for Tajiks. For these activists, Russia's provision of employment to more than a million Tajik labor migrants was tantamount to protecting Tajiks' rights.

The second change was a shift under Kabiri away from electoral politics. Elections in Tajikistan had never been entirely free or fair, but now they increasingly looked like a farce. Instead, Kabiri focused on generating a broad social appeal regardless of whether this translated into seats in parliament. In 2007 this principally took a form that again mirrored the Turkish example: the IRPT proudly and clearly championed the rights of women to wear the hijab in educational institutions—something the regime worked to prevent.[108] In addition, Kabiri noted his desire to protect Tajik traditions (such as the norm that traditional weddings are lavish and extravagantly expensive) from the encroachments of the regime. Though the regime could prevent the IRPT from translating its popular appeal into seats in parliament, it was at pains to prevent the party from appealing directly to the public. In this sense, it had once again become more a social movement than a political party contesting power.

The IRPT was not alone in appealing directly to the public. Hizb ut-Tahrir was increasingly a competitor and one that, by taking an uncompromising stance vis-à-vis officialdom, positioned itself as a principled alternative to the existing order (an order that HT depicted as condoned and supported by the United States). In fact, the northern Soghd region—one of the areas of the country most prone to opposition for having been largely been left out of the political settlement that ended the civil war—saw active competition between the two.[109] Recognizing HT's increasing popularity especially in that region, the IRPT emphasized that HT's radical ideas could turn adherents toward violence and away from the real message of Islam.[110] The fact that Kabiri, unlike his party forebears, was from a younger generation more accustomed to making such direct appeals, enhanced this approach.[111]

In sum, the shift in the nature of symbolic America created a moderate liability for the IPRT. It deeply complicated the party's efforts to maintain a political space based on a tenable position that democracy and religious devotion were not just compatible, but in fact necessary for each other to thrive. Party rhetoric shifted in orientation, but with European and Turkish models not completely separate from American ones, the symbolic legs on which the party stood had begun to wobble.

This meant shrinking room for maneuver. No longer seen as the durable guarantor of Islamic values, the IRPT was widely considered ill equipped to defend pious Muslims, who defected to other groups. And the regime in turn used the radical rhetoric and increasing visibility of those other groups as evidence that all political Islam was dangerous. The IRPT had become an all-purpose scapegoat. In 2010 party activists were blamed for a jailbreak and uprising led by a former civil war commander in the Rasht Valley.[112] Similarly, in 2015 the party was blamed when a deputy defense minister led a small group that took up arms against the regime. This was enough of a pretext to shutter the party entirely and to initiate a crackdown on party members and their families—a crackdown that included attempts to persecute activists who lived in exile in Europe.

Just a few months before the regime banned the IRPT, the government-run Islamic Center revived a pithy slogan from the civil war era: "If Islam needed a [political] party, the Prophet Muhammad would have established one."[113] Putting aside the fact that the Prophet Muhammad did not live in an era of party politics, this signaled the end of an experimental period in Central Asian politics. A religious party had not only participated in political life; it had played a central role in that politics.

The IRPT represents an unusual case. First, on a scale of movements from narrow-cast to broad-cast, it shifted over time. It began in the late Soviet period as a fairly narrow-cast movement very much interested in becoming broader, but the Tajik Civil War precluded this. Instead, the movement came to be associated with its combat role before emerging as an elite-level partner in the post-conflict settlement. It was clearly oriented to broadening its appeal first as a contender for parliamentary seats and the presidency and later via direct appeals to social issues. In the end, increasing pressure from the regime limited the party's ability to broadcast its message and ultimately ended it entirely.

Second, the party was unusual because of its stance on democratic protections for religious liberty in general and on the United States as a model in particular. By becoming associated with the US, however, a shift in the overall nature of symbolic America generated a moderate liability for the party, complicating its efforts to survive in an inauspicious environment.

Islamic Movement of Uzbekistan

Finally, let us turn to a very different Islamist group: the Islamic Movement of Uzbekistan (IMU). Whereas HT professed peaceful if radical change, the IMU embraced violence. While HT benefited from a broad membership, the IMU was a cabal of militants. HT existed well before the return of Central Asian ambivalence about symbolic America, but the IMU was founded in 1998, amidst the return of this ambivalence. In one key way, however, the IMU was like HT: it offered an ideology that hinged on a negative evaluation of the United States. It used this negative evaluation to invigorate and inspire its core adherents, in a process of frame "amplification."

The major figures involved in the IMU's creation were Tahir Yuldashev and Juma Hojiev (Namangani), both unsatisfied with the moderate Islamic path taken by others[114] and both involved in a short-lived 1991 effort to establish some version of sharia law in the Uzbek city of Namangan under the banner of the Adolat movement.[115] After providing a few empty promises to the young Islamists, Uzbek premier Karimov quickly reversed himself and initiated a brutal crackdown on pious Muslims that continued unabated until his death in 2016.[116] In the meantime, Yuldashev and Namangani found themselves in exile in Afghanistan and Tajikistan. Namangani, a former Soviet paratrooper who had served briefly in Afghanistan, gained prominence as a field commander during the Tajik Civil War. By 1998, the two had formed the IMU and staged violent incursions into Kyrgyzstani territory in 1999 and 2000.

In retrospect, there were two foundational moments for the IMU's ideology. The first was the government crackdown and ban on Adolat in March 1992,[117] which produced in Yuldashev and Namangani an enduring anti-Karimov orientation. *Uzbekistan* was their target, even if they were willing to take full advantage of porous borders with neighboring Kyrgyzstan and Tajikistan. A failed effort to broaden their orientation and rebrand the IMU as the Islamic Movement of Turkistan illustrates the point: they lacked the ability to mount a wider militant effort.

The second moment came in 1998, as the IMU formalized as an organization in Taliban-controlled Kabul at precisely the moment when Osama Bin Laden and the Taliban's Muhammad Omar enjoyed intensifying relations. Some reports suggest that Namangani was appointed head of a military unit consisting of pro-Taliban foreign mercenaries who would fight the Northern Alliance. Thus, at precisely the moment when the IMU came into existence, a negative depiction of the United States was available as a viable frame; the IMU in fact was incubated in an environment that would have a lasting impact on its ideology. The IMU would be designated a foreign terrorist organization by the United States in 2000, shortly after four American mountain climbers were taken hostage in Kyrgyzstan.

Once created, the IMU began to advertise its cause actively. In one 1999 document obtained by Naumkin, the organization offered this call:

> Instead of bringing back Islamic life . . . we have allowed tyrannical apostates to seize power. They had been fighting against Islam; their preceptors had shed more Muslim blood than the Bolsheviks; they had jailed, deported, and killed the 'ulama. They had been oppressing young Muslims with particular cruelty. They had closed the mosques of Allah, forbidding the mention of Allah's name. In former times, they had been serving Communist interests in Uzbekistan. History knows that on the territory of Uzbekistan they are pursing the policies of Israeli Jews and enemies of Islam in America.[118]

In another 1999 leaflet reacting to the bombings in Tashkent, the IMU wrote:

> Let them know those who received advice and assistance from the external anti-Islamic forces who oblige our ancient Muslim people to live according to the laws of the infidels, who slanderously attack Islam, who are the enemies of Islam. . . . The Creator will reward the Muslims for these torments in the afterlife, but the new generation is moving away from its faith and veneration

of Allah, being imbued with Western culture. This is where the real trouble lies.¹¹⁹

Similarly, Olcott and Babajanov cite what they call "terrorist notebooks," one of which enjoins followers "to make a declaration of the fact that unbelievers and the government are oppressors; that they are connected with Russians, Americans, and Jews, to whose music they are dancing; and that they don't think about their people."¹²⁰

Yuldashev himself offered in a 1999 interview:

> A despotic and apostate group have become the rulers of the country. They have waged war against Islam. They have massacred more Muslims than their Bolshevik teachers. They have sent religious scholars to jails and they have persecuted and killed. They have exerted severe oppression, particularly against young Muslims. They have closed God's mosques and forbidden the name of God to be uttered there. If it was written in the pages of history that they served the communists' interests in the past, now they are carrying out in Uzbekistan the policy of Israeli Jews and the American enemies of Islam.¹²¹

Karagiannis notes that Iran's state radio made itself available to disseminate IMU's messages:

> The IMU has also promoted anti-U.S. and anti-Jewish frames. In April 1999, for example, Iran's state radio station broadcast a statement on behalf of the IMU that described Karimov and his government as acting "in the forefront of U.S. and Israeli attempts to enslave the peoples of Central Asia, to plunder their wealth [and] to build military bases." The statement repeatedly framed Karimov as "Jewish" and "unbeliever" seeking to secure privileges for Judaism and Christianity in Uzbekistan, to the detriment of Islam.¹²²

Did this master frame enhance the IMU's cause? We do know that such depictions were used in recruitment. Rotar describes his travels to the Karategin Valley of Tajikistan in 1999, where "trainees were shown footage featuring the struggles of Islamic militants with the 'unfaithful' the world over,"¹²³ though we cannot know for certain to what extent such depictions resonated with potential recruits.

It is clear that the IMU at least tried to be attuned to its audience by referring to the Soviet period. Thus, it claimed that the Karimov regime continued the policies of its "Bolshevik teachers" by repressing Islam.¹²⁴ In another call, the IMU referred to Lenin:

> What did Lenin do? He was with the people all the time. The one who is going to topple a state should always be with the people. For example, the Decembrists all came from the intellectual milieu. They lost their struggle. The revolution was made by the Jews on Lenin's behalf. But the people do not understand anything. Like sheep, [they] can only eat. [They] will not even ask: "Where are you leading me?" The Americans are also like sheep, as they have no faith and ultimate goal.¹²⁵

Although not particularly burdened by logical consistency or evidence, and although the IMU in general allowed itself a fairly frontal criticism of the Sovietization of Central Asia,¹²⁶ it is likely that references to Soviet-era ways of thinking were a tactical move designed to attract a greater following. And there is at least some evidence that local Muslims were oriented to Soviet-era references.¹²⁷

It is impossible to know if such efforts would have borne fruit. No sooner had the IMU begun its image-making efforts than it executed a series of terrorist acts to which the region's states answered with force. Any boost to recruitment that might otherwise have come from image-making alone did not happen. The IMU remained a tiny, fringe terrorist group that with each passing year found its room for maneuver within Central Asia more restricted. In 2001, Namangani was killed as NATO-led troops occupied Afghanistan. The IMU continued to exist but fled, shifting its operations to the borderlands between Pakistan and Afghanistan, relatively more distant from ex-Soviet states. Yuldashev was killed in a NATO airstrike in 2009, after which IMU activities were severely diminished (in spite of predictions to the contrary).¹²⁸

In short, what impact did rising ambivalence about the United States have on the IMU? Since it did not exist as such before this ambivalence arose, its very emergence owes something to the shift in symbolic America. Even as the United States and its Central Asian allies moved to actively disrupt the financing and organizational capacity of the IMU, it continued to exist. A small movement of militant zealots might not rely heavily on image-making, but the availability of negative depictions of the United States provided it sustenance. In short, the IMU would likely have been less destructive and less capable in the absence of a deteriorating symbolic America. Comparative evidence from other post-Soviet contexts confirms this interpretation of what might have been.[129]

Conclusion

Islamist trajectories owed much to the changing symbolic politics surrounding the image of the United States. HT and the IRPT made broader appeals to the general public and thus relied significantly on image-making; they were more affected than the IMU, which appealed to a narrower array of potential members. HT and the IMU attached a negative valence to the United States and therefore stood to benefit from the deteriorating US image, whereas the IRPT initially attached a positive valence to symbolic America and therefore experienced this shift as a liability.

Thus far, I have left unaddressed one potentially important actor: the state. Does state action structure the possibilities for social mobilizers? The short answer is that these secular authoritarian regimes have all been poised against Islamist mobilization, treating it as a political and social threat. In the cases of Turkmenistan and Uzbekistan, the principle lever for exercising influence has been repression. State action in the softer authoritarian contexts of Kazakhstan, Kyrgyzstan, and Tajikistan hinges on persuasive as much as on coercive measures. These latter regimes actively sought to shape Muslim identity and channel religiosity via state-sponsored institutions.[130] Thus, the ability of Islamist movements to recruit was in part a function of how well the official, state-sponsored alternatives were able to recruit.

In Central Asia, the official muftiates stressed the rectitude of the Hanafi tradition that dominated in the region, while making some allowance for Sufi rites.[131] Theologically, this official Islam was intended to counter Salafism, the approach to Islam that denied the relevance of Sunni Islam's major schools of jurisprudence and that instead sought inspiration in the revelations and life of the Prophet himself. A highly professionalized and well-trained religious establishment might have succeeded in steering the pious away from Salafism and toward mainstream Hanafi Sunni Islam.

While there was some variation across Central Asian contexts, official Islam largely failed to gain the sympathies of broad religious publics, as the public generally found it theologically wanting. This took extreme form in Uzbekistan under Karimov, where the central government dictated the content of Friday sermons.[132] Popular disenchantment also prevailed in Kazakhstan, especially when in 2000 Nazarbaev appointed Absattar Derbisaliev, a secular scholar in the Soviet Orientalist tradition, as grand mufti.[133] Derbisaliev replaced Ratbek Nysanbaev, who had been accused of corruption. Replacing a corrupt official with an unqualified one did little to endear the pious to official Islam.

A lack of religious knowledge generated perceptions that the official religious establishment had priorities other than religion. D. V. Makarov describes for Dagestan what equally fits for Central Asia: "Against the backdrop of fairly close ties between religious officialdom and the unpopular ruling regime involved in corruption scandals, the political non-conformism of the Salafis looks especially attractive to the youth."[134] Efforts to enlist the support of major independent religious figures, such as Mohammad Sodik in Uzbekistan and Akbar Turajanzoda in Tajikistan, brought some credibility to the official religious establishment,[135] but, on the whole, the state's efforts fell flat.

As a consequence, Central Asia's states were in no position to change the dynamic generated by symbolic America and the politics of image-making. The outcome resonates with what Quintan Wiktorowicz describes for Arab states; he says that Jihadi discourse

> argues that Western influence over Arab governments through foreign assistance, International Monetary Fund loans, military connections and political alignments renders these governments "puppets" of the West and its Zionist allies in the Middle East. In Algeria for example, Islamist rebels went to considerable effort to frame the government as a French surrogate intent on preventing society from fully realizing its Islamic potential.[136]

Although it was not foreordained, Islamism became an idiom through which those with a negative evaluation of the United States and its assumed surrogates could express their "genuine grievances, both domestic and international." This amplified their political effect far beyond what narrow membership in Islamist groups might suggest; Islamists could claim to represent the interests of and be supported by all Muslims.[137] In the meantime, those Islamists with a positive evaluation of the United States increasingly stood on shaky discursive ground.

Wiktorowicz is correct to emphasize that framing requires "considerable effort." Before turning to labor activism, where such an effort failed to be considerable, let us first examine the activism of human rights groups.

HUMAN RIGHTS TRAJECTORIES

Moderator: OK, what can you say about America?
Taalai: Americans, they know how to defend the interests of their citizens. But what they are doing in Iraq, in Yugoslavia, this is already globalization. From a purely economic [point of view] why should cigarettes be just Marlboro and Camel? Why should people feed themselves with these hamburgers?
Dasha: And they are generally uncultured; they dress, eat, and behave in public in ugly ways.
Larisa: And they impose their policies on everyone, starting from the election of [our] national leaders and ending with what we should eat.
>   Focus group, Bishkek, Kyrgyzstan, 1 March 2006

Moderator: What do you think? What kind of country is the US?
Khakim: A country that wants to be first.
Zurab: A real democratic state.
Rakhmatullo: [It] wants to take over the world [tsel' ovladet' mirom].
Farkhad: I had a completely different opinion of America before George Bush. But after Bush came to power, after the war against Afghanistan, Iraq, and now the attempt to start a war against Iran, my positive opinions changed in a negative direction.
Ibrakhim: America is a cunning state. It puts its nose into others' business. It makes mountains out of molehills [iz mukhi slona delaet].
Khakim: A developed state.
>   Focus group, Osh, Kyrgyzstan, 9 April 2006

ONE COULD OFFER a simple story about human rights activism in Central Asia. At the height of American power after the Soviet collapse in 1991 and before the Iraq War in 2003, funding from abroad for activists was plentiful, political opportunities were ample, and the language of individual rights was universal even if the practice of defending those rights was not.[1] The United States served to inspire these processes until September 11, 2001, when much changed. Quickly mired in a "security-first" foreign policy, the United States fought two major wars that undercut its ability to pursue a robust and credible human rights agenda.

The simple story is not factually wrong. Western actors could no longer afford the economic and political costs of promoting human rights in places like Central Asia.[2] The securitization of US foreign policy indeed did complicate the pursuit of a human rights agenda. Yet, how fully can we understand these politics if we solely focus on US material power visible from thirty-thousand feet? There is no doubt that American power and its relative decline had an impact on human rights trajectories, but its impact is best understood by descending to the ground.

In Central Asia human rights activism traveled two paths. The first was classic mobilization in the streets. By its magnitude, street protest in Central Asia might not impress. The numbers involved could not compare to those in Serbia in 2000, Georgia in 2003, Ukraine in 2004 and 2014, or Egypt, Libya, and Tunisia in 2010–12. Nonetheless, given its much smaller population, mobilization was sizeable—in fact large enough to contribute to the overthrow of two presidents in Kyrgyzstan (Askar Akaev in 2005 and Kurmanbek Bakiev in 2010). A second path involved advocacy not on the streets but more quietly through personal and professional networks. These human rights activists operated via close familiarity and engagement with both international and domestic law. Whereas street mobilization relied strongly on image-making efforts by activists, these professional advocates relied less on them. Changes to symbolic America had a greater effect on the former than on the latter.

This chapter uses the extended example of Kyrgyzstan, where both kinds of mobilization occurred. After providing background on the country's relatively liberal moment in the 1990s, I consider the frames that mobilizers used in 2005 and 2010. The chapter shows that, while events in 2005 and 2010 should not be understood as democratic revolutions, they nonetheless would have been impossible without a discursive environment saturated with the language of human rights. Symbolic America played directly and consequentially into this mobilization. I then turn to the advocacy increasingly practiced by seasoned human rights defenders, showing how their activism was also affected, though to a lesser extent, by shifting symbolic America.

Kyrgyzstan: From Liberal Moment to Careening Authoritarianism

It speaks volumes about our optimism for Central Asian states that Western analysts once described Kyrgyzstan as an "island of democracy."[3] From independence in 1991, the Akaev regime provided enough reason for hope; its relatively more open polity stood in stark contrast to the sultanistic regime of Niyazov's Turkmenistan and the closed authoritarianism of Karimov's Uzbekistan. If it failed to consolidate its nascent democratic institutions, it nonetheless looked good by comparison.

Especially impressive was Kyrgyzstan's media environment and commitment to press freedom. Notwithstanding the many evident shortcomings of the state's political institutions, freewheeling debates projected images of a Kyrgyzstan firmly on the path toward greater liberalism.[4] Akaev "talked the talk" of a seemingly committed democrat,[5] whereas his counterparts in Uzbekistan and Turkmenistan seemed both bedeviled by autocratic paranoia and inspired by a deep social and political conservatism. Inclined to quote Thomas Jefferson and to invoke the ostensibly democratic instincts of Kyrgyz nomadic tradition,[6] Akaev endeared himself to the West by announcing his apparently liberal plans for the country's future. This plan clearly materialized on the economic front; in a highly touted moment, in 1998 Kyrgyzstan became the first post-Soviet state to join the World Trade Organization.

With Kyrgyzstan's relative openness projected internationally through its remarkable media, the West took note, as donor organizations and Western governments opened their purses. In most years from 1993 through 2007, Kyrgyzstan received more foreign aid per capita than did the other four Central Asian states combined.[7] Much of this supported nascent civil society groups. Like its space for free expression, the space for NGO activity was impressive, with a wide variety of actors attempting to offer public goods previously provided by the state.[8] Seemingly against the odds, this small, poor, mountainous, and landlocked country in the middle of Eurasia emerged with surprisingly vibrant linkages to the West.

Kyrgyzstan's relative political openness would not last. By the mid-1990s, it was showing signs that its commitment to meaningful democratic standards was dubious. Already in 1994, the regime had conducted a highly flawed presidential referendum that authorized the dissolution of parliament. This was followed in 1996 by another constitutional referendum that effectively "gave Akaev the right to appoint all state ministers, administrators and—critical to the further consolidation of executive power—judges."[9] Authoritarian backsliding continued, with increasing pressure on opposition figures—principally Bakhyt Beshimov, Feliks Kulov, and Zamira Sydykova—exerted by a pliant judiciary that generally supported Akaev's increasingly autocratic rule.[10] Hard to discern amidst the overall optimism about Kyrgyzstan's democratic prospects, such quiet backsliding did not go entirely unnoticed. Parliamentary elections held in 2000 were widely criticized as deeply flawed.[11] An OSCE report summarized:

> Both rounds of the 2000 parliamentary elections in the Kyrgyz Republic were characterised by a series of negative trends, that ultimately prevented a number of political parties and candidates from competing in the election on a fair and equal basis. The pre-election period was marred by a high degree of interference in the process by state officials, a lack of independence of the courts, resulting in a selective use of legal sanctions against candidates, and a bias in the state media.[12]

American officials rarely took notice of backsliding in aspiring democracies, though there were exceptions. Representative Christopher Smith (R-New Jersey) offered this appraisal in a 2001 US congressional hearing:

> Since disappointment is a function of expectations, I think it would be fair to say that Kyrgyzstan, under the leadership of Askar Akayev, is the most disappointing country in the former USSR. For years, Kyrgyzstan was considered the most democratic country in Central Asia. At one point, President Clinton's Deputy Secretary of State, Strobe Talbott, even called Akayev, "the Thomas Jefferson of Central Asia." . . . Today, nobody would use such language.[13]

Notwithstanding Smith's disappointment, the growing list of shortcomings mattered little for international aid. As long as Kyrgyzstan distinguished itself so dramatically from its neighbors, the money continued to flow. As long as donors continued to give, a deteriorating human rights record and intensifying authoritarianism seemed politically inconsequential.

Such arrangements can have pernicious effects on political order. Kept afloat in part by foreign aid, Kyrgyzstani political institutions faltered. None of the country's political practices—authoritarian or democratic—crystallized into well-functioning formal institutions; informal pressure groups and organized criminal networks suffused political life.[14] The word that best characterizes this situation is *careening*, which Dan Slater defines as "unpredictable and alarming sudden movements, such as lurching, swerving, swaying, and threatening to tip over" and "endemic unsettledness and rapid ricocheting."[15] While Slater uses the term to refer to unconsolidated democracies, Kyrgyzstan shows that authoritarian regimes can suffer from the same enduring defect; Kyrgyzstan was "struggling but not collapsing."[16] Its inability to consolidate authoritarian rule in the 2000s and 2010s was chronic.

This lack of consolidation matters much for post-Soviet politics and in fact may be more substantial than regime type, the influence of external actors, or popular preferences, as the following pages detail.

Street Protest and Symbolic America in 2005 and 2010

Analysts tend to describe street protest in one of two ways. Either it is "people power" fueled by genuine and legitimate grievances, or it is the product of outside actors who manipulate the local playing field to pursue their geostrategic goals. Let us steer clear of these two common depictions as we consider the mobilization that toppled Akaev in 2005 and Bakiev in 2010.

First, although one might paint with a broad brush, lumping mobilization in Kyrgyzstan with superficially similar events in Serbia, Georgia, and Ukraine as "color revolutions," the term *revolution* is a poor match for the Kyrgyzstani case. In fact, the events that led to the 2005 ouster of Akaev were largely elite-driven. As Scott Radnitz expertly documents, mobilization occurred because aggrieved economic elites had lost rent-seeking options. To remedy this loss, they moved to supplant the ruling Akaev clique by mobilizing their followers through robust patronage networks. Most of these followers in 2005 were rural, poor, and largely disconnected from national-level political concerns, so it took a translocal alliance of wronged "big men" to challenge the central regime. To be sure, elites used the language of bottom-up democracy (as we shall see below), but Radnitz convincingly shows that the dynamics were fundamentally top-down.[17] The 2010 ouster of Bakiev displayed a similar pattern.[18] Henry Hale describes such cycling as the normal political dynamics of Eurasian states: what seems to be a change in regime is in fact just the replacement of one political-economic patron with another.[19]

Second, claims about the influence of outside actors pursuing their geostrategic interests are often overstated.[20] Post-Soviet publics who were critical of the West by the early 2010s often opined that the United States highly influenced or indeed orchestrated all anti-regime mobilization. This logic had some resonance. After all, it is true that the United States preferred democracy (for a combination of normative and strategic reasons) and enjoyed vibrant linkages with Kyrgyzstan in particular. But, in the end, the West had surprisingly little direct impact on Kyrgyzstan's political trajectory. As Steven Levitsky and Lucan Way remind us, *linkage* between advanced industrial democracies and their nondemocratic counterparts is distinct from any *leverage* such advanced industrial democracies might have over these counterparts.[21] Commentators who assumed that American financing for civil-society groups equaled an American ability (and desire) to foment revolution made leaps of logic and evidence likely to convince only those already inclined to believe in conspiracies. In reality, if civil society in Kyrgyzstan was an America-supported fifth column, it was a strikingly ineffectual one. Not only were American monies poorly coordinated and occasionally misspent by a privileged local elite, but the NGO sector that received American financing was too weak to drive major political change.[22]

All of this suggests a need to clarify what we mean by America's role, with a clear view of its symbolic power. As I suggest below, the United States was a symbolically relevant touchstone for broad swathes of Central Asian populations from the 1990s well into the 2010s. It was on this symbolic plane that the (relatively) liberal moment had an important impact. The language of democracy by itself did not cause mobilization, but it was an essential feature for such mobilization to emerge.[23]

2005: Akaev's Fall

Any understanding of Akaev's ouster should begin with a stolen election.[24] Even though citizens recognized that their elections had not yet been fully free and fair, they nonetheless believed that the ballot box could usher in substantive change. Thus, even flawed contests served as the perfect focal points around which those inclined to oppose the status quo could coordinate their expectations. While other events could potentially serve this function, elections indexed democratic voice and packed symbolic punch.²⁵

The language of democracy, human rights, and symbolic America had permeated political life in Kyrgyzstan, especially among the members of a varied opposition. Opposition-leaning publications put this on display in the years preceding Akaev's ouster. One student writing in *Tribuna* in May 2001 averred, "In the USA any idea, any student claim [suzhdenie] is inevitably heard out; initiative, independent thought and originality are welcomed."²⁶ Kyrgyzstan, this perspective implied, could only aspire to the robust protection and encouragement of free speech found in the United States.

A 2003 article decried how Kyrgyzstani officials abused libel laws to intimidate journalists, in explicit contrast to the United States.

> In Kyrgyzstan, a journalist may be tried under two articles of the Criminal Code—for insult and for defamation. But, there are no concrete standards [to determine] what is an insult to honor and dignity, and what is defamation. These notions are rather vague. In the USA, when a bureaucrat plans to sue the media, he must meet high standards for these terms and prove that the truth was deliberately distorted.²⁷

Opposition newspapers reproduced on their pages the reports of the US State Department and articles from US newspapers critical of the Kyrgyzstan's ruling elites.²⁸ Representing an embrace of symbolic America, these decisions to republish were also an endorsement of the quality of work done by American officials and journalists. Occasionally, newspapers would issue a direct appeal to American policymakers to come to the aid of opposition figures facing persecution.²⁹ Throughout the 1990s and into the 2000s, opposition newspapers tended to refer to the United States in salutary terms even if the US did little to assist opposition figures persecuted by an increasingly authoritarian regime.³⁰

While the glowing depiction of American *domestic* policy and political life continued unabated, American *foreign* policy was a different matter. Opposition newspapers did not shy away from offering barbed critiques of the Bush Administration's decisions, especially the fateful one to invade Iraq in 2003, as well as the excesses committed by American soldiers and contractors in the conduct of that war. Yet, opposition papers carefully distanced themselves from wholeheartedly anti-American positions.

By the early 2000s, the situation had begun to shift, with the opposition facing the front end of an emerging dilemma. America continued to inspire via its domestic political model, but its foreign policy initiatives generated growing criticism, resentment, and in some quarters outrage. To the extent that human rights activism was linked in the public eye to an aggressive US foreign policy and an unpopular war in Iraq, mobilizers were tarnished by association. Yet, activists had few options; they were not well served by biting the symbolic hand that fed them. Instead of shifting their depictions of the United States in the face of rising ambivalence about US foreign policy, the opposition criticized the Akaev regime for exploiting the rise in popular anti-Americanism for political gain. A March 2002 article accused officialdom of using anti-Americanism to distract the Kyrgyzstani public from "its problems that the government has not resolved" (svoi, nereshennye pravitel'stvom, problemy).[31]

The language of democracy and human rights was broadly accepted; it infused the statements of those contesting Akaev's rule. For example, well-known civil-society activist Tolekan Ismailova wrote in 2002 that the Akaev regime sought to discredit activists, claiming, "We also intend to turn to Kyrgyzstani society and to international organizations to begin a large-scale campaign for defending the rights of human rights defenders and representatives of civil society."[32] After Akaev's ouster in 2005, his successor, Kurmanbek Bakiev—who at the time still appeared to be a committed democrat—wrote, "The Kyrgyz always governed the state with the help of people's democracy [pri pomoshchi narodnoi demokratii]. Our people had people's democracy even a thousand years ago. The Kyrgyz never allowed themselves to be subjected to a dictatorship or the usurpation of power."[33] That Bakiev himself would soon succumb to greater dictatorial excesses than Akaev's did not prevent him from embracing the language of human rights and democracy.

It is testimony to the hegemony of human rights frames that even those without identifiable democratic credentials would use them. Consider the opposition figure Feliks Kulov. A Russophone Kyrgyz initially trained as a police officer, Kulov generally preferred law-and-order themes and stressed the value of close relations with Russia (rather than the West).[34] Yet, even though he maintained a strong geopolitical orientation toward Russia, he suggested that if Kyrgyzstan was supposed to be an "island of democracy," it should act like one.[35] Arrested first by the Akaev regime and then by the Bakiev regime, his public image had transformed into that of a victim of authoritarian rule and therefore—by the seemingly self-evident logic of the time—someone with impeccable democratic credentials.

In short, through the early 2000s, the language of democracy and human rights was hegemonic, even sacrosanct (though the practice of protecting democracy and human rights was a separate matter). This hegemony would not last. As the image of the United States shifted, so too did the nature and power of human rights activism.

2010: Bakiev's Fall

Just five years after Akaev was overthrown, a second authoritarian regime would fall in Kyrgyzstan. On the surface, the two cases were similar. In each, an elected president succumbed to authoritarian backsliding and eventually fled the country in the wake of sustained protests. On a deeper level, key differences between the two hint at a shift that had occurred to symbolic America.

Bakiev was an unlikely democrat. A member of the Soviet Communist Party and a factory director, he had started his political career in the southern Kyrgyzstani coal town of Kok Yangak in 1990, eventually rising to become prime minister in 2000. Two months after police shot four demonstrators in the Aksy district in 2002, he resigned his post, claiming that he "must bear responsibility for moral reasons."[36] For most of his career, he worked squarely within the political system. His reemergence in 2004 among the figures actively opposed to Akaev's rule did not change this simple fact. Indeed, his written reflections are rife with comments complimentary to Akaev's leadership, as I discuss below.

Yet, this consummate political insider was typical of elite Kyrgyzstani politicians in rhetorically embracing democracy and human rights, linking them especially to the United States, while claiming for them a basis in Kyrgyz nomadic tradition. In an extended set of personal reflections, he wrote in 2003 that "Americans teach us democracy," but he also reminded readers, "Even before civilized humanity even knew about the existence of America, and in those faraway times when slavery thrived in Europe, the Kyrgyz people lived by the laws of kin-based societal democracy [po zakonam rodovoi, obshchinoi demokratii (sic)]." He elaborated, "We should keep in mind the existence in nomadic societies of Asia of a democratic tradition, as we approach [the question of] deepening democratic norms and institutions in an Asian society."[37]

Facing an evident tension between supporting the increasingly authoritarian Akaev and embracing the language of human rights and democracy, Bakiev was untroubled. For him, Akaev had "started in 1990 the pivotal turn [nachal... novatorskii povorot] toward a democratic society." Any deficiencies in Kyrgyzstan's democracy were natural, given that "only a couple of electoral campaigns" had occurred since the Soviet period. Moreover, "the practice even of countries with developed democracy shows that their electoral mechanisms now and then give rise to serious system failures." Referencing the Bush-Gore election in 2000, he added as if with an exclamation point, "It is enough to recall the recent presidential elections in the USA." Trying to thread the needle between apologizing for authoritarianism and overzealously embracing democracy, he summarized, "He who absolutizes democracy is doomed to disappointment, and he who does not accept it [is doomed] to slavery."[38]

On the narrower question of human rights protections, Bakiev was rhetorically unwavering, writing, "For a transitioning society, human rights and the mechanisms of defending these rights are the epicenter of all societal processes." Kyrgyzstan, he admitted, fell short: "On the whole, the constitutional status of an individual still is realized far from fully; constitutional rights and freedoms are often ignored and violated." He then listed foreign actors and states that "offer us serious assistance in the matter of guaranteeing human rights," the first of which is the United States. He ended his discussion of human rights by appealing directly to anyone who "works with the population" to "understand the principles and ethics lying at the heart of human rights standards and feel connected to their spirit [chuvstvovat' soprichastnost' s ikh dukhom]."[39]

Well known among Kyrgyzstanis for avoiding public pronouncements,[40] Bakiev remained quiet until 2004, when he cofounded the People's Movement of Kyrgyzstan. Subsequently earning the support of another opposition figure, Roza Otunbaeva (who would become president in 2010), the movement "had little in the way of a common platform beyond supporting fair elections and urging that Akaev follow through on his pledge to step down in October 2005."[41] While one should not expect from Bakiev a robust indictment of the Akaev regime for its authoritarian practices, this did represent a rhetorical embrace of key democratic principles. He talked the talk of democracy and human rights.

Of course, talk can be cheap. Bakiev's use of democratic tropes did nothing to ensure that he would rule as a democrat. Yet, before we declare his rhetoric meaningless, it is worth re-emphasizing the nearly universal optimism about democracy's (eventual) triumph so common to the period. If regimes were authoritarian, they were considered by definition illegitimate, corrupt, and unlikely to survive; if regimes were democratic but with flawed institutions, they were still considered by definition superior to their authoritarian counterparts; if regimes were democratic and with consolidated institutions, they were considered by definition virtually immune from backsliding. In this context, the expectation was that toppling an authoritarian leader would necessarily move politics in a democratic direction. Democracy was assumed to be a normal and natural end point; the rest was detail.

Once in office, Bakiev succumbed to the temptations of his post, proving himself an unambiguous authoritarian. As early as May 2005, even would-be allies such as the head of the Ar-Namys Party declared him worse than Akaev.[42] Gradually, the new regime assumed a confrontational stance toward civil society and sought to cement power by creating a large pro-regime umbrella party called Ak Jol.[43] Systematic harassment of journalists and opposition figures followed, along with an overwhelming victory in compromised elections held in 2009. Kyrgyzstan under Bakiev could no longer even pretend to be Central Asia's "island of democracy."

Not a democracy, the new regime likewise was not a consolidated authoritarian regime. Rather, it was careening, penetrated by organized crime and suffering from tottering patronage structures.[44] This regime was akin to a building with a "rotten door,"[45] all but waiting for challengers from the opposition to push open and install themselves in power. As it happened, Bakiev received his "comeuppance"[46] in April 2010, when steeply rising utility prices spurred protests first in Talas, then in the capital, Bishkek. The regime deployed snipers, and about seventy-five people died as Bakiev first sought cover in the southern city of Osh before fleeing to Belarus,[47] where he remained in exile as of 2020.

Symbolic America

In this way, Kyrgyzstan distinguished itself as the sole post-Soviet Central Asian state to experience regime change, doing so twice in a five-year span. Yet, there was one key difference between the two sets of events. By 2010 the power of symbolic America to rouse support for democracy was on the wane. Indeed, if the spark for protests in the past had been human rights abuses (Aksy in 2002) and unfair electoral practices (in 2005), by 2010 protests were disconnected from these issues typical of pro-democracy mobilization. Instead, they focused on corruption in the regime (which had become demonstrably worse under Bakiev) and poor economic performance.

The Kyrgyzstani public came to view increasing nepotism and the rising cost of living as two sides of the same coin. In October 2009, Bakiev appointed his son Maksim to head the powerful Central Agency for Development, Investment, and Innovation, raising the specter that he was grooming Maksim to succeed him as president.[48] This move was followed by an official announcement that electricity rates would rise in January 2010, and that the electricity distribution company Severelektro would be "privatized" (at firesale prices) by a company under the junior Bakiev's control. Protests began in January and continued until 7 April 2010, when the opposition seized the Kyrgyzstani White House.[49] President Bakiev had apparently forgotten his pledge, made upon assuming power in 2005, that "now a real people's power has been established. . . . I will not allow my family to interfere in the affairs of the power structures; I will fight to raise the living standard of the population."[50] His evident hypocrisy seemed to invite organized opposition.

Over the course of five years, members of the opposition on several occasions had forwarded demands to the Bakiev regime. While they continued to call him out for violating democratic principles, their tone began to shift. Instead of democracy and human rights, increasingly they were interested in good governance. They assumed, as do most committed democrats, that good governance results when a polity is built upon democratic principles. Yet, elections and individual freedoms were no longer sufficient. In 2006, the opposition issued a united call for "democratic reforms for the flourishing of Kyrgyzstan," which combined demands for constitutional reforms to limit the power of the presidency with "a guarantee of real economic competitiveness, a prohibition on the use of state power to oust economic competitors, the elimination of the practice of 'family' business, and the protection of independent entrepreneurs from pressure by criminal forces."[51]

By 2008, the message was even clearer. A graver sin than Bakiev's authoritarianism was his regime's poor governance. A "memorandum" signed by a wide array of opposition organizations and actors attested:

We, seriously concerned about the catastrophic deterioration of the socio-economic situation of the majority of the country's citizens caused by the incompetence of the authorities, believe that the main cause of the crisis, generating corruption, the criminalization of the state, and all the other problems and maladies of society is [Bakiev's] perverse [porochnaia] system of government. The system leads to irresponsibility and impunity in the higher state power in the person of the presidents of Kyrgyzstan and their closest circle.[52]

The opposition did not need to call out Bakiev by name. His inability to pursue good governance was clear and more objectionable than was any violation of democratic principles.

This shift in framing was not incidental. A "democracy fatigue" had set in, complicating the claim made by Kyrgyzstani NGO leaders that human rights were universal and deserved robust protection as a result. As one observer colorfully described it, "It seems that the West is already tired of this masquerade, this clown show [klounada] with the same performers who first and foremost take care of their own pockets under the guise of defending sacred human rights."[53]

In spite of the country's freewheeling media environment, even the word *journalism* began to acquire pejorative connotations, implying sensationalist profit- and attention-seeking, rather than being a robust and welcome watchdog of political processes.[54] Alla Piatibratova of the Osh Media Resource Center claimed that the change was understandable, since ordinary people's support for a free media had always been tenuous, and state employees had long had to toe the politically correct line for fear of being fired.[55] At least some NGOs had acquired a reputation for operating as businesses pursuing in-kind profits, with the United States as their principal patron, rather than as not-for-profits committed to creating public goods.[56] Natalia Ablova of the Bureau of Human Rights and the Rule of Law indicated that after the shooting of Alexander Ivanov (which opens this book), human rights activists themselves became disillusioned and lost trust in the US embassy. She further remarked that the quality of personnel sent by the West to Kyrgyzstan was high in the 1990s and much lower thereafter.[57] Likewise, the liberal newspaper *Respublika* quietly called into question aspects of the American political model in its coverage of the US presidential election.[58] If those who normally tapped the resonant resources represented by symbolic America now sought distance from it, this represented an important change in the landscape of political possibilities.

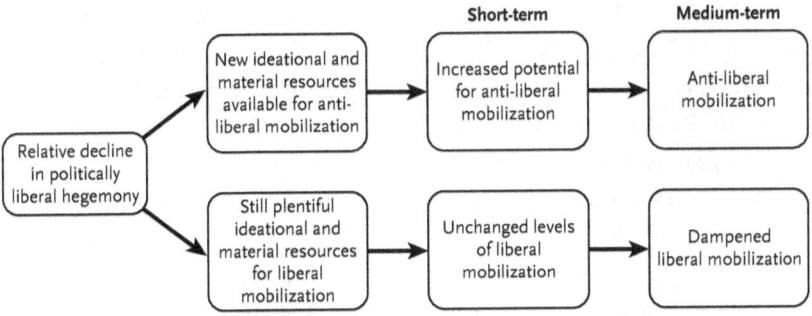

FIGURE 4. Short- and medium-term effects of the erosion of politically liberal hegemony.

Lagged Effects: Human Rights Activism and Global Hegemony

As the previous chapter detailed, Islamic activism received a boost when the content of symbolic America began to shift, first slowly in the late 1990s and then more quickly in the early 2000s. So, why did the rising ambiguity in popular views of the United States not have a dampening effect on democratic and human rights activism in the late 1990s? Why did this dampening effect come later, in the mid-2000s?

Consider the broad environment in which these two movements operated. Under a politically liberal hegemony in which the US was symbolically resonant, an anti-hegemonic movement—like many of the Islamist movements covered in the previous chapter—could receive new inspiration due to proliferating symbolic possibilities. But in that same politically liberal hegemonic environment, a pro-hegemonic movement possessed precisely the same symbolic resources it had enjoyed before. Figure 4 illustrates.

As the overall image of the United States shifted, novel ideational and material resources became available to anti-liberal groups fairly quickly, while the shift more gradually affected the possibilities for human rights advocates. This shift in symbolic America thus had a lagged effect in one area (human rights) and a more immediate effect in another (Islamic activism).

In this regard, the example of the Islamic Renaissance Party of Tajikistan (IRPT) is instructive. The IRPT offered both an Islamic-values platform and a human rights agenda emphasizing freedom of conscience. While human rights groups in Kyrgyzstan were not particularly hampered in the early 2000s by shifting symbolic resources, the IRPT began to suffer from the shifting symbolic America earlier. Why did these Western-oriented Islamists suffer politically almost immediately under shifting symbolic America, whereas the non-Islamist liberals suffered more gradually?

First, an entire industry and global infrastructure had emerged in the 1990s to support human rights activism, as long as that activism was conducted in a legibly Western way. Unlike secular pro-human rights activists, the IRPT operated on a razor's edge, having to convince outsiders that it advocated human rights as much as its counterparts who did not focus on freedom of conscience. The IRPT explicitly contested elections; unlike NGOs that were agnostic about who had political power as long as power was used appropriately, the IRPT was partisan. Supporting specific political parties as such was not something that the global donor infrastructure available to human rights groups could do.

Second, the regime in Kyrgyzstan used the hegemonic language of political liberalism (even though its practice fell well short of the ideals espoused); it was to a considerable degree constrained by its own discourse. By contrast, the IRPT operated in Tajikistan in an environment where the language of stability, order, and conflict prevention was dominant.[59] Ongoing instability in neighboring Afghanistan reiterated the importance of these values. As long as the IRPT was understood to be on the side of conflict prevention and order, it had a seat at the table and indeed a role in government. Ultimately, as the rhetoric of Islamist "threats" heated up, the authoritarian Rakhmon regime made a decisive move against its erstwhile partner, depicting it as no more than the proverbial wolf in sheep's clothing.[60]

Finally, while Kyrgyzstan generally enjoyed much space for civil society to mobilize on a variety of issues, Tajikistan had little. In fact, the Rakhmon regime did much to discourage mobilization that might upset a precarious post–civil war peace.[61] In short, human rights groups were both materially and ideationally empowered in Kyrgyzstan into the early 2000s, whereas the equivalent groups in Tajikistan enjoyed much less access to these material and ideational resources. When symbolic America shifted in the 1990s, the IRPT was predisposed to losing political momentum quickly, whereas Kyrgyzstani NGOs were predisposed to maintaining their political influence at least for some time.

TABLE 2. *Respublika*'s evaluation of the United States

Average evaluation of US (6-point scale)	Period	Number of articles
4.09	1992–1996	11
4.21	1997–2001	18
3.47	2002–2006	32

Note: On the 6-point scale, 1 was strongly negative, and 6 was strongly positive.

This lag in the changing evaluation of the United States is visible in the pages of the newspaper *Respublika*, which was well known for its pro-democracy editorial stance. Consider how these depictions changed over time, from 1992–2006. Each mention of the United States was evaluated on a six-point scale, with 1 strongly negative, and 6 strongly positive. The early part of the period covered shows positive evaluations of the United States in the references made to the US. That would change by the latter period. Table 2 groups these evaluations by five-year period.

While there is some arbitrariness in the temporal cutoff between periods, there is no doubt that by the 2000s evaluations of the United States had become more common and generally more ambivalent.

Professionalized Advocates

Activism comes in many varieties. One of them involves what Margaret Keck and Kathryn Sikkink call *transnational advocacy networks* (TANs), which are "organized to promote causes, principled ideas, and norms, and they often involve individuals advocating policy changes that cannot be easily linked to a rationalist understanding of their 'interests.'"[62] Among the central distinguishing features of such networks is their ability to mobilize opinion outside any given state, with the intent to eventually exert pressure on said state.

The number of TANs globally rose dramatically in the 1990s, for a variety of reasons. Politically liberal hegemony meant that advocates were both empowered with a sense of mission and unencumbered by complicating ideological alternatives. The ability to effect liberal ideals across the globe was viewed largely as a practical, rather than an ideological, question; it was simply a matter of mustering adequate will and resources to do the job. Second, because the United States was unwilling to provide truly transformative government-to-government aid (à la the postwar Marshall Plan for Europe) for post–Cold War Eurasia, a patchwork of Intergovernmental Organizations (IGOs), International Nongovernmental Organizations (INGOs), and other actors from the private sector picked up the slack. Finally, the 1990s were the heyday of what at the time appeared to be radically diminishing national sovereignty and even what seemed to be a wholesale retreat of the nation-state as a political formation in the face of an overwhelming new wave of globalization.[63] On an operational level, the ease with which people, communications, finances, goods, and services could now cross political borders made the creation and operation of such TANs much simpler than ever before. On an ideational level, these changes abetted new ways to imagine global communities operating by common principles.

Robust, active, and ready to transform Eurasia, these TANs did not always work according to plan. In spite of great funding and good intentions, their ability to penetrate local governments and societies was often more limited than the language of communism's "collapse" might imply. Many analysts wrongly equated the demise of state socialism as a system with the wholesale disappearance of its constituent parts, as if one of the most significant experiments in the history of humanity could vanish without a trace.[64]

In actual fact, this was not a tabula rasa. As Sarah Henderson vividly describes:

> For the majority of funded organizations, the offices remained unvisited and the publications usually sat on a shelf with a multitude of other brochures, newsletters, bulletins, guides, and directories that had been published and distributed only to the same circle of NGOs. Rather than actually engaging the population, administrators, or legislators in a dialogue, NGOs often organized a conference around a topic for other NGOs and published a pamphlet about it.[65]

One could forgive local populations for occasionally concluding that civil-society actors were unaware of, or uninterested in, local realities.[66] NGOs could be considered to be composed of strangely irrelevant if ultimately benign forces,[67] or they might be construed as dangerous in their fundamental ignorance of local societies, which undermined the local provision of public goods. It took only a modicum of paranoia to extend the logic to conclude that outside forces by their very nature were engaged in a conspiracy to subjugate local populations.[68] In retrospect, the difficulty of translating "not-for-profit" into local languages should have hinted at the problem: many Central Asians wondered how those who received handsome salaries from Western-funded NGOs could not be *profiting* from this arrangement. The leap to imagining a vast Western plot with NGOs as the foot soldiers positioned to encircle Eurasia becomes slightly less baffling from this perspective.

The TANs that operated in Eurasia quickly adjusted to these realities, becoming what—to emphasize their distinctiveness in the region—I call *professionalized advocates*. By the late 1990s, the advocates who worked in Central Asia began to do so as quiet, elite-oriented, behind-the-scenes actors disconnected from broader local societies. They were professionalized in two senses. First, they were trained individuals with specialized skills well suited to building careers in the NGO sector. Second, they operated by the norms and practices of their profession.

These professionalized advocates engaged in a variety of activities. In addition to writing reports for public dissemination, they (1) provided legal counsel to those challenging practices that failed to meet international standards, (2) monitored criminal trials where political figures stood accused, and (3) encouraged local officials to become aware of and abide by national and international legal obligations. In short, these professionalized advocates sought to play a quiet watchdog role not necessarily played by other actors under authoritarian rule.[69]

Were they effective? It is true that NGOs in general and human rights NGOs in particular did not produce massive transformations in Central Asian regimes. It may be that even when local NGOs proliferate in number under authoritarian rule, they remain unlikely to thrive in any qualitative sense.[70] It also may be that a culture of paternalism on the part of NGOs fundamentally undermines their efficacy.[71] And it might be that "neighborhood effects" make Central Asian terrain basically inhospitable to the growth of democratic values and robust human rights protections.[72]

Yet, if we look at individual instances, there is no doubt that the quiet advocacy of professionals can work to effect. Consider the case of Alexander Sodiqov. A Tajik national and young scholar at a Canadian university, Sodiqov in 2014 found himself incarcerated in Tajikistan and charged by Tajik authorities with espionage and high treason. A sustained and decentralized campaign conducted with the crucial participation of professionalized advocates ultimately produced his release and return to Canada to continue his studies. While many factors, including the good will of specific members of the Tajik government, produced the outcome, there is no doubt that transnational professional advocates, with their specialized skills, worked behind the scenes to engage legal processes while allowing space for those who risked embarrassment to "save face" instead.[73]

Shifts in Symbolic America

While promoting universal values on *behalf* of ordinary people, these professionalized advocates of human rights protections did not require the active support of ordinary people. As a result, such groups were less affected by shifts in ideational resources such as those represented by symbolic America. Yet, there is no question that the shift in symbolic resources complicated their efforts.

Lawyers working in the human rights area reported the rising difficulty in pursuing cases with human rights dimensions. One prominent lawyer in Dushanbe described in an interview the stalling and stonewalling that he encountered when pursuing such cases. Whereas in the past, government bureaucrats were reasonably responsive, by 2006 they behaved in palpably different ways.[74] A prominent lawyer who defended the rights of Hizb ut-Tahrir activists accused of crimes was herself accused of using "human rights" as a cover for pursuing an agenda of "Islamization."[75]

Yet, professionalized advocates often could continue to do their work; the shift did not fundamentally undercut their efforts. NGOs like Human Rights Watch continued to monitor trials of opposition figures. As one prominent Tajik human rights lawyer contended, sometimes press coverage and even attention from monitors like the Organization for Security and Cooperation in Europe (OSCE) could spur officials in Tajikistan to engineer crackdowns to avoid embarrassment.[76] The corollary was also true: human rights activists who operated quietly below the radar screen could be fairly effective in getting their work done. Similarly, Cai Wilkinson found that LGBT activists in Kyrgyzstan benefited from the "passive" approach of Europe—an approach based on "being, rather than doing"—as they continued to quietly advocate under challenging circumstances.[77]

Conclusion

In a simple version of the story, US foreign policy of the 2000s privileged security over human rights, undercutting the traction that rights activists could gain. Yet, this version is wanting.

While US foreign policy blunders clearly complicated activism, the trends in fact started much earlier. Well before the election of Donald Trump as US president in 2016, and in fact well before the 2003 Iraq War, the widely criticized incarcerations at Guantanamo, and the revelations about illegal "extraordinary renditions" and the atrocities committed by Americans at Abu Ghraib—all of which tarnished the global reputation of the United States—the human rights activism that was so vibrant in the 1990s had begun to peak. Even without those palpable US foreign policy gaffes, symbolic America already had shifted. It had already become much harder to deploy America as a symbol of human rights protection and a paragon of moral rectitude.

Moreover, the simple story misses the important, slow-moving processes of sedimentation. In Kyrgyzstan, Askar Akaev relied strongly on liberal democracy as a legitimizing discourse even as his rule backslid into an ineffective authoritarianism. In the hands of a more adept authoritarian ruler, like Kazakhstan's Nursultan Nazarbaev, perhaps the Kyrgyzstani regime under Akaev could have survived.[78] But the shift in symbolic America gave voice to opposition critiques of Akaev's hypocrisy. Just as a distance had appeared between America's proclaimed values and its policies around the globe, Akaev was not making good on the promises of liberal democracy. This was a slow-moving process, but one with real political import by the time of Bakiev's ouster in 2010.

Recognizing such slow-moving processes reveals important complexities involved with activism. Thus, it is a mistake to assume that anti-liberal Islamist activism and pro-liberal human rights activism are necessarily engaged in zero-sum competition, in which a gain in traction for one spells a loss in traction for the other.[79] While these kinds of activism did travel roughly in opposite directions in the 2000s, human rights activists were able to muster ongoing support and be effective in their efforts, given an ongoing politically liberal hegemony. Moreover, because some human rights activists operated as professionalized advocates, they could often continue quietly to pursue their agendas, if to marginally diminished effect. Because these

TABLE 3. Effect on efficacy by movement type

	Broad-cast movement	Narrow-cast movement
Critical orientation	Immediate, significant	Immediate, modest
Laudatory orientation	Delayed, significant	Delayed, modest

professionalized advocates operated in networks of limited scope and did not particularly require popular support, their activities were less dramatically affected by a shift in symbolic America.

In short, in Central Asia in the 1990s and 2000s, human rights trajectories were affected by shifts in symbolic America. But how this liability played itself out was a function of whether mobilization required ongoing popular support or could continue without such explicit support. Table 3 summarizes.

With the shift in symbolic America, new political possibilities as raw material for mobilizational framing was now available across the political spectrum. Those inclined to criticize the United States now had a resonant vocabulary available, and those inclined to laud the United States retained the symbolic resources to do so. A critical broad-cast movement could immediately and strongly benefit from the newly available symbolic raw material. A critical narrow-cast movement could also benefit immediately but to a lesser extent. In the meantime, a laudatory broad-cast movement would experience a significant impediment to its efforts, and a laudatory narrow-cast movement would experience a lesser impediment to its efforts. The two latter movements experienced this with a delay because their laudatory stance still dovetailed with the globally hegemonic language of political liberalism.

It is tempting to conclude that human rights activism was dying as of 2016. After all, with the rapid upsurge in populist rhetoric in North America and Europe and with the clear authoritarian backsliding in places like Russia, Turkey, Hungary, and Venezuela, the human rights agenda faced unprecedented global headwinds. But just because a particular version of a political principle begins to ring hollow does not mean that the principle itself evaporates. The discourse of democracy and liberalism at least in Central Asia had promised far more than it delivered, and expectations were dashed. By 2016 it had become rarer to see Central Asians arguing for serious human rights protections, free press, and fair political competition, yet these values did not disappear without a trace. Nor did the people who shared these values simply vanish. To the contrary, they had already left a profound mark on a generation of Central Asians. In the longer run, it may be that human rights activists who distance themselves from symbolic America will stand the best chance of success.

4

LABOR, DISORGANIZED

> "Is there any point to which you would wish to draw my attention?"
> "To the curious incident of the dog in the night-time."
> "The dog did nothing in the night-time."
> "That was the curious incident," remarked Sherlock Holmes.
> — Arthur Conan Doyle, "Silver Blaze"

AS THE SHIFTING FORTUNES of Islamist and human rights activism highlight, symbolic politics matter because they change the horizons of the possible. With the 1990s giving way to the 2000s, newly sedimenting social meanings provided mobilizers with changed raw material for their framing efforts. Certain actors were empowered while others were disempowered, and the political terrain consequently shook.

In this chapter, I take stock of a third and final type of activism: labor. By all appearances, labor was in a position to take full advantage of shifts to symbolic America. In Central Asia, as across post-socialist space more generally, societies had experienced dramatic macroeconomic contraction and massive dislocation in the aftermath of the Soviet collapse. Labor protections that had been robust and explicit were quickly dismantled or hollowed out, as economies and budgets shrank. Ordinary people suffered greatly, and labor—the notional cornerstone of state socialism—had ample grievances.

In the meantime, Western consultants, NGOs, international financial institutions, and governments promoted rapid marketization on the logic that such shock therapy would prove good medicine. Instead, the record on such transformations was—at best—mixed, and the region's publics began to view Western advice as something between well-intentioned but naïve and eminently sinister. The fact that local governments had been more than willing to take Western advice did little to change how publics viewed the scorecard. In short, not only did labor have ample grievances; it also had ample reason to launch criticism of the United States in particular and the West in general, as it pursued local agendas.

And yet, as I detail below, symbolic America was strangely quiet in an issue area where it might have been quite prominent. Labor activists in Central Asia were well aware of the United States. They knew its economic and political power. They knew that the US was the architect of the global economic order, yet they did not tap into its symbolic power. Why not? How should we understand this negative case?[1]

Nonbarking Dogs

To appreciate Central Asia's important peculiarities, let us put its experience into a broadly comparative framework. In what would become the advanced industrial West, states historically developed healthy labor protections, largely due to pressure from strong unions. Likewise, in Latin America, the preexisting power of unions ultimately forced the incorporation of the working class and its interests into the political system.[2] In the parts of East Europe and Eurasia that would constitute state-socialist space, the pattern was different: labor generally lacked autonomous power but found its agenda nonetheless pursued by a state intent on promoting workers' interests.

Labor's dependence on the state was rooted in the region's history. On the eve of the Bolshevik revolution, the proletariat was small in European Russia and barely existed in other parts of what would become Soviet territory. In Central Asia, this led to a peculiar outcome: the party-state championed a working class that it still needed to create.[3] Thus, whereas in Latin America and West Europe, the question was how labor and its interests would be incorporated into politics, in Soviet space there was precious little to incorporate in the first place. As a result, the labor we see today is best understood as created by the Soviet party-state.

Indeed, the seventy-year Soviet experiment left a deep imprint. Of course, the self-proclaimed workers' paradise had failed to make good on Marx's predictions and Lenin's promises, instead offering a suffocatingly paternalistic commitment to the working class.[4] Further, the Soviet Union ultimately would collapse under the weight of unmet promises, its efforts hollowed out by overreach, mismanagement, and simple venality. At the same time, the Soviet state did in fact engineer substantial material improvements for the working class that it both created and championed: universal education and literacy, guaranteed employment, wage equity, and nondiscrimination in the workplace, as well as cradle-to-grave social welfare protections. The Soviet collapse did not erase the Soviet legacy.

Whatever its accomplishments on this front—and it is worth repeating that the rhetoric easily outpaced the reality—they were achieved without a meaningful role for labor unions. And who needed them, when the party-state was apparently so radically attuned to the interests of the proletariat? Beginning with Stalin, unions had been "effectively turned into transmission belts for carrying out directives of party leaders . . . [by] assisting managers and planners in maintaining labor discipline and fulfilling plan targets."[5] This subservience to the party-state would weaken after Stalin's death and the Soviet Union's return to the International Labour Organization (ILO) in 1956,[6] but the essential structural arrangement remained. As the USSR approached its ultimate demise and citizens poured into the streets to advocate for systemic change, labor activism was more muted than other types of activism, as workers' interests were widely assumed to be adequately represented by definition.[7]

One measure of this structural arrangement's ongoing influence is its prominence, even in state-socialist cases far from Central Asia where major change might have been expected to occur. Consider Poland, where the Solidarity movement emerged amidst labor unrest in 1980 as an independent trade union. With it contributing so centrally to political change and eventually forming the country's first post-socialist government in 1990, one might have reasonably expected unions to become politically powerful and independent. Yet, as David Ost puts it, "That was not to be. Solidarity leaders, now heading the government, as well as those still heading the union, pressed workers to accept radical neoliberal reforms and give up rights in the workplace. This ideological promarket behavior was a legacy of the fight against communism: the enemy's enemy became a friend."[8]

If this occurred in Poland, there was little reason to expect a robust labor movement elsewhere. Across the region, with GNP contracting through

1993 in East Central Europe and through 1996 in former Soviet space,[9] macroeconomic conditions were hardly conducive to the emergence of labor power. Yet, labor weakness continued well after macroeconomic recovery began in the late 1990s. Indeed, the pattern that Ost summarizes had been set: "Trade unions fared poorly in postcommunist Eastern Europe. Everything about them declined: their membership, workplace authority, collective solidarity, enterprise responsibilities, and political influence."[10] Labor's "consent and collaboration [were] not essential for policy adoption or implementation," writes Paul Kubicek.[11] Labor barked very little across post-socialist space.

Something was afoot in the broader global economy that dampened labor's chances: the hegemony of a particular vision of economic virtue that prioritized global investment, capital mobility, consumer-driven growth, and corporate profits. In that event, labor found it hard to articulate a case for its rightful place amidst such circumstances—a point to which I return in the chapter's conclusion.

Central Asian Circumstances

It is worth drilling down into Central Asia's specific economic conditions. Consider first some features common to all five of the region's states.

All states of the region began with high union density. Turkmenistan and Uzbekistan were at one end, with swollen formal membership in official trade unions of ambiguous utility. The Turkmen National Centre of Trade Unions almost seemed ready to burst with a reported 1.1 million members out of a total population of over 5.5 million.[12] Similarly, in Uzbekistan the Federation of Trade Unions reported a membership of 5.9 million members out of a total population of about 29 million.[13] In these two cases, post-Soviet practices so closely resembled Soviet-era ones that we should be forgiven for viewing them as unchanged. By some contrast, Kazakhstan, Kyrgyzstan, and Tajikistan experienced significant institutional rupture, although Soviet legacies reared their head, with large fragments of Soviet institutional arrangements recombining in novel form and distinctively Soviet cultural schemata and parameters of the "thinkable" reasserting themselves.[14]

A second major commonality was the prevalence of informal economic relationships—this too a Soviet legacy. In closed economies with a commitment to providing full employment, nominal employment levels mask declines in the real value of wages, and employees may experience significant

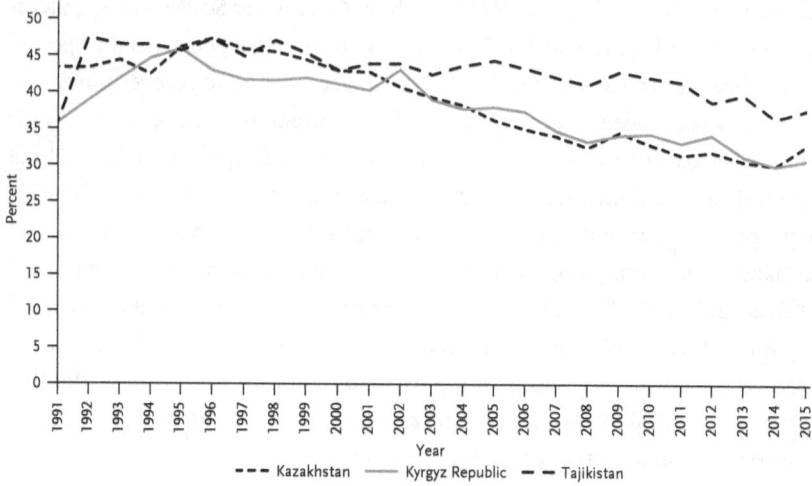

FIGURE 5. Shadow economy as percent of GDP.

wage arrears. In Uzbekistan, until 2017 much labor was simply conscripted from state employees and even schoolchildren for the annual cotton harvest, which dominated that country's political economy.[15] Under such conditions, it was entirely normal for individuals to shift to the economy's informal sectors. But even in the relatively more open economies of Kazakhstan, Kyrgyzstan, and Tajikistan, enormous portions of GDP continued to flow through the informal shadow economy (figure 5).[16]

With so much occurring in the shadows, it was hard to imagine labor gaining traction. Indeed, even in post-socialist East and Central Europe, tripartite arrangements that on paper seemed to formalize a central role for labor were nothing more than "illusory."[17]

Yet, while the general pattern of structural forces undercutting labor's ability to organize and bargain was evident, the region exhibits important variations that invite our attention. Consider Turkmenistan and Uzbekistan. If we focus only on their respective economic profiles, some demand for labor might have been expected to materialize. Compared to the other states of the region, Turkmenistan's workforce has the highest percentage employment in industrial sectors and the lowest in agricultural ones. Uzbekistan is in the middle of the pack in agricultural employment and the second-highest in levels of industrial employment. Uzbekistan's trajectory might also predict a rise in activism, as the country has become more reliant on industrial labor since the Soviet collapse.[18]

But Turkmenistan and Uzbekistan were not just industrial economies; they were politically closed industrial economies with scant space for civil society. Hard authoritarian regimes, they broached no independent mobilization unless that mobilization was explicitly and unequivocally pro-regime. Labor did not exist as an autonomous entity in any meaningful sense in either of these two contexts, which had experienced minimal political change since the Soviet era.

By contrast, Tajikistan saw major institutional change due to civil war and the partial breakdown of the state.[19] Enormously and stubbornly reliant on agricultural labor (at over 50 percent of the employed labor force), its low employment in industry rapidly declined further with the onset of civil war, never to recover (as of 2018 data).[20] In the meantime, Tajikistan became increasingly dependent on remittances sent from relatives working abroad, principally in Russia. This reliance became particularly noticeable in the mid-2000s, as figure 6 shows.[21]

Thus, for reasons different than what we see in scarcely changed and authoritarian Turkmenistan and Uzbekistan, Tajikistan was also deeply unlikely to see labor mobilization of any significance. Moreover, the weakly consolidated but clearly authoritarian Tajik regime did little to empower unions. As a report by the International Labour Organization (ILO) prescribed for

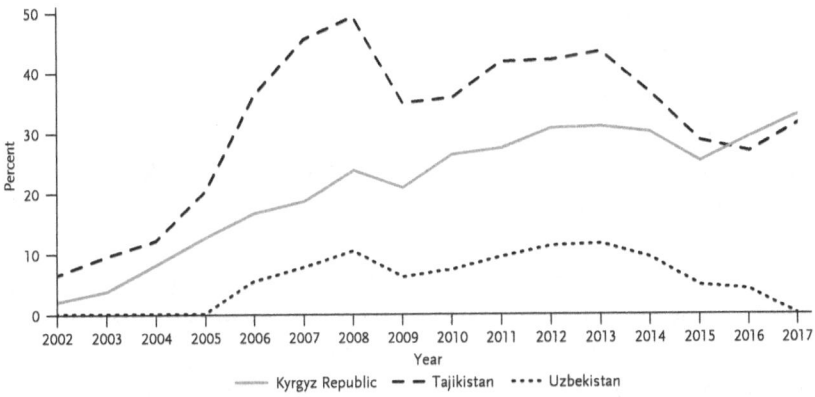

FIGURE 6. Personal remittances, received (% of GDP). Note: Kazakhstan and Turkmenistan reported negligible remittances. They are omitted from the figure.

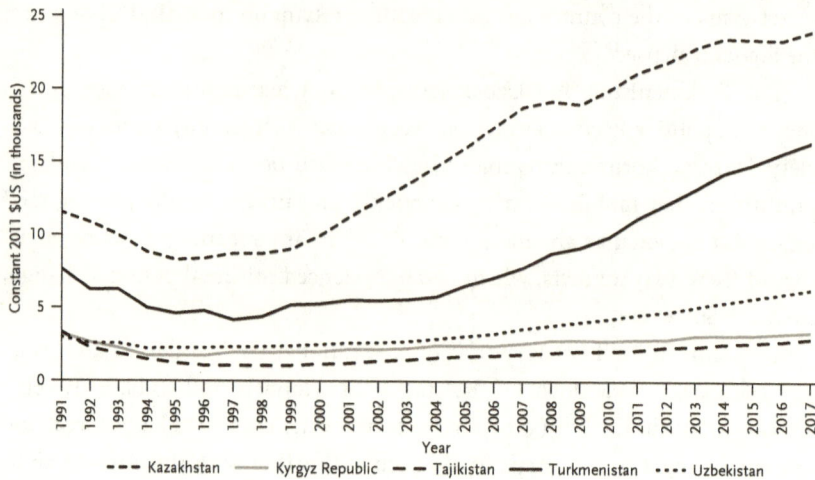

FIGURE 7. GDP per capita (constant 2011 international $).

Tajikistan, "The trade union movement needs a major overhaul, in particular in order to adapt organizational structures to current needs and changing economic activities and employment patterns."[22] Next to Turkmenistan and Uzbekistan, the regime could point to some reform, but in reality it was quite minimal, cosmetic, and scarcely implemented.[23]

Kyrgyzstan's economic profile bore some similarities to Tajikistan's. For example, it too relied heavily on remittances (figure 6). Yet, Kyrgyzstan had undergone significant reform, with myriad changes to its labor and related laws, including a new labor code created in 2004 with significant international involvement. The problem in Kyrgyzstan was that labor had few resources to mobilize. As the ILO flatly described, "Unions' capacity seems to be rather weak . . . [and] there are a lot of people (both in leadership and staff of the Federation and branch/sectoral unions) who are quite often lacking vision, positive thinking and a proactive approach."[24] Moreover, given the dominance of the informal economy,[25] organizing presented acute challenges. In such unpropitious circumstances, problems in labor relations were addressed ad hoc, if they were addressed at all. Asel Doolotkeldieva describes the class of brokers that emerged to act as intermediaries between workers, on the one hand, and management, unions, and the state, on the other. These brokers were in an ambiguous position; they often advocated positions protecting their brokerage role rather than representing the interests of labor as such. And the very informality of this arrangement seriously undermined any effort to create a durably productive relationship between labor and management.[26]

In the meantime, the broader Kyrgyzstani economy recovered from the 1990s decline, but growth rates remained anemic, putting downward pressure on wages and benefits and undercutting labor's position. Figure 7 shows GDP per capita in the five countries of the region from 1991 to 2017.[27]

Overall, in Central Asia demand for labor activism was dampened by rapid and pervasive deindustrialization, high levels of real unemployment, and high levels of employment in the informal sectors of the economy. Moreover, most Central Asians in the 1990s faced concerns more immediate than organizing around labor issues. As scores of interlocutors told me in the late 1990s, they felt lucky just to get bread on the table. The underpaid and underemployed found themselves expressing little beyond gratitude for being paid and employed in the first place.

These were the generally inauspicious circumstances for labor. In this context, Kazakhstan was something of an outlier.

Labor Activism in Kazakhstan

In addition to boasting a growing economy (figure 7), Kazakhstan was in other ways a state where some labor mobilization was to be expected. First, the country's mass privatization significantly shifted ownership away from the state, but the process in Kazakhstan was deeply flawed, giving rise to widespread impressions of "crony capitalism."[28] In the meantime, a receding social safety net, episodic currency devaluations, and industrial wages that struggled to keep pace with inflation were in tension with broad state narratives about the imminent arrival of broad-based prosperity. Even as economic growth continued in aggregate for Kazakhstan, the distribution of gains was highly uneven, generating resentment against individuals who ostentatiously displayed their wealth and questions about large-scale and enormously expensive state projects such as the creation of a new capital city.[29] Combine all this with a fairly permissive, soft-authoritarian political environment[30] and concerns about stagnant wages and substandard working conditions, and Kazakhstan was the Central Asian state most likely to witness mobilization.

Perhaps Nazarbaev recognized this potential, for his regime seemed determined to prevent it from materializing. Indeed, it is worth having a close look at the specific measures taken to ensure that labor's initial weakness generally reproduced itself.[31]

Reinforcing Labor's Weakness

In Kazakhstan, a variety of factors—some old and some new—served as ongoing constraints on activism.

First, at the national level, the state maintained a near monopoly on official union activity. After the uncertainty and ferment of the 1990s came to an end, the Federation of Trade Unions of the Republic of Kazakhstan (Federatsiia profsoiuzov Respubliki Kazakhstan, or FPRK) resurrected the basic role of the Soviet-era All-Union Central Council of Trade Unions. From 1991 until 2015, the Confederation of Independent Trade Unions of Kazakhstan (formerly Confederation of Free Trade Unions of Kazakhstan) sought to carve out space for autonomous unions, but it was constantly under pressure from the regime before ultimately being deregistered in 2015.[32] In the meantime, the FPRK's near monopoly generated virtual sectoral monopolies and ensured the pliancy of unions within most enterprises.[33]

Labor's subordinate role was thus cemented, as Elena Maltseva describes, through fairly crude enticements: "In return for maintaining social stability, trade union representatives were offered funds and office space to present the image of a well-functioning organization; unions also received bonuses and salaries for permanent staff. As a result, trade unions supported management." As Maltseva shows, this support was repeatedly made manifest, with unions supporting management during various miners' strikes against Arcelor Mittal, Kazakhmys, Karaganda Metal Works, the Ural'sk Metallist Plant, and the Irtysh Chemical Metallurgical Plant. Similarly, unions backed management in labor disputes by construction workers in Astana and Almaty and by workers at Kazakhstan Railways. "Most of these initial worker actions," Maltseva adds, "were sparked by unpaid wages or significant wage cuts, poor work conditions, low safety standards, or frequent work-related injuries; however, few of them received adequate support from official trade unions."[34]

Taking the side of management thus was entirely normal for official trade unions. Even after a massacre at Zhanaozen (discussed below) brought international condemnation and consequent pressure on the regime to improve working conditions, new legislation did nothing to change labor's fundamental orientation. A 2014 law reproduced the marginalization of truly independent unions. In 2016, a new labor code went into effect, simplifying the process of laying off workers and limiting protections for organizing on behalf of labor.[35]

Perhaps as important as these macro-structural constraints were the myriad micro-obstacles that labor organizers faced in their efforts, as the state and management worked together to ensure that the playing field privileged pro-regime interests.[36] In some cases, this began with the very physical location of enterprises. By siting enterprises strategically, the state in alliance with the employer could control access and monitor activities. For example, Kazakhstan's Tengiz oil field, which was launched in the late 1980s but given new life via a massive oil deal with Chevron in 1993, was located far from population centers. To complete Tengiz's isolation from broader Kazakhstani society, a series of nearby residential settlements was subsequently removed entirely. From the barbed wire surrounding the site to the strictly enforced control over the comings and goings of workers, to the near total exclusion of outsiders from the site, Tengiz came to resemble a correctional facility as much as an industrial enterprise.[37] In 1996, Tengiz workers began to mobilize, forming an unofficial union of 3,300 members and advancing workplace demands; a combination of coercion and cooptation continually quashed their efforts.[38]

Coercive dirty tricks at Tengiz and many other sites across Kazakhstan staunched the appetite for labor organizing, producing among workers an attitude that one interviewee called "fatalism."[39] Meaningful regulation of subcontractors (which were sometimes fly-by-night firms) was absent; predictably, this exerted downward pressure on wages and undercut workplace protections for health and safety. For their part, subcontractors were also kept in line, as secretive bidding processes for lucrative contracts could easily exclude companies making unusual or expensive demands. Reportedly, subcontractors were "expected to provide an obligatory kickback upon the contract signature."[40]

Contractors and subcontractors routinely shared with each other any emergent information about nascent labor organizing. It is hard to describe such sharing as innocent. Lists would informally circulate throughout the Tengiz region about individual workers tagged as "troublemakers"; these individuals were informally barred from obtaining work. "Troublemaking" included disseminating printed material about labor protests elsewhere, informing employees about their legal rights, and advising individuals about any embryonic organizing.[41] When being informally barred was not enough to deter would-be organizers, legal roadblocks could suddenly appear, such as that erected in 2007 by the management of the copper mining company Kazakhmys, which claimed in court that activists had used an illegal name for their independent trade union and were therefore breaking the law.[42] A similar tactic was used in 2012, when pro-regime actors created a "ghost" trade union with the very name that organizers had created for their union. The existence of another trade union with the same name prevented organizers from legally registering in 2013. This was the eighth unsuccessful attempt by this particular union to register itself with the authorities.[43] The cumulative effect of such individually minor obstacles was to deter organizing by independent labor.

Rumors abounded that employees acted as paid informants, apparently reporting to management on the activities of would-be agitators.[44] The resulting atmosphere of secrecy produced paranoia, such that it may have mattered less whether such informants *actually* existed than the fact that they were *believed* to exist. If confronted, the regime and management of course could deny everything, arguing that individuals who were against independent labor had every right to voice their personal opinions. Indeed—they might claim—the voicing of honest differences of opinion on labor relations was itself evidence of an emerging pluralism that the regime would want to protect, not quash.[45]

The judiciary was friendly to the state and management. Although nominally autonomous, judges faced enormous pressure to toe a pro-regime line. As already described, the regime expected compliant local courts to find reasons to deny legal registration to nascent labor unions, as occurred at Kazakhmys in 2001.[46] For their part, enterprise directors knew that judges would generally side with management. Thus, during the 2008–2009 financial crisis, which hit Kazakhstan relatively hard, enterprises by law were prohibited from laying off workers. Some nonetheless found space for creativity, opting to grant employees "unpaid leaves," after which they would be eligible to return to work. If this violated the spirit of laws ensuring job security, many enterprise directors were unfazed, as they could cut costs without contributing to the ranks of the officially unemployed, all the while remaining in the regime's good graces.[47]

Naturally, there were no ironclad guarantees. With its soft authoritarianism, Kazakhstan's political economy was littered with myriad actors always influenced by, but not entirely controlled by, the regime. In the judiciary, courts did not always take the side of management. In a few cases, company lawsuits against employees were dismissed.[48] Nonetheless, broad pro-regime patterns were unmistakable. Moreover, rarely did courts refrain from using their power; even when their interventions were ill informed from the perspective of the law itself, the courts routinely and actively inserted themselves into labor relations.[49]

While the regime could deny involvement in orchestrating everyday dirty tricks, and while it could point to parchment protections such as a labor code that met international standards,[50] in reality working conditions were usually poor. Migrants were often mistreated.[51] The regime circumvented legal labor protections by bringing criminal charges against labor activists and even the lawyers who represented them.[52] The situation would deteriorate further by 2017, as unabashed harassment of workers descended to new lows.[53] Russia's reassertion of its authoritarian influence in former Soviet space, as well as declining leverage in Central Asia for international actors such as the ILO, meant that many hitherto sub-rosa techniques by which the regime undermined labor would come into the open.

The Occasional Power of Disorganized Labor

Given that labor was comparatively disorganized and clearly constrained by an oppressive political regime well connected to global capital flows, one might expect the sounding of the death knell for Kazakhstani labor. This would be premature. A pattern of disruptions, exemplified by those in 2011 that culminated in tragedy in Zhanaozen, highlights the potential for labor in Kazakhstan. Often weak and disorganized, labor nonetheless was a social and political force. Put differently, it is worth listening to the noises made, however faintly, by nonbarking dogs. Doing so reveals that activists missed important framing opportunities presented by shifts to symbolic America.

Let us trace the patterns of protest since the Soviet collapse. The wave of activism that had engulfed the late Soviet state touched Kazakhstan as well, with coal miners joining strikes in the Karaganda region in 1989. This pattern, by miners who labored in atrocious working conditions, with low pay and long hours, would continue into the 1990s. Led by self-declared independent trade unions, miners would halt work in 1992, 1994, and massively in 1995, as they joined forces with workers from the Ekibastuz region. Workers advanced sector-specific demands, as well as demands for wages that were in arrears.⁵⁴ Further disruptions occurred in southern Kazakhstan in the towns of Kentau (1997) and Zhanatas (1997–98), in an ore refinery and a phosphorus plant, respectively. The Zhanatas protests included fifty hunger strikers, threats of self-immolation, a blockade of a railway line, and a police crackdown. All of these strikes were curtailed by regional authorities through a combination of coercion and limited concessions.⁵⁵

Among the next disruptive episodes was that in Glubokoe in 2003, a small East Kazakhstan town that had hosted one of three copper smelting plants for the company Kazakhmys. With significant ownership by the state (25 percent in 2002) and by South Korea's Samsung (32 percent in 2002), Kazakhmys sought to close the plant and move operations to other regions.⁵⁶ This led to a standoff, as an advocate for workers' rights described in real time:

> A lockout by workers [zakhvatnaia zabostovka] is underway in the village of Glubokoe in the East Kazakhstan region against the attempt by the management of the transnational company Kazakhmys to dismantle and remove the valuable equipment of the Irtysh Copper Smelting Plant [ICSP]. The authorities are actively promoting attempts by foreigners to destroy the plant and are involving intelligence agencies to seek reprisals against the leaders of the ICSP workers. . . . Workers demand nationalization. Every day, residents of the town of Glubokoe hold meetings in different neighborhoods [v raznykh kvartalakh]. Self-defense detachments [comprised of] workers and youth have been created to confront the police and strikebreakers.⁵⁷

To resolve the standoff, authorities arrived in Glubokoe and signed a memorandum committing to resettle newly unemployed workers in Zhezkazghan (about 1,400 kilometers away), where a new smelting operation would open. Authorities appeared uninterested in keeping their promises.⁵⁸

In far western Kazakhstan in 2004 and 2005, the Tengiz oil field was the site of protests and heightened tensions between workers and the management of a major oil subcontractor.⁵⁹ The conflict assumed an interethnic dimension, because aggrieved lower-paid workers were Kazakhs while management and higher-paid workers were often Turkish. In the end, the protests produced physical altercations but little substantive change beyond a marginal boost to wages. In the meantime, management created a new state office, the Tengiz Department of Relations with Enterprises, with the express purpose of hearing workers' grievances individually. The office would be radically understaffed and entirely overwhelmed. Predictably, this arrangement did little to address the underlying conditions at Tengiz, and violence erupted again in October 2006. This time, more than one hundred Turkish workers were hospitalized,[60] and rumors began to circulate that some Turks had been killed. Even if unfounded, such rumors illustrate how tense the atmosphere was where identity politics and labor relations were complexly intertwined.[61]

The disruptive power of labor would find its full expression in a tragedy that unfolded in 2011 about seven hundred kilometers from Tengiz. In retrospect, it is clear that conditions in Zhanaozen specifically and the Mangistau region more generally had been ripe for unrest. As Maltseva details, "Harsh climatic conditions that made local agriculture difficult, a lack of basic infrastructure, . . . poor quality housing and living conditions, and hazardous industrial working conditions made the life of ordinary residents expensive, depressing, and unhealthy."[62] Add to that the influx of thousands of ethnic Kazakh repatriates from China and Mongolia, a high birthrate, and high youth unemployment, and life in Zhanaozen was a "struggle for survival, with many residents angry, frustrated, and disappointed."[63]

During a broad strike of oil workers against the firm OzenMunaiGaz (and other subsidiaries of the state-controlled oil and gas company KazMunaiGaz), demands varied and evolved over time, but a central theme was inadequate pay and insufficient protection of collective-action rights.[64] With striking workers occupying Zhanaozen's central square from May through December 2011, authorities sought to clear the space for an Independence Day celebration on December 16.[65] Frustrated that striking workers refused to move, authorities ultimately opened fire, killing somewhere between fifteen (the official tally) and one hundred (unofficial accounts). Strikers had not been armed, and video footage clearly shows regime forces treating protestors and bystanders with impunity, even firing on fleeing individuals. The regime immediately declared a state of emergency. Evicting independent journalists from the region, it intended to control the narrative produced by these embarrassing and tragic events.

The narrative promoted by officialdom included apparent "lessons" drawn from the Zhanaozen tragedy: poor socioeconomic conditions can contribute to social unrest, oil wealth does not distribute itself to the broad population, and sound public policymaking is therefore required. In the massacre's aftermath, central authorities developed a series of programs designed to boost regional development in the Mangistau region in particular and in neglected villages, towns, and regions across Kazakhstan more generally. The diagnosis was that regional officials had been insufficiently enlightened in their approach to the striking workers; further enlightenment would prevent further tragedy. In the end, the regime prosecuted labor activists accused of contributing to the explosive confrontation, in addition to local authorities deemed to have committed acts of corruption that had exacerbated social tensions.

Yet, while the regime's narrative indicated a pragmatic interest in avoiding unrest, officials showed no interest in altering the basic structure of labor relations. Organizing continued to be viewed with great suspicion, as if independent labor by definition could not represent worker interests better than could an enlightened authoritarian regime that had rededicated itself to improving socioeconomic conditions. As before, workplace problems continued to be addressed ad hoc, and whether or not they were successfully addressed was largely a function of the goodwill of management. Proposed solutions were really tinkering to improve management's ability to forge enlightened public policy, such as the suggestion that better "personnel management" would improve worker motivation.[66] While subsequent labor disputes did not see a return to such tragic violence, the situation for labor after Zhanaozen in fact deteriorated.[67] Under such conditions, it was the very disorganized nature of labor that elevated its potential to be socially explosive. Not surprisingly, disruptions continued, including one a few hours' drive from Zhanaozen in Qalamqas, which was still unresolved as of 2018.[68]

If the pattern of increasing mobilization and disruptiveness was on display in Kazakhstan, it was more muted but also visible in Kyrgyzstan and Tajikistan. In Kyrgyzstan, a metallurgy union struck at the Kumtor gold mine in October 2010, ultimately resulting in a modest wage increase.[69] A traders' union at the enormous Dordoi bazaar in the capital city of Bishkek was effective, usefully bridging individual traders and management.[70] In neighboring Tajikistan in 2012, teachers went on strike in the northwest city of Penjakent, despite the regime's extremely strong pressure on teachers to refrain from any kind of concerted, disruptive action.[71] In short, while it is impossible to provide a complete catalog of unrest, labor enjoyed potential to disrupt normal politics. In the meantime, the material conditions that generated grievances, such as those concerning acute housing shortages, showed no sign of improving.[72]

Framing American Capitalism

As previous chapters showed, framers who avail themselves of resources provided by symbolic America may change the efficacy of their movements. Below I analyze the words of high-profile labor activists to address two issues. First, how did they frame local concerns and what interpretative schemata did they deploy? Second, to what extent and in what ways did activists link local concerns to extralocal ones? To what extent did they deploy master frames and what did any such frames consist of? While there was some variety in approach and style, activists typically showed awareness of the United States in particular and the West more generally, but they stopped short of making an explicit link to anti-American master frames.

Three Types of Frames

Social movement theorists divide frames into three types: diagnostic, prognostic, and motivational.[73] *Diagnostic frames* define a problem, making claims about its contours and attributing blame or responsibility. *Prognostic frames* offer a forecast about how best to address the problem, providing a plan of action. *Motivational frames* entail a call to action, offering a message designed to inspire. Though in practice the three frame types overlap, I separate them for analytic purposes.

Framing logically starts by defining the problem; problems do not speak for themselves. To make the point clear, imagine a few alternative frames about poor working conditions. Perhaps workers "deserve" poor conditions, given their natural place in the order of the universe. Perhaps poor conditions amount to "just punishment" visited upon workers by a vengeful deity. Maybe such conditions are a temporary, if unfortunate reality for those who fail to understand that the market demands that they find new work elsewhere. Perhaps such working conditions grease the wheels of economic growth, benefiting society as a whole, keeping operating costs and consumer prices low. Or maybe poor working conditions are a morally unacceptable byproduct of capitalist enterprise that requires remedy. I imagine tremendous variety in which of these frames would appeal to which framers under which circumstances. There is nothing automatic about how a problem is defined or to whom blame is attributed. Framers make choices.

In the case of Kazakhstan, activists diagnosed the problem as coming from the state. They typically depicted low wages, long hours, and poor working conditions as caused by the corruption and greed so common in the authoritarian politics of the region. Thus, the activist Ainur Kurmanov described the authorities' approach to labor mobilization in the Kentau region in 2003 this way:

> The social catastrophe that broke out as a result of the neoliberal policy of the government forces destitute people to fight for their life and the life of their children, to whom the authorities leave no future. And these citizens who do not want to die quietly of hunger, cold, and disease are labeled as among the worst enemies of the state, a state that serves the interests of a narrow circle of officials and their relatives/entrepreneurs. Authorities' violence [nasilie vlasti] against the resisting elements of the oppressed classes is increasingly acquiring the character of undisguised state terror. And this shows even more vividly the intensification of social contradictions and instability, in a country trying to convey its successful example of liberal economic reforms to other CIS [Commonwealth of Independent States] republics.[74]

It was specifically the "government," the "state" and the "authorities" that were engaged in violence and self-serving behavior. Further, Kurmanov diagnosed a fair bit of fakery, because what authorities claimed to be a model for other countries to emulate was in fact a trap that left people with "no future."

Prognostic framing varied. On the one hand were frames that depicted the solution as largely a technical one that simply required political will. Thus, activists regularly called upon authorities to revisit the coefficients underlying the calculation of wages. Issues of inequality and injustice were always beneath the surface, but the solution was described as a practical one. Outrage was not particularly required, and confrontation was ill advised. Only reasoned argument was needed to address grievances. Thus, in Zhanaozen in September 2009 and March 2010, workers' demands centered on changing the remuneration system, rather than on a wider array of issues.[75] Only later would demands broaden, when the protests in Zhanaozen began to mount in May 2011.

Other prognostic frames called out management practices. The typical framing contended that objective, material conditions were appalling but that management did everything to deny the objective facts on the ground. For example, in a dispute between Kazakhmys and workers in Karaganda in 2007, an informal labor leader argued that no solution was possible until management stopped being "disingenuous" (lukavstvo) and "openly propagating disinformation" (otkrovennaia dezinformatsiia obshchestvennosti).[76] His plan for combatting the problem centered on *likbez*, a Soviet-era abbreviation for the "liquidation of illiteracy." In other words, workers simply lacked knowledge; providing it was the solution.[77]

Some prognostic frames targeted the system of labor relations that prevented truly independent unions from operating. This kind of framing was becoming more common in the 2010s, and especially after Zhanaozen. The analyst Yevgeniy Zhovtis suggested that

> Zhanaozen demonstrated the vital necessity for independent trade unions to exist.... [I have in mind] the existence of organized representatives of workers, whom they would trust, who would coordinate social activity, who would be able to conduct a dialog on an equal basis with employers and the representatives of state power, who would have the authority and the competence to resolve labor disputes.... Zhanaozen should sound the alarm.[78]

Still others called out the regime itself. Thus, in the months that eventually led to the tragedy at Zhanaozen in 2011, striking oil workers resigned en masse from the ruling Nur Otan Party—the dominant, pro-presidential political party that nearly all workers had joined, if only for fear of losing their jobs.[79] This mass resignation made workers particularly vulnerable to varied forms of retribution by officials. Whether or not the move worked to effect, it underscores the fact that their target was the domestic political establishment.

Most pointedly, some posited that responsibility lay with the repressive apparatus of a coercive, authoritarian regime, suggesting that citizen resistance was the answer. Thus, over the years Kurmanov spent much time in prison on politically motivated charges (and he was not the only such activist).[80] Increasingly, his rhetoric was difficult to distinguish from that of other opposition actors who had identified the "regime of personalized power" (one of several widely recognized pseudonyms for Nazarbaev and his regime) as the source of Kazakhstan's broad array of problems. As workers began to strike in Mangistau in June 2011, Kurmanov wrote:

> In spite of all these attempts of the fake [zheltye] trade union bosses, the activities of Kazakhstani oilmen are already worldwide in nature, since they are already projecting on the territory of the Central Asian country all the workers'

discontent with the robbery by transnational corporations. In fact, this is the first conscious and broad movement of workers in the CIS with clear goals, and in many respects acquired a genuinely political dimension [politicheskaia okraska]. And first of all, this was possible because of the active antagonism by employers in the face of the Chinese company CITIC and the monster KazMunaiGaz, which is in the hands of the middle son-in-law of the president, Timur Kulibayev, as well as because of unprecedented repression against strikers launched by the special services and the government of the country.[81]

Finally, what did activists do to inspire the rank-and-file to participate and thereby take on risks that they might normally avoid? Motivational framing had two dimensions. First, activists deployed language focused on raising workers' consciousness of their comparatively disadvantaged position, of their legal rights, and of the obstacles to availing themselves of such rights. The language of outrage of course crept into activists' framing, but more typically it was a quiet language calling for fairness rather than a loud language announcing indignation.

Some of this language was simply a call for workers to organize, as Workers' Movement of Kazakhstan activist Sakhib Zhanabaeva wrote in 2003:

> The West bartered: democracy in exchange for the export of primary commodity resources and of Capital [sic]. Western countries themselves do not conduct deadly [chelovekoubiistvennye] reforms [in their own countries] because these countries have a people that can stand up for itself. We are demonstrating the silence of lambs. All crimes can be committed only with the silent agreement of indifference. . . . Let's get organized! We [the Workers' Movement of Kazakhstan] do not receive grants or other sponsoring help. Our allies are not tainted by state offices and corruption. And we do not grovel [ne presmykaemsia] before the money bags of America and Europe.[82]

While Zhanabaeva mentions the "money bags of America and Europe" and the West's preference for "primary commodity resources," she falls short of blaming them. Rather, the crux of her call is to overcome the "silence of the lambs" and instead to demonstrate agency by organizing. Like the Soviet-era *likbez*, hers was an appeal to raise consciousness in order to take action.

Second, activists deployed Soviet-style rhetoric concerning the struggle of the proletariat. Consider the platform of the Socialist Party (operating largely from exile), which includes a commitment to widespread nationalization:

We have in mind the nationalization of all strategic sectors of the country's economy, specifically the mining industry, metallurgy, energy, transport, major commerce, scientific institutions, and other economic sectors of key importance for society—[all] under the control of established workers' committees [pod kontrolem sozdavaemykh rabochikh komitetov].

Nationalization is unthinkable without moving the entire banking sector and financial system of the country... into the hands of the workers and the state. The most important element is the question of introducing a state monopoly on foreign trade.

Nationalization is only a means in the hands of organized workers and workers' parties for changing the balance of class forces in society through fundamental socioeconomic and political transformations and broad democratic reforms in the economy. The nationalization of enterprises that are in the hands of Nazarbaev oligarchs and foreign capitalists is a necessary step towards democratization; that is, access of workers to a portion of national wealth through the control and management of production.[83]

It is hard to know how effective such framing was, but it clearly ran against the grain of promarket understandings of the post–Cold War era.[84] It is not terribly surprising that activists more typically depicted their cause in quite local terms. "Even when massive strikes were organized such as the 1995 coal miners' strike in Karaganda," Steve Hess explains, "claimants continued to focus on specific material grievances, such as unpaid wages to coal miners, and did not adopt widened and more-inclusive frames that might incorporate citizens in other economic sectors into a common identity."[85]

What framing might have successfully widened the discussion and included other citizens, generating a broader-based movement for change? What opportunities for frame bridging were available that might have made a difference?

Missed Opportunities

The United States was not absent from the imagination of labor organizers. One coal miner widely known for his activism in the Karaganda region wrote in his personal memoirs about a trip to the United States, in which he was amazed by the pristine and safe working conditions at an Illinois mine. After describing the situation in great detail (with a running contrast to conditions in Kazakhstani mines), he added: "American miners don't have sweat under their arms. I checked. Each of them has signed a 300-page contract with the company. . . . They do drink [p'iut oni prilichno] but the vodka [tastes like] plastic. And they 'lose touch' quickly ['otkliuchaiutsia' oni bystro]." The working conditions and lifestyle of American miners impressed him deeply, even if their capacity for alcohol did not.[86]

Not everyone was so taken with the American model. Thus, when one activist from Glubokoe visited Russia for a 2003 conference of the Siberian Social Forum, he attended one panel that addressed the "widespread Americanization that suffocates national cultures and traditions both of the peoples of Russia and of Kazakhstan" and another that discussed the "deadly investments" made by foreign corporations.[87] The activist Sakhib Zhanabaeva from the Worker's Movement of Kazakhstan described the difficulty of her material situation, saying, "I have a big family: a husband and three children. They all have a higher education. They didn't graduate from Cambridge, but they have diplomas from ELITE Soviet universities that are no worse than Harvard."[88] The implication was that *their* Cambridge and Harvard are wrongly held up as the sole standard-bearers for education; *our* own Soviet institutions should not be forgotten.

With symbolic America not far from activists' imaginations, they might have forged explicit links to an anti-American master frame. I see little evidence that activists in Central Asia sought to create such master frames or link their struggles to already existing ones. In November 2012, a fire in Dhaka, Bangladesh, engulfed a factory that produced garments for export to the United States, among other Western countries; the fire killed more than 110 people and was widely attributed to unsafe working conditions. Similarly, police killed thirty miners and four protesters during a strike at a platinum mine in South Africa in August 2012. These incidents might have been redescribed as part of a pattern; a frame claiming that the greed of American and Western capitalists imperils or kills workers might have been resonant in parts of Central Asia.

One Kazakhstani academic hints at what such a frame might have looked like. Reacting to the tension between Turkish management and Kazakh workers at Tengiz, he claims that the US stands behind it all:

> The not-insignificant presence of Turkish companies and businessmen in this [the oil and gas] sphere is explained not so much by their high competitiveness,

as—to repeat—by the promotion of their interests by official US policy and by American capital in our country. In fact, in Kazakhstan today there is not a single major project with the participation of Americans or simply Western companies where Turks are not present as partners, contractors, subcontractors, or simply personnel as middle managers. The Americans, who evidently position themselves as the "big brother," with persistence that approaches crying indecency, have imposed and continue to impose upon us Turks as the new "older brother." And the citizens of Turkey who come here, for the most part try to behave towards local people accordingly. Hence, all the problems.[89]

The Zhanaozen massacre in particular had the potential to bridge to anti-American master frames, as Western multinational corporations remain deeply involved in oil extraction and export. Activists seemed to have avoided such a framing, perhaps in part because the specific companies against which workers struck were not Western ones.

A master frame would have had to go further than the claims made above by the Kazakhstani academic. It would have had to bridge to proliferating discourses critical of global capitalism, which Donatella della Porta and her colleagues call the "global justice movement."[90] Starting with widespread and highly visible protests at the 1999 Seattle conference of the World Trade Organization (WTO), a global cycle of protest started to emerge that targeted the WTO, the International Monetary Fund, the World Bank, and the European Union.[91] While these actors were not synonymous with the United States, they were the products of the American postwar political economic order. Activists held them responsible for the plight of the global working class that was suffering under rapacious capitalism. The master frame of this disparate movement was "neoliberal globalization," which subsumed themes like "social justice, democracy from below, ethics, and environmental justice."[92]

Any such links to anti-American master frames would have been valuable for labor's mobilizational efforts. They would have lifted some of the blame for poor working conditions from the regime, deflecting it to a remote and abstract global hegemon. By depicting itself as against American-style global capitalism rather than against the regime per se, labor potentially might have decreased antagonism between labor and the state. Blaming the United States would also have supplied the regime with ammunition as it sought to renegotiate its position vis-à-vis foreign multinationals. The 2000s were a period of rising economic nationalism,[93] and the regime in Kazakhstan in particular often deployed environmental regulations for example to force the renegotiation of ownership in major oil consortia.[94] If labor had loudly demanded better working conditions than American-style capitalism seemed capable of supplying, the regime might have been in a position to come to labor's defense.

Would any of this have made a difference? I am skeptical that developing or deploying a master frame would have raised salaries, improved benefits, or changed working conditions in any specific factory or enabled a positive-sum resolution in any specific labor dispute. But that is the wrong thing to expect from a master frame. Instead, tapping into symbolic America might have opened possibilities for movement activists to engage in frame bridging—an effort to link collective action frames to each other. In turn, this would have improved movement efficacy.

Conclusion

If the immediate post–Cold War era witnessed the global hegemony of liberalism in both its economic and political variants, the economic variant remained secure even as its political counterpart became much less so. To the contrary, the collapse of the Soviet bloc meant that one pole orienting ideological debates about economic affairs fell precipitously from the public imagination. China, the last of the major if only nominally socialist states, rapidly embraced capitalist enterprise. Of course, debates about political economy continued, but once the 1990s faded, they came to center on what types of state intervention into markets were appropriate to maximize corporate profits and ensure robust economic growth. With these as the overriding aims of policymakers, labor was an afterthought and was continually caught flat-footed. In this sense, the globe had become economically "American"—something that undermined most efforts at anti-American framing on the economic front.

There were exceptions—that is, places where criticisms of American-style capitalism helped to shift the political terrain. In his efforts to build an authoritarian state, Vladimir Putin, for example, took full advantage of a backlash against Western consultants, experts, and interventions that were associated in the popular imagination with Russia's economic decline in the 1990s. Putin would not undermine the essentially capitalist contours of Russia's political economy, but he would use anti-American tropes to shift it in an unabashedly dirigiste direction. The powerful president of a powerful state was more than able to tap into symbolic America for his own purposes.

Central Asia's labor activists were less powerful than Russia's president. Operating from a position of structural weakness, they faced ongoing dirty tricks that kept their ambitions low, their framing efforts modest, and their sights generally away from symbolic America. But there is a "but." If the global rise of populism in the late 2010s meant anything, it signaled that those who felt left behind in the new global political-economic order would find alternative ways to have their views represented. Whether this would occur through labor mobilization or other means in Central Asia remained unclear.

For its part, China had by 2019 made strong inroads into Central Asia, investing an estimated US$136 billion via its so-called Belt and Road Initiative, largely in mineral and petroleum exploration and processing, energy connectivity, and rail and road connectivity.[95] As a result, Chinese firms had the potential to displace other economic actors from the region, and thus to shift how Central Asians related to the outside world. Having said this, it is worth recalling that much of the symbolic power of the United States hinges on its universalizing ambitions. If China demonstrates similarly universalizing ambitions, it may in the future become a symbolic touchstone for Central Asians and one with potential to shift movement trajectories.

CONCLUSION

Shaping the Slow Politics of Anti-Americanism

AMERICA IS A RESONANT SYMBOL with shifting social meanings that travel great distances. What are the implications of these symbolic travels? In this conclusion, I first recap the Central Asian story before asking about the ultimate impact of slow anti-Americanism. Then, in Leninist fashion, I ask, "What is to be done?" What changes might shape how symbolic America affects global publics and global politics? While policymakers pay attention to the substance of their policies and sometimes pay attention to communicating their policies, they rarely concern themselves with matters of credibility. As research on framing effects suggests, however, the credibility of the messenger is crucial to effective public diplomacy and therefore essential to affecting how symbolic America shapes political dynamics.

Symbolic America and Social Movement Trajectories

As this book has argued, when processes of sedimentation shift the stock of available images, the possibilities for social mobilization consequently change. This statement encapsulates a twofold departure from normal thinking about anti-Americanism. First, the metaphor of a rising tide of public anti-Americanism that swamps policymakers and compels them to alter bilateral relations with the United States is misleading. It might fit the case of Iran on the eve of the Islamic Revolution, but it is a poor match for most other times and places. Second, whereas many discussions of anti-Americanism are concerned with discrete outcomes usually understood in binary terms (e.g., does popular anti-Americanism in Country X cause its leadership to reverse policy?), this symbolic politics approach suggests a more complex relationship between social forces, on the one hand, and bilateral relations with the United States, on the other. Any such relationship is traceable, observable, and important, but it is also indirect and multifaceted, producing outcomes best described in shades of gray rather than black and white.

As I have underscored, two important factors—namely, a social movement's initial evaluation of the United States and whether it is a broad-cast or narrow-cast movement—crucially shape the ultimate impact that shifts to symbolic America have on social mobilization. As chapter 2 described, different Islamist movements highlight this variation. Groups like Hizb ut-Tahrir (HT) and the Islamic Movement of Uzbekistan (IMU) harbored negative views of the United States, while the Islamic Renaissance Party of Tajikistan (IRPT) after the civil war came to have a positive view. HT was the movement most interested in broadcasting its message, while the IMU was interested in narrow-casting its message to a small number of committed supporters and the IRPT was a political party operating under major constraints that permitted only a moderate ability to spread its message. HT benefited greatly from the shift to symbolic America; the IMU benefited somewhat from this shift; and the IRPT suffered somewhat.

As chapter 3 covered, human rights activists harbored strongly positive initial views of the United States. Activists oriented toward street protests found their activities hampered by shifts to symbolic America, while the professionalized advocates involved in transnational networks found their activities hampered to a lesser degree. Finally, as the coverage of labor activism in chapter 4 reminds us, successful framing does not spring automatically from circumstances; it takes a concerted effort by activists to frame their efforts in ways that benefit from shifts to symbolic America. The effect of image-making politics depends in part on the creative agency of movement activists. Table 4 summarizes.

In short, the politics of image-making has a starker impact when membership is broad, participation is based on abstract rather than face-to-face relationships, and activists seize political opportunities presented to them. The impact may be immediate or lagged since powerful structural

TABLE 4. Symbolic America and shifting mobilization in Central Asia

Movement	Initial evaluation of United States	Broad-cast or narrow-cast movement?	Efficacy
Hizb ut-Tahrir	Negative	Broad	Strongly benefits
Islamic Movement of Uzbekistan	Negative	Narrow	Benefits
Islamic Renaissance Party of Tajikistan	Positive	Medium	Inhibits
Democracy protesters	Positive	Broad	Strongly inhibits
Transnational advocates	Positive	Narrow	Inhibits
Labor	n/a	Broad	n/a

forces are at play across the globe. Either way, this impact is remarkable and important.

Anti-Americanism, Redefined

As the vignette in the Preface describes, many expected that the shooting of Aleksandr Ivanov by an American serviceman in 2006 would become a test of anti-Americanism's political impact. Would the rising tide of anti-Americanism swamp the government of Kyrgyzstan, compelling it to push back against the United States? Or would this tiny state facing an insurmountable power imbalance steer clear of controversy to avoid alienating the global hegemon?

As it turned out, these were the wrong questions to ask because the impact of changes to symbolic America occur gradually and often subtly. To be sure, US foreign policy matters. If the United States had not invaded Iraq in 2003 on the false information that the latter had weapons of mass destruction, a key fount of the US's deteriorating global image would never have materialized. Similarly, if the United States had not scuttled long-standing norms of free trade as it did under the Trump administration in 2018, a major source of concern about the US as a global actor would not have appeared. Yet, if we seek to find unmediated, direct consequences of anti-Americanism's rising tide, we will be disappointed. Most shifts to symbolic America occur slowly, their effects churning slowly over time.

Geologic metaphors are helpful. *Sedimentation* suggests that orientations about the United States flow across frontiers of social class, cultural difference, and physical space in ways that are difficult to contain. When Central Asians traveled to Russia or consumed Russian media, when ethnic Uzbeks in Uzbekistan, Tajikistan, or Kyrgyzstan communicated with their co-ethnics in a neighboring state, and when iconic American brands like Marlboro, Levi's, and Coca-Cola first made inroads into post-Soviet consumer markets, this shifted the array of images to which Central Asians were exposed. Sedimentation likewise suggests that a shift in attitude about the United States has the potential to become part of the layered bedrock of social meanings. These meanings, in turn, can be quarried by social mobilizers. Such processes per se do not cause policy change, but they do provide raw material for such a possibility.

These processes together produce shifts in symbolic America with potentially dramatic effects. The Central Asia we saw by 2020 was not the same Central Asia from a decade or two earlier, in significant part because the types, scope, and dynamics of social mobilization had shifted. The region now had a consolidated pattern of politics: repressive and secular authoritarian regimes countenancing little opposition and fearful of civil society activism, especially from Islamist movements.[1] The political landscape was different.

Islamist movements had become more active and more anti-liberal. Enjoying extremely little space for domestic expression, they increasingly operated in the political shadows or in exile. In the meantime, larger numbers of Central Asians were intrigued by these movements and their promise to replace the status quo with a social order based on justice. In turn, the appetite for Islamist solutions generated an even stronger appetite for repression among Central Asia's secular, authoritarian regimes. This dynamic generated bizarre if fairly widespread rumors, such as the one popular among ordinary Central Asians that the West had installed and promoted radical Islamists in Central Asia in order to justify its meddling in a region where it did not belong.[2] Uzbekistan was the early riser, with the IMU and President Islam Karimov stoking each other's paranoia. By the mid-2010s, Tajikistan would lead the charge, with its severe and politically motivated crackdown on the Islamic Renaissance Party. Shifts to symbolic America by themselves were not responsible for this dynamic, but they did make it more likely to emerge. In the end, none of the region's states would escape it.

Simultaneously, shifts to symbolic America served to undercut human rights activism and the broad normative power of Western political ideals. Instead of wide-ranging commitments for ongoing political and economic reform and instead of multifaceted relationships covering a variety of social, economic, and political issues, Central Asia's political ties to the West were reduced to carefully delimited obligations secured largely on a bilateral basis or left in the realm of high-minded if anodyne pronouncements of common interest. As the West retreated, Russian and Chinese models of political and economic development filled the gap. This was enormously consequential for the architects of US foreign policy, who could no longer exercise American "soft power" in a region of crucial importance to US interests. Central Asia's engagement with the West did not disappear, but it was now a shadow of its former self. The change would have been even more dramatic if labor activists, who largely eschewed anti-American framing, had instead developed and deployed master frames critical of the United States. Nevertheless, the cumulative impact of shifts to symbolic America on Central Asian politics was significant and warrants our continued attention.[3]

What Is to Be Done?

Given these broad patterns, anti-Americanism is best understood as a pronounced tendency to deploy negative evaluations of symbolic America in social and political life. This tendency is as much sociological as it is psychological since it is built into collective constructions and collective identities. While behavior may be patterned, it nonetheless is prone to change as novel influences—some traveling great distances—become sedimented. Rooting out anti-Americanism where it has become bedrock might be a tall order, but there remains an important margin within which to affect this anti-American tendency.

To identify political dynamics is one thing; to intervene and influence them, another. Thus, we must conclude by posing a very Leninist question. Just as the Bolshevik leader underscored that the need for change does not necessarily produce that change, policymakers should not resign themselves to the macro-structural forces seemingly beyond their control.

Shaping symbolic America for political effect might seem a Sisyphean task. After all, even were it beneficial to craft a globally appealing US foreign policy, policymaking is not a popularity contest. Moreover, one need not be a "realist" to recognize that the very language of realism—that is, that states engage in the rational pursuit of national interest—pervades Washington. To shape symbolic America must not mean slipping into an idealism with little chance of gaining traction among policymakers.

It would be equally naïve to suggest that US foreign policy needs no attention, yet naiveté is in ample supply. We sometimes learn that improving the US image is simply a matter of improving communication or a question of effectively conveying America's great qualities. That was President George W. Bush's approach in October 2001:

> How do I respond when I see that in some Islamic countries there is vitriolic hatred for America? I'll tell you how I respond: I'm amazed. I'm amazed that there is such misunderstanding of what our country is about, that people would hate us. I am, I am—like most Americans, I just can't believe it. Because I know how good we are, and we've got to do a better job of making our case.[4]

For Bush, the problem was nothing more than a colossal and tragic misunderstanding. The solution was to set the record straight in "some Islamic countries." Emblematic of this approach was an advertising campaign launched after 11 September 2001. Depicting Arab Americans as leading happy and successful lives in the United States, the campaign was beautifully produced but coolly received. As it turned out, while the message was supposed to underscore the compatibility of Arab values and American values, audiences on the receiving end instead resented Arab Americans for their success abroad.[5] If viewers were unable to appreciate how welcoming American society in fact was to people of Arab descent, the problem was more than miscommunication. The problem was that different social environments give rise to perfectly valid, yet entirely different perspectives about the United States.

Misdiagnosing the problem, Bush's approach prescribed the wrong remedy. The premise underlying his statement and many like it is that policy shifts are inadvisable; US policy is morally correct and politically effective, by definition.[6] The only question is how to convey the essential and unfailing wisdom of US policy. Such an approach is deeply risky, since if communication is received as so much propaganda, voices decrying American hypocrisy become louder. Communication failures are thus not just the wrong medicine; they are potentially toxic.

Communicating effectively is a challenge; doing so across cultures is even more difficult. This is what those engaged in public diplomacy seek to do.

Does Public Diplomacy Work?

Public diplomacy is "a communication instrument used in governance broadly defined" that has multiple dimensions, writes Bruce Gregory.

> It differs from education, journalism, advertising, public relations, branding, and other ways in which people communicate in societies. However, it imports methods and discourse norms from civil society and depends on thick relationships with civil society to succeed. Because it is open communication, dependent on the practical benefits of truth and credibility, public diplomacy requires structural arrangements that protect imported norms (e.g., decisions based on academic merit in educational exchanges and journalism values in international broadcasting) and firewalls that separate it from covert instruments and deception techniques also used by political actors. Public diplomacy operates th[r]ough actions, relationships, images, and words in three time frames: 24/7 news streams, medium-range campaigns on high-value policies, and long-term engagement.[7]

Given this welter of factors, many of which are beyond the immediate control of policymakers, what indeed can be done? What is the margin for conducting effective public diplomacy?[8]

Research that I published with Renan Levine explores this scope for effective public diplomacy in Central Asia.[9] We were interested in hypothetical efforts to affect Central Asian attitudes about the United States. To gain analytic traction, we conducted a survey experiment and focus groups with 121 citizens of Kyrgyzstan and Tajikistan. In the survey, we randomly assigned particular frames and particular frame attributions to participants. The intention was to isolate the effect of public diplomacy efforts, controlling for other factors that influence how people view the United States. After the survey experiment, participants then engaged in free-ranging focus group discussions about the United States.

We built our analysis around a central frame, which depicted the United States as a place in which Muslims can openly and productively practice their faith:

> America rejects bigotry. We reject every act of hatred against people of Muslim faith.... America values and welcomes peaceful people of all faiths—Christian, Jewish, Muslim, Sikh, Hindu and many others. Every faith is practiced

and protected here because we are one country. Every immigrant can be fully and equally American because we're one country. Freedom of worship is an American value, and more than two million American Muslims are associated with more than 1,200 mosques in the United States.[10]

Some participants received the frame, while others received nothing. Those who did receive it also received various attributions. In some cases, it had no attribution; in others it was variously attributed to President Bush, to the US ambassador, or to an ordinary American. We then posed "feeling-thermometer" questions about the United States to see if exposure to frame and attribution affected participants' average responses.

Our evidence speaks directly to the question "What is to be done?" First, we found that the frame depicting the US as a good place to be a practicing Muslim had by itself little effect on subsequently expressed attitudes about the United States. That is, the groups receiving the prompt reacted similarly to those who received no prompt. Even though the frame had been carefully designed to improve expressed opinions of the United States, the frame alone made little difference. Second, the message also failed to "prime" participants to discuss the issue further. Priming is the process by which exposure to a particular topic renders it particularly salient in participants' minds. In the focus groups that followed the survey experiment, participants who had received the frame were no more likely to discuss religiosity and religious freedom than those who received no prompt. By themselves, frames had little impact.

In the real world, a message does not emerge from nowhere; it necessarily has a messenger. When we provided an attribution to the frame, this had a clear and important effect on subsequently expressed attitudes. Attributing the statement to President Bush or to the US ambassador (to Kyrgyzstan or Tajikistan, as appropriate)—who might be considered authorities on the United States—caused respondents to be *less* receptive to the message. That is, we found a deleterious "Bush effect." Pollsters had long noted that global publics had a low opinion of Bush during his presidency, but our finding is more dramatic. Central Asians did not merely *discount* a statement attributed to someone who for them lacked credibility. Instead, their suspicions caused the expected framing effect to be *resisted* and *reversed*.

Scholars have noted the importance of messenger credibility,[11] but it may be more important than ever. In the face of innumerable distinctive frames vying for attention, publics lean on trustworthiness to cut through the morass. If the goal is to communicate in order to persuade, then creative efforts to promote credible messengers must be central to public diplomacy. Moreover, since the "Bush effect" also affected how the fictional "ambassador" framing was received, we must be attuned to what psychologists call an "anchoring bias," in which individuals rely on ties to the US government as they evaluate any new piece of information.

Finally, the research that Levine and I conducted shows that context matters enormously. Consider the context of multiple, competing framing efforts. We designed our survey experiment to control for confounding factors. Doing so allowed us to identify the framing effects above. In the real world, however, framing occurs in contexts thick with social meanings; in our research, we held focus groups after each survey experiment to approximate the rough-and-tumble discussions that are the normal stuff of social interaction. After the focus groups concluded, we returned to "feeling-thermometer" questions about the United States. We found that the framing effects that had been observable during the survey experiment diminished in power after discussion with peers occurred. That is, as time passed and participants conversed with their peers, the framing effects became much weaker and in some cases evaporated. This may not be surprising, but it is nonetheless important: efforts at public diplomacy comingle with many other opinions, frames, and attempts at persuasion. To be effective in such contexts, they must compete with these alternative renderings.

Also consider the context of preexisting opinions. In the specific context of a particular social setting, what is the array of opinions of the United States held by individuals? Our research found that when an individual engages in discussion in a group with high average starting opinions of the United States, his or her opinion of the United States generally becomes even more positive. This makes sense, since one can imagine that persuasive attempts pushing in the same direction will have a cumulative effect. By contrast, if opinion ranges widely from negative to positive, this has the effect of lowering opinions of the United States even when a positive frame of the US is presented. In sum, there is a ceiling on how influential any positive message will be on views of the United States when less-positive information is available.

Implications

Public diplomats do not have carte blanche to influence the opinions of global publics. Opinion is malleable, but representatives of the United States government are constrained by existing attitudes toward the United States and by the credibility of the messenger. In Central Asia, the US government's poor reputation affected how individuals apprehended the United States as a global and regional actor. The impact of the frame attributed to the ambassador, while more tempered, nonetheless suggests that the consequences of Bush's poor reputation for American credibility would outlast the change in administration. The global controversies that first arose during the Bush administration had downstream effects, limiting the capacity of US government officials seeking to pursue effective public diplomacy.

If the advertisements for commercial products are any guide, frames would likely have to be deployed (1) with sensitivity to the background characteristics of the target population, (2) repeatedly, and (3) by credible messengers to be durably effective. First, frames that work generally in a country context might fail (or even have an adverse effect) within specific communities. Here, the injunction for public diplomacy is easy to state: start by knowing the context—not only at the level of countries or regions within countries but at the most micro level possible. Some scholars have already taken a step toward greater contextuality, disaggregating images of the United States into multiple types: "ally," "enemy," "dependent," "barbarian," and "imperialist." While this does not exhaust the possibilities, it is indeed essential to examine "the full range of potential international images,"[12] lest a message be woefully miscalibrated or misdirected.

Second, one-off framing efforts are likely to be lost in the welter of alternative images and other communicative efforts that Central Asians experience. Repetition is a potential strategy to overcome this challenge, though saturating the information space might not be practical. Our research raises an alternative possibility: that wide-ranging discussions about the United States conducted among local individuals may be more effective in shifting opinions than are simple framing efforts. Such wide-ranging discussions may touch upon many aspects of the United States; they may trigger a shift in attitude more effectively than a narrowly targeted frame would.

Third, credible messengers are crucial. We often assume that the message matters more than the messenger. Whether because of confirmation bias or because we are in fact correct, we tend to believe our own messages and find it inherently strange that someone else might be skeptical. Yet, research shows that the choice of messenger is crucial. To mount effective, proactive public diplomacy that stands a chance of shaping the slow politics of anti-Americanism, we should be well attuned to this possibility.

What might this entail? One option is to recruit individuals from the country in question who have already proven themselves to be persuasive with the target audience. These could be esteemed religious figures, venerated elder statespeople, or other figures prominent in the public eye. The risk is that such an indirect approach could trigger images of America's history of covert intervention. Thus, when reports surfaced that the US Department of Defense was considering a secret program to "discredit and undermine the influence of mosques and religious schools that have become breeding grounds for Islamic militancy and anti-Americanism," it was reasonable to question whose voices would be coopted for this purpose. As Muhammad Qasim Zaman put it, "That such initiatives would dislodge extreme interpretations of Islam more effectively than they undermine the effort to locate and justify 'moderate' ones remains, at best, uncertain."[13]

A more promising avenue is to promote US government spokespeople with deep knowledge of the language, history, and culture of specific world regions. Such area-studies knowledge would supply a simple and useful test of how palatable a message might be. If such people cannot effectively translate the essential wisdom of US policy into language that persuades their target audience, it might be time to revisit the policy itself or, at a bare minimum, to prepare for a strong negative reaction when such a policy is deployed.

The Politics of Traveling Images

It has become a commonplace that we live in an interconnected world in which images travel easily and quickly. What happens on one side of the globe can and indeed often does have an impact a world away. If this much is clear, the implications for social and political life are harder to discern. This book has laid bare one particular story—a story showing how changes to symbolic America shift trajectories for social mobilization in post–Soviet Central Asia. One example among many, it nonetheless suggests more general lessons.

First, policymaking that ignores symbolic politics is naïve. The solution is to bring these considerations into the mainstream. We might think by analogy. With gender mainstreaming, policymakers are tasked to weigh in advance the likely implications for gender relations of any policy being developed. With environmental risk assessments, many states require an advance estimate of the impact that a policy choice will likely have on the natural environment. Similarly, policy choices have downstream effects on symbolic America, and these effects can and should be estimated in advance. We would not want to reduce policy considerations to their psychological dimensions,[14] but to ignore how symbolic shifts alter political trajectories can lead to policy that ultimately proves self-defeating.

Second, the transnational dimension of symbolic politics is not new, but global connectivity brings novel forms of interaction that are "polycentric" and can abet rapid cascades of political change.[15] States will retain their preeminent role in shaping symbolic politics, but, without a monopoly on the process, they will be smart to take stock of the variety of ways in which images travel and the equal variety of factors that mediate their impact. Images of consumer products, pop superstars, political violence, natural and human-caused disasters—and the list surely does not end here—circulate widely, move quickly, and have clear social and political import.

Third, for all the variety and unpredictability of transnational symbolic politics, images do not travel willy-nilly and their impact is not random. Some environments are more receptive than others to the sedimentation of particular images. In the Central Asian contexts covered in this book, Kazakhstan and Kyrgyzstan in a macro sense enjoyed spaces more open to transnational influences than did Tajikistan, Turkmenistan, and Uzbekistan. At a more micro scale, we should not study traveling images in an institutional or cultural vacuum. The social movement framework used here is one way to take stock of the impact of traveling images in concrete contexts.

Fourth, power plays a crucial role in how images travel and what impact, if any, materializes. This has been a study of symbolic *America* for a variety of reasons, the first of which is that the United States in this period was globally hegemonic. An immense power disparity made it more natural to study symbolic America and its impact on Central Asia, instead of symbolic Central Asia and its impact on the United States. It is nonetheless worth emphasizing that hegemony exists at multiple scales. The images of regional hegemons like Brazil, China, India, and Russia inevitably play into the politics of their respective neighborhoods in ways that deserve more attention. One could go further, considering how the images of capital cities like Washington or

Moscow play into respective politics at a smaller scale.[16] Thus, as we address traveling images, we should maintain a clear view of the power politics this necessarily entails.

Finally, as we consider symbols and their travels, we will be smart to maintain a sense of proportion and even intellectual humility. Symbols and their travels clearly shape, nudge, cajole, and influence, but rarely do they *determine* political outcomes. Empirical patterns emerge, but specific outcomes will remain unpredictable. Central Asia is a changed place in part because of shifts to symbolic America, even though we would be hard pressed to accurately predict in advance the impact this will have on elections, on regime type, on policy outputs, or on other variables that tend to pique the interest of political analysts. The study of symbolic politics may sometimes confound our scientific ambitions, but it affords us a clearer view of a crucially important dimension of politics that we ignore at our analytic, and sometimes practical, peril.

APPENDIX
Reflections on Methods and Methodology

Academic books famously take long to write. This one took even longer than normal, in part because I wanted to study America's image from multiple angles. Turn it ever so slightly, and symbolic America reveals yet another facet. It also took longer because my dissatisfaction with the concept "anti-Americanism" doomed me to a significantly inductive study, moving from the complex realities of a messy world to theory building. If *doom* seems too strong a word, it does have the virtue of conveying how deeply befuddled one can be when faced with open oceans of evidence. Turning befuddlement into a book was never going to be easy.

I had become something of an advocate for political ethnography in the discipline,[1] and I spent many months trying to design this research with extended participant observation as its central component. Yet the exigencies of professional and personal life intervened, making that hard to execute. In the end, I nonetheless think that this book operates with an ethnographic sensibility, taking seriously (if not necessarily at face value) the perspectives of my Central Asian interlocutors themselves. I do wonder what book would have emerged from an ethnographically immersive study of a few research sites.

In general, my approach takes its inspiration from Rudra Sil and Peter Katzenstein's "analytic eclecticism." Their approach makes

> intellectually and practically useful connections among clusters of analyses that are substantively related but normally formulated in separate paradigms. It rests on a pragmatic set of assumptions, downplays rigid epistemic commitments, and focuses on the consequences of scholarship for concrete dilemmas. It challenges the analytic boundaries derived from paradigmatic assumptions, and refuses to carve up complex social phenomena solely for the purpose of making them more tractable to a particular style of analysis.

> Instead, it identifies important substantive questions that have relevance for the real world, and it integrates empirical observations and causal stories that are posited in separate paradigm-bound theories or narratives.[2]

I am drawn to their desire to move away from "paradigm-bound" thinking, which can be limiting, to forge analytic connections between the previously unconnected, and to resist creating research agendas that privilege what is considered easily researchable. Feeling liberated, I have gathered whatever evidence made sense and used whatever method made sense, all under conditions not of my own choosing. Let me start by addressing these conditions before I turn to evidence, methods, and methodology.

Conditions

Had someone replaced me with another researcher, this would have become a different project. First, I have been interested in Central Asia for more than twenty-five years, and I have been interested in perceptions of the United States for even longer. In this sense, the research question that this book tackles is very much *my* research question. My task was to make it interesting and intelligible to others who otherwise are drawn to other matters. Second, I was trained in the use of qualitative methods, so privileging focus groups, interviews, and document analysis was natural. Even when I use numerical data, I present them largely for descriptive purposes (chapter 1) or rely on a co-investigator (Renan Levine, in the Conclusion) to analyze statistical patterns on a narrowly defined matter for which other evidence is unavailable.

There are many more personal characteristics that might matter: I am white, of Jewish upbringing, male, a tenured professor, relatively economically privileged, married with children, a dual American-Canadian citizen, and so on. These things made it easier for me to approach certain people, harder to approach others. They made it easier for me to ask certain questions, harder to ask others. In conversations with Central Asians (covered below), I always followed the advice of Timothy Pachirat, who encourages us simultaneously to become aware of and embrace our partiality.[3] There is no "view from nowhere."[4] Had the gods dispatched someone else to do the work, they would have been commissioning a different project.

Over the life-span of this research (2002–2018), certain broad research conditions quietly left their mark. Turkmenistan always had been off-limits for serious data collection on political questions. In 2005, after a massacre of protestors in Andijan, Uzbekistan, and the subsequent souring of relations between the West and Uzbekistan, my planned fieldwork in that country became impossible. References to field-based data from Uzbekistan and Turkmenistan are therefore absent. I did get access to Hizb ut-Tahrir activists in neighboring Kyrgyzstan, but any ground-level view of how the Islamic Movement of Uzbekistan operated was precluded. My family was pleased to learn that I would remain at a safe distance from militants.

Access in Kazakhstan, Kyrgyzstan, and Tajikistan was generally good. Of course, access is not a binary, but a sliding scale. As a Westerner sympathetic to a human rights agenda, I had no problem speaking with Kyrgyzstan's pro-democracy civil society actors; I had poorer access to Kazakhstan's labor activists in the oil sector, since the sector carefully monitored the comings and goings of outsiders. In Tajikistan, I spoke with members of the Islamic Renaissance Party of Tajikistan (IRPT), but everything in Tajikistan changed in 2014, when Tajik authorities arrested a Tajik-passport-holding University of Toronto PhD student doing research, charging him with high espionage and treason. He was eventually able to return to Toronto, but thereafter the climate for researchers in Tajikistan deteriorated quickly. For me in particular, research in Tajikistan has not been thinkable since. For Tajik scholars still in the country, I fear for their livelihood if not their lives. In 2015, the IRPT was banned, its leadership and even ordinary members harassed, prosecuted on politically motivated charges, and pursued globally.

For many, if not most, social science topics, I strongly believe that we should aim to be comprehensive and exhaustive without dismissing evidence that falls short of that ideal. Likewise, we should seek evidence that is accurate but not throw out material that does not lend itself to face value interpretation. The virtues of systematic research are not lost on me, but, given the enormous weight of circumstances beyond my control, it was hard to imagine being anything other than truly catholic in my approach.

Evidence and Methods

This eclectic approach had six main components.

First, I had the pleasure of reading scores of terrific academic works on Central Asian politics and society. The past decade has seen a steady rise of research conducted at close range in Central Asia by scholars with exceptional language skills, cultural knowledge, and analytic acumen—many of them from the region itself. We scholars always "stand on the shoulders of giants," but perhaps particularly so in this case because my topic ranges across the region and across social movement types. I am grateful to the community of scholars who continue to inspire.

Second, I read and analyzed innumerable documents, journalistic accounts, and reports. Some of this amounted to background reading on Central Asian social movements and therefore has not been cited. It may seem awkward to mention work that I do not reference directly, but I am convinced that how we interpret the world is a function of what we are exposed to, not solely of what makes it into our final manuscripts. As Michael Polanyi aptly puts it, "we can know more than we can tell."[5]

Documentary sources that I "can tell" are many. Because change over time was important to my analysis, I tried to reconstruct how Central Asians were viewing the United States across the span of decades. I read Radio Free Europe / Radio Liberty reports assiduously. I also read the accounts in newspapers from the region. For Kazakhstan, I read *Kazakhstanskaia pravda* and *Panorama*. For Kyrgyzstan, I read *Delo nomer* and *Respublika*. For Tajikistan, I read *Najot* in English translation and *Aziia-Plius* in Russian. Given heavy-handed state censorship, newspapers were unlikely to be helpful in Turkmenistan and Uzbekistan. I limited my systematic reading on this score to articles that made some mention of the United States or things understood as "American."

I read reports by nongovernmental organizations, government bodies, and international actors that had some bearing on the three social movement types of interest or on views of the United States more generally. This was of necessity a broad-gauge effort since I could not know in advance where information of utility might present itself.

Aside from the coding exercises which had a distinctive logic (see below), I tried to imagine the French historian Marc Bloch as my intrepid guide to interpretation. Bloch counsels historians to be aware of the audience, intended and otherwise, for a given document, as well as any absences and silences: "Ordinarily, we prick up our ears far more eagerly when we are permitted to overhear what was never intended to be said."[6] Since our documents do not speak for themselves, they must be properly questioned. He writes, "From the moment when we are no longer resigned to purely and simply recording the words of our witnesses, from the moment we decide to force them to speak, even against their will, cross-examination becomes more necessary than ever."[7] Of course, some "cross-examinations" are narrow, with a particular end in mind, while others are broader and more open-ended, but the key is to coax the material into "speaking."

Third, I spoke to Central Asians. I call most of these conversations "interviews" in the endnotes because I usually had my own research topic in mind as I conducted them, but I approached them with maximum flexibility. In most cases, I was happy to let the conversation evolve because that is what conversations do, though I would always seek ways to nudge them, slowly if necessary, back to my topic. They were decidedly unstructured affairs. For the topics that I research, I have never seen great value in taking an invariant approach when the relationships with our interlocutors vary so tremendously. Their formal designations—social movement activist, member of the political opposition, government official, and so on—run the gamut, but recognizing that only scratches the surface of variation in relationships between research and researched.

Some interlocutors viewed the world quite differently than I did. I never saw it as my role to change anyone's mind. So, when a local, educated Hizb ut-Tahrir activist described to me a vast, global Jewish conspiracy to encircle Central Asia, I was taken aback by the ease with which he deployed anti-Semitic tropes in conversation with someone of Jewish origin. Instead of correcting him or others who might not possess all the relevant facts, I always tried to proceed with an ethnographic sensibility, asking, "Why might this person view the world as he or she does?"

To the extent that interviews are in fact conversations, it would also be unnatural to be silent. To be sure, some people prefer the sound of their own voice, but most interlocutors have some curiosity about the researcher and expect to learn a bit about him. Without trying to convince or challenge, where appropriate I would invite them to refine, elaborate, consider alternatives, or tell me where they got their information from. I always tried to remain open-minded even if I had no reason to believe this approach was being reciprocated. I cannot prove that these efforts paid dividends, but they felt natural to me and productive for my research project.

There are many approaches to interviews in the social sciences;[8] mine approximates that of my late colleague Lee Ann Fujii. I was always struck by how close our methodological sensibilities were. Regularly, Lee Ann put into words what I could not adequately conceptualize. She taught us to take seriously "metadata," which are "informants' spoken and unspoken thoughts and feelings which they do not always articulate in their stories or interview responses, but which emerge in other ways."[9] She implored us to develop relationships with interviewees based on mutual respect, an approach she would call "relational interviewing."[10] Social science is richer for her varied and important contributions, and social science will be in all senses better if it takes them seriously.

For this project, interviews were conducted with activists, mobilizers, ordinary people, and government officials, yet they were not the primary source of face value data on framing. I quickly discovered that many framing choices are not made consciously, and, to the extent that I was interested in such choices made over time, actors often could not recall the specifics of their diagnostic, prognostic, and motivational framing efforts.[11] Interviewees were selected purposively, that is, with an eye to what their expected testimony could contribute to our understanding of the phenomenon, given their social/political position. This is very different from interviews based on "sampling" techniques designed to generalize from a small number of interviewees to a larger population.

Fourth, I organized focus groups in a variety of locations. For this purpose, I decided to make myself scarce. I calculated that my very presence in front of a group summoned to discuss "foreign affairs" (the generic title we gave in our recruitment calls) could throw a proverbial wet towel on the conversation and make participants less likely to criticize the United States. Instead, I conducted trainings for focus group leaders from Kazakhstan, Kyrgyzstan, and Tajikistan, providing them detailed instructions.[12] I am certain that this guidance helped them to produce better data, though it must also be true that a different moderator would have altered the dynamic. Knowing this, I paid close attention to the gender and language competence of each focus group leader in selecting groups for each to lead.

Eighteen focus groups were conducted, with six each in Kazakhstan, Kyrgyzstan, and Tajikistan. The groups were as follows, with an emphasis on capital city/region, level of education, and gender:

Focus group #1
1. Conducted in [capital city] with 12–15 participants.
2. *All* participants have a higher education.
3. Even distribution of men and women.

4. Even distribution by age between 21 and 55.
5. Even distribution of birthplace, by region of [the country].
6. Everyone should speak [the titular language].

Focus group #2
1. Conducted in [capital city] with 12–15 participants.
2. *No* participants have a higher education.
3. Even distribution of men and women.
4. Even distribution by age between 21 and 55.
5. Even distribution of birthplace, by region of [the country].
6. Everyone should speak [the titular language].

Focus group #3
1. Conducted in [regional city] with 12–15 participants.
2. All participants have a higher education.
3. Only *men*.
4. Even distribution by age between 21 and 55.
5. Approximately even distribution of birthplace, by region of [the country]. It was acceptable to have slightly more participants who were born in the region in which the city is located.
6. Even distribution by rural/urban residents.
7. Everyone should speak [the titular language].

Focus group #4
1. Conducted in [regional city] with 12–15 participants.
2. All participants have a higher education.
3. Only *women*.
4. Even distribution by age between 21 and 55
5. Approximately even distribution of birthplace, by region of [the country]. It is acceptable to have slightly more participants who were born in the region in which the city is located.
6. Even distribution by rural/urban residents.
7. Everyone should speak [the titular language].

Focus group #5
1. Conducted in [regional city] with 12–15 participants.
2. *No* participants have a higher education.
3. Only *men*.
4. Even distribution by age between 21 and 55.

5. Approximately even distribution of birthplace, by region of [the country]. It was acceptable to have slightly more participants who were born in the region in which the city is located.
6. Even distribution by rural/urban residents.
7. Everyone should speak [the titular language].

Focus group #6
1. Conducted in [regional city] with 12–15 participants.
2. *No* participants have a higher education.
3. Only *women*.
4. Even distribution by age between 21 and 55.
5. Approximately even distribution of birthplace, by region of [the country]. It was acceptable to have slightly more participants who were born in the region in which the city is located.
6. Even distribution by rural/urban residents.
7. Everyone should speak [the titular language].

This represents significant variety, though it must be emphasized that focus groups per se should not be used to generalize to a larger population. Instead, they allow us to generalize to a process. That is, they provide a window onto how politics is made and remade in social situations. Focus groups are not organic social situations, but they do a serviceable job of simulating them.

Fifth, with the help of research assistants, I engaged in a series of coding exercises, used to establish broad patterns and explore change over time. Central was the coding of mentions of the United States in coverage by Radio Free Europe / Radio Liberty (RFE/RL; chapter 2). I coded every news item from each Thursday's RFE/RL *Newsline* from 1991 through 2001. About 7 percent of the more than 17,000 items coded describe an event in which a societal or governmental actor expressed an attitude about the United States. Thus, public statements, protest demonstrations, legislation pending or enacted in local parliaments, news conferences, leafleting efforts, diplomatic negotiations, and a whole series of other reported events all contained information about how actors felt about the United States. I judged each relevant news item on a 6-point scale: a 6 was strongly pro-US; 1, strongly anti-US. The daily scores were averaged and then aggregated into quarters. I coded news items not only on Central Asia but on the entire ex-USSR. I employed two coders for this exercise, and I verified their coding for one hundred items.

More limited coding exercises were conducted with the regional newspapers (above), two each from Kazakhstan, Kyrgyzstan, and Tajikistan. In the latter case, newspaper availability was too spotty to get a clear view of longitudinal patterns. The basic parameters for coding were the same as for the RFE/RL exercise.

Sixth, the final method of data collection was a survey experiment conducted on the heels of each focus group (above). Of the three countries, the data on Kyrgyzstan and Tajikistan did not suffer from inexplicable anomalies. Unfortunately, I was not able to use the data on Kazakhstan because of such anomalies. Thus, we recruited 121 people (nearly evenly split between the two countries) through the personal networks of moderators and their contacts. In ex-Soviet societies, where network-based behavior is typical,[13] broadly advertising a study to recruit a room full of diverse strangers could make participants reticent to share their views and compromise the validity of responses.[14] Instead, we recruited from several different communities so that the views expressed within each discussion might reflect those of groups found in the broader population to provide a demonstration proof of how framing effects work. While we hoped that our participants would be broadly representative of their communities, our hypothesis testing required only that we randomly assign individuals to treatments to observe differences among them.

Research was conducted in two locations in Kyrgyzstan: Bishkek and Osh. Tajikistan had three sites: Dushanbe, Khujand, and Kulob. Each location has distinctive characteristics. Bishkek and Dushanbe are capital cities. They are more densely settled, more urban, more linguistically and culturally Russified, and have denser personal, cultural, and communication links with the West than do the other cities. Osh is Kyrgyzstan's second-largest city and Khujand is Tajikistan's second-largest city. Compared to the capital, each has closer ties to agriculture, is less Russified, and is linked by physical geography and ethnic composition to Uzbekistan. In short, Bishkek and Dushanbe share some principal similarities, while Osh and Khujand share other crucial similarities.

In Kyrgyzstan, we recruited 29 respondents in Bishkek and 32 in Osh. In Tajikistan, 19–21 respondents participated in focus groups conducted in Dushanbe, Khujand, and Kulob. Eight to 12 people participated in each group.

All but one group contained at least one member assigned to each experimental condition; 7 out of 12 groups contained at least two participants assigned to each condition. The sole exception was an 8-person discussion in Dushanbe that did not include a respondent assigned to the no-quote control (below).

In total, we randomly assigned 25 participants in all the locations to read the statement attributed to President Bush. Twenty-five participants read the statement attributed to the ordinary American, and 26 read the statement attributed to the US ambassador. Twenty-three read the quote without any attribution, and 20 were randomly assigned to the control. Of the 121 respondents, 118 provided an answer to at least one of the prediscussion questions used to calculate the index. And 113 participants also provided an opinion of the United States after the discussion.

Our sample was not necessarily representative of the population. For example, ethnic minorities were underrepresented. According to the *CIA World Factbook*, about 80 percent of Tajikistan is Tajik, and 65 percent of Kyrgyzstan is ethnically Kyrgyz. In our sample, 55 respondents identified as Kyrgyz, 54 as Tajik, 4 as Russian and 5 as "other." The largest minority in each country is Uzbek. Russians make up 12.5 percent of Kyrgyzstan. Seventy-five percent of our respondents identified themselves as having a religion. All were Muslim except four Christians—three in Kyrgyzstan and one in Tajikistan. This is broadly similar to the populations, as 90 percent of Tajikistan and 75 percent of Kyrgyzstan is Muslim. On average, the groups recruited in Kyrgyzstan were less religious than those in Tajikistan. Our sample was relatively well educated, with three-quarters having graduated from college. Most discussion groups were entirely or almost entirely composed of college-educated people. College-educated respondents were in the minority only for one group in Osh. The average age of our sample was thirty-two, older than the median age for each country (twenty-four for Kyrgyzstan, twenty-one for Tajikistan).

If all of this eclectic data-gathering seems like too much work for one person, it was. I relied heavily on the good judgment and terrific contributions of many research assistants over the years. The book was literally impossible without them, and I owe them an enormous debt of gratitude.

Methodology

All this disparate evidence presented ample opportunity to "triangulate," confirming conclusions—large and small—via multiple sources of data wherever possible. But having a multitude of data is no guarantee that they speak to each other. This returns us to the question of methodology.

It has become received wisdom that scholars of comparative politics should use "multiple" or "mixed" methods. Typically, this is understood to mean employing both quantitative and qualitative evidence. The conceit is that, since each approach has its shortcomings, only a combination can provide an accurate account of the research topic. In reality, I doubt that many social scientists have ever believed it best to rely on one method to produce knowledge. Certainly, many individuals have made careers by deploying their well-honed skills in one technique, but even they typically view their work as being in conversation with work produced via other techniques. The injunction to "mix methods" strangely assumes that multiple methods are unusual and therefore a special argument needs to be made on their behalf. In my experience, a participant-observer might also conduct unstructured interviews. An interviewer might also scour available quantitative datasets. An historical institutionalist might also take into account the insights of game theorists. I too employ multiple methods of inquiry.

But we should ask, Under what conditions is mixing methods productive, and under what conditions is it counterproductive? Sil and Katzenstein, arguing for analytic eclecticism, suggest that incommensurability of approaches is "not as severe as is frequently assumed."[15] I am less sanguine. To me, the autonomous, profit-maximizing individual of rational-choice theory cannot be easily reconciled with the neuron-driven individual of neuroscience or with the role-playing individual of sociological science. The fact that we use a single term ("individual") in all three cases does not make it advisable to mix approaches from each. If this is true for concepts, it is also true for methods. It might be possible to reconcile some kinds of participant observation with some kinds of interviewing, but if you try to combine interpretivist participant observation with structured, positivist interviewing, you may just produce an analytic mess.

Perhaps it is a bit like baking: before you throw everything into a mixing bowl, it might be useful to know a thing or two about proportions, sequencing, and what ingredients in fact work well together. If some ingredients simply should not be mixed into the same batter, you could still consider distinct preparations before serving them on the same plate. At the extreme, flavors simply clash. For those cases, best to prepare them for different meals.

Leaving (as I should) the actual cooking and additional metaphor-making to those more capable, I suspect that no research project mixes methods in equal portions; instead, most rest upon a dominant approach. This is the case because, while methods can be used in the service of different methodologies, there is what Max Weber called an "elective affinity" between particular methods and particular methodologies. Today, a typical ethnography rests upon interpretivist tenets. Today, a typical election study relies upon neopositivist assumptions. That these affinities are neither permanent nor perfect does nothing to diminish their importance.

The more incommensurate the ultimate philosophical underpinnings of two given methods, the more that "mixing" in fact is subordinating one method to the other. One might profitably embed a mini-research question undergirded by positivist assumptions within, and therefore in the service of, a larger interpretivist research project. That is what I sought to do. My goal was to elucidate what might shift Central Asians' perceptions of the United States. To gain traction, I employed a survey experiment in the context of focus group discussions, provisionally accepting assumptions about statistical controls and causality widely used in neopositivist social science. But many of the broader questions about Central Asians and their exposure to, and use of, political images are better captured by the slow-moving metaphor of sedimentation and the epistemological apparatus that accompanied it. In the end, I believe that this study is best read as one in which interpretivist methods and sensibilities are dominant and neopositivist ones are provisionally adopted for narrow questions embedded within. I am comfortable serving them together on the same plate.

NOTES

PREFACE

1. Tyntchtykbek Tchoroev, "Kyrgyz Political Circles Split on Manas Decision," *Radio Free Europe / Radio Liberty*, 9 February 2009.
2. Manas closed in 2014, largely without any groundswell of opinion.
3. Flaws were understandable in the aftermath of the 9/11 attacks and the sensemaking scramble that ensued, but today we have the luxury of an unrushed and sober evaluation. For insightful early evaluations, see Shibley Telhami, "Why Do They Hate Us So Much?," presented at "Political Islam: Challenges for U.S. Policy," Aspen Institute, Washington, DC, 27 June–3 July 2003; and Marc Lynch, "Taking Arabs Seriously," *Foreign Affairs* 82, no. 5 (2003): 81–94.
4. Bernard Lewis, "The Roots of Muslim Rage," *Atlantic Monthly* 266, no. 3 (1990): 47–60; Samuel P. Huntington, *The Clash of Civilizations and the Remaking of World Order* (New York: Simon & Schuster, 1996).
5. Islamic political thought became concerned with the West only in the late nineteenth century. See Charles E. Butterworth, "Political Islam: The Origins," *Annals of the American Academy of Political and Social Science* 524 (November 1992): 26–37.
6. Examples include Noam Chomsky, *Rogue States: The Rule of Force in World Affairs* (London: Pluto Press, 2000); and Timothy Mitchell, "American Power and Anti-Americanism in the Middle East," in *Anti-Americanism*, ed. Andrew Ross and Kristin Ross (New York: New York University Press, 2003), 87–105. For a polemic against French anti-Americanism, see Jean François Revel, *Anti-Americanism* (New York: Encounter Books, 2003). A sober-minded treatment is Sophie Meunier, "The Distinctiveness of French Anti-Americanism," in *Anti-Americanisms in World Politics*, ed. Peter J. Katzenstein and Robert O. Keohane (Ithaca: Cornell University Press, 2007), 129–56.
7. Proposing that to undercut anti-Americanism is to pay too high a cost, Ajami writes, "To maintain France's sympathy, and that of *Le Monde*, the United States would have had to turn the other cheek to the murderers of al Qaeda and engage the Muslim world in some high civilizational dialogue." See Fouad Ajami, "The Falseness of Anti-Americanism," *Foreign Policy* no. 138 (September/October 2003): 57.

8. Joseph Nye, *Soft Power: The Means to Success in World Politics* (New York: Public Affairs, 2009).

9. Throughout this book, I use "America" as a shorthand for the United States. This is consistent with ordinary parlance in post-Soviet space.

INTRODUCTION: SLOW ANTI-AMERICANISM

1. Robert Snyder, "Explaining the Iranian Revolution's Hostility Toward the United States," *Journal of South Asian and Middle Eastern Studies* 17, no. 3 (Spring 1994): 19.

2. Marco Aponte-Moreno and Lance Lattig, "Chávez: Rhetoric Made in Havana," *World Policy Journal* 29, no. 1 (Spring 2012): 40.

3. James A. McCann, "Ideology in the 2006 Campaign," in *Consolidating Mexico's Democracy: The 2006 Presidential Campaign in Comparative Perspective*, ed. Jorge Domínguez, Chappell Lawson, and Alejandro Moreno (Baltimore: Johns Hopkins University Press, 2009), 268–84.

4. Case-studies abound. On anti-Americanism in Germany, see Mary Nolan, "Anti-Americanism and Americanization in Germany," *Politics & Society* 33, no. 1 (March 2005): 88–122. On South Korea, see Yongshik Bong, "Pragmatic Anti-Americanism in South Korea," *Brown Journal of World Affairs* 10, no. 2 (Winter/Spring 2004): 153–65. On Europe generally, see Serio Fabbrini, "The Domestic Sources of European Anti-Americanism," *Government and Opposition* 37, no. 1 (2002): 3–14. On the Arab world, see Abdel Mahdi Abdallah, "Causes of Anti-Americanism in the Arab World: A Socio-Political Perspective," *Middle East Review of International Affairs* 7, no. 4 (December 2003): 62–73; for a flip-side discussion about how Hollywood films depict Arabs and Muslims, see Jack G. Shaheen, "Reel Bad Arabs: How Hollywood Vilifies a People," *Annals of the American Academy of Political and Social Science* 588, no. 1 (July 2003): 171–93.

5. Peter J. Katzenstein and Robert O. Keohane, "The Political Consequences of Anti-Americanism," in *Anti-Americanisms in World Politics*, ed. Peter J. Katzenstein and Robert O. Keohane (Ithaca: Cornell University Press, 2007), 275.

6. Katzenstein and Keohane, "Political Consequences of Anti-Americanism," 276.

7. For one treatment of a foreign policy lobby, see John J. Mearsheimer and Stephen Walt, *The Israel Lobby and U.S. Foreign Policy* (New York: Farrar, Straus and Giroux, 2007), as well as a trenchant rebuttal by Robert Lieberman, "The 'Israel Lobby' and American Politics," *Perspectives on Politics* 7, no. 2 (2009): 235–57.

8. Alan McPherson, *Yankee No! Anti-Americanism in U.S.—Latin American Relations* (Cambridge, MA: Harvard University Press 2003), 167.

9. Parag Khanna, "Waving Goodbye to Hegemony," *New York Times Magazine*, 27 January 2008; Fareed Zakaria, *The Post-American World* (New York: W. W. Norton, 2008). The phrase "the indispensable nation" comes from Bill Clinton's remarks on international security issues, George Washington University, 5 August 1996,

https://www.presidency.ucsb.edu/documents/remarks-international-security-issues-george-washington-university.

10. See Alexander Cooley and Daniel Nexon, *Exit from Hegemony: The Unraveling of the American Global Order* (New York: Oxford University Press, 2020).

11. Cédric Jourde, "'The President Is Coming to Visit!': Dramas and the Hijack of Democratization in the Islamic Republic of Mauritania," *Comparative Politics* 37, no. 4 (July 2005): 421–40; Jason Brownlee, *Authoritarianism in an Age of Democratization* (New York: Cambridge University Press, 2007); Jennifer Gandhi and Adam Przeworski, "Authoritarian Institutions and the Survival of Autocrats," *Comparative Political Studies* 40, no. 11 (2007): 1279–301; Lisa Wedeen, *Ambiguities of Domination: Politics, Rhetoric, and Symbols in Contemporary Syria* (Chicago: University of Chicago Press, 1999); Lisa Wedeen, *Peripheral Visions: Politics, Power, and Performance in Yemen* (Chicago: University of Chicago Press, 2008); Edward Schatz, "The Soft Authoritarian 'Tool Kit': Agenda-Setting Power in Kazakhstan and Kyrgyzstan," *Comparative Politics* 41, no. 2 (January 2009): 203–22; Lisa Blaydes, *Elections and Distributive Politics in Mubarak's Egypt* (New York: Cambridge University Press, 2011); Steven Levitsky and Lucan A. Way, "Why Democracy Needs a Level Playing Field," *Journal of Democracy* 21 no. 1 (2010): 57–68; Dan Slater, *Ordering Power: Contentious Politics and Authoritarian Leviathans in Southeast Asia* (New York: Cambridge University Press, 2010); Milan W. Svolik, *The Politics of Authoritarian Rule* (New York: Cambridge University Press, 2012).

12. J. Paul Goode, "Redefining Russia: Hybrid Regimes, Fieldwork, and Russian Politics," *Perspectives on Politics* 8, no. 4 (2010): 1055–75.

13. Katzenstein and Keohane, "Political Consequences of Anti-Americanism," 303.

14. Peter J. Katzenstein and Robert O. Keohane, "Varieties of Anti-Americanism: A Framework for Analysis," in Katzenstein and Keohane, *Anti-Americanisms in World Politics*, 12.

15. Mark Blyth, "The Politics of (Mis)-Representation: Constructing (and Destructing) Europe in Discourses of Anti-Americanism," paper presented to Comparative Politics Workshop, University of Toronto, 12 April 2007, 8.

16. For one consideration of "pro-Americanism," see Anne Applebaum, "In Search of Pro-Americanism," *Foreign Policy* 149 (2005): 32–41.

17. On categories of analysis and categories of practice, see Rogers Brubaker and Frederick Cooper, "Beyond 'Identity,'" *Theory and Society* 29, no. 1 (2000): 1–47.

18. As Simon introduced, human rationality is deeply bounded by "access to information and the computational capacities that are actually possessed by organisms, including man, in the kinds of environments in which such organisms exist." Herbert A. Simon, "A Behavioral Model of Rational Choice," *Quarterly Journal of Economics* 69, no. 1 (1955): 99. Yet, even thick accounts of rationality are wedded to an ontology favoring human choice (however bounded). Normatively attractive in a liberal society, this does not make them descriptively accurate. See Kenneth J. Arrow,

"Methodological Individualism and Social Knowledge," *American Economic Review* 84, no. 2 (May 1994): 1–9. Attempts to re-describe human agency without liberalism's assumptions about individual choice include Hans Joas, *The Creativity of Action* (Chicago: University of Chicago Press, 1996); and Mustafa Emirbayer and Ann Mische, "What Is Agency?" *American Journal of Sociology* 103, no. 4 (January 1998): 962–1023.

19. Katherine Cramer Walsh, "Scholars as Citizens: Studying Public Opinion through Ethnography," in *Political Ethnography: What Immersion Contributes to the Study of Power*, ed. Edward Schatz (Chicago: University of Chicago Press, 2009), 165–82. See also John R. Zaller, *The Nature and Origins of Mass Opinion* (New York: Cambridge University Press, 1992).

20. Patrick R. Miller, "The Emotional Citizen: Emotion as a Function of Political Sophistication," *Political Psychology* 32, no. 4 (2011); Marcel Zeelenberg, Rob M. A. Nelissen, Seger M. Breugelmans, and Rik Pieters, "On Emotion Specificity in Decision Making: Why Feeling Is for Doing," *Judgment and Decision Making* 3, no. 1 (January 2008): 18–27.

21. Hauke R. Heekeren, Sean Marret, and Leslie C. Ungerleider, "The Neural Systems That Mediate Human Perceptual Decision Making," *Nature Reviews Neuroscience* 9, no. 6 (June 2008): 467–79.

22. In *Anti-Americanisms in World Politics*, Katzenstein and Keohane conceptualize anti-Americanism as "polyvalent," but when they bring evidence to bear, they rely principally on opinion surveys.

23. David O. Sears, "Symbolic Politics: A Socio-Psychological Theory," in *Explorations in Political Psychology*, ed. Shanto Iyengar and William J. McGuire (Durham, NC: Duke University Press, 1993), 113–49; David O. Sears, "The Role of Affect in Symbolic Politics," in *Citizens and Politics: Perspectives from Political Psychology*, ed. James H. Kuklinski (New York: Cambridge University Press, 2001), 14–40.

24. Schemata are defined as "the highly organized and generalized structures in memory that guide cognition and memory recall." See M. L. Morgan and D. L. Schwalbe, "Mind and Self in Society—Linking Social Structure and Social Cognition," *Social Psychological Quarterly* 53, no. 2 (1990), as paraphrased in Kristen Renwick Monroe, James Hankin, and Renée Bukovchik Van Vechten, "The Psychological Foundations of Identity Politics," *Annual Review of Political Science* 3 (2000): 423. They distinguish "schemata" from "social representations," which are understood to be intersubjective and social, whereas schemata are treated as subjective and individual-based.

25. David O. Sears, "Symbolic Politics: A Socio-Psychological Theory"; David O. Sears, "The Role of Affect," 32–33. On emotion at a level beyond that of individuals, see Janice Bially Mattern, "On Being Convinced: An Emotional Epistemology of International Relations," *International Theory* 6, no. 3 (2014): 589–94; Todd Hall, "Sympathetic States: State Strategies, Norms of Emotional Behavior, and the 9/11 Attacks," *Political Science Quarterly* 127, no. 3 (2012) 369–400; Murray Edelman, *The Symbolic Uses of Politics*, 2nd ed. (Urbana: University of Illinois Press, 1985), 31; and

David Kowalewski, "The Protest Uses of Symbolic Politics in the USSR," *Journal of Politics* 42, no. 2 (1980): 439–60.

26. On the heritability of political traits, see John R. Alford, Carolyn L. Funk, and John R. Hibbing, "Are Political Orientations Genetically Transmitted?," *American Political Science Review* 99, no. 2 (May 2005): 153–67; James H. Fowler, Laura A. Baker, and Cristopher T. Dawes, "Genetic Variation in Political Participation," *American Political Science Review* 102, no. 2 (May 2008): 233–48; James H. Fowler et al., "Genes, Games, and Political Participation," in *Man Is by Nature a Political Animal*, ed. Peter K. Hatemi and Rose McDermott (Chicago: Chicago University Press, 2011), 207–23.

27. Work that treats the social realm as consisting of fixed attributes of individuals cannot appreciate such shifts. For example, one study that considers how religious identity affects one's views of the United States reduces religion to answers to a feeling thermometer question. See Michele G. Alexander, Shana Levin, and P. J. Henry, "Image Theory, Social Identity, and Social Dominance: Structural Characteristics and Individual Motives Underlying International Images," *Political Psychology* 26, no. 1 (February 2005): 27–46.

28. Trevor Purvis and Alan Hunt, "Discourse, Ideology, Discourse, Ideology, Discourse, Ideology," *British Journal of Sociology* 44, no. 3 (September 1993): 485. See also Ferdinand de Saussure, *Course in General Linguistics*, trans. Wade Baskin, ed. Charles Bally, Albert Sechehaye, and Albert Reidlinger (London: Fontana, 1974).

29. Emile Durkheim, *The Division of Labor in Society*, trans. W. D. Halls (New York: Free Press, 1984); Clifford Geertz, "Ritual and Social Change: A Javanese Example," in *The Interpretation of Cultures*, ed. Clifford Geertz (New York: Basic Books, 1973); Edelman, *Symbolic Uses of Politics*. More recent work in this tradition includes Jan Kubik, *The Power of Symbols against the Symbols of Power: The Rise of Solidarity and the Fall of State Socialism in Poland* (University Park: Penn State University Press, 1994); Michael Schatzberg, *Political Legitimacy in Middle Africa: Father, Family, Food* (Bloomington: Indiana University Press, 2001); Wedeen, *Ambiguities of Domination*; Lisa Wedeen, "Conceptualizing Culture: Possibilities for Political Science" *American Political Science Review* 96, no.4 (2002): 713–28; and Wedeen, *Peripheral Visions*. Discourse-analytic work, such as that done in international relations (IR), represents one offshoot. See Michael Shapiro, "Introduction II: Textualizing Global Politics," in *International/Intertextual Relations: Postmodern Readings of World Politics*, ed. James Der Derian and Michael Shapiro (Lexington, MA: Lexington Books, 1989), 11–22; Roxanne Doty, *Imperial Encounters: The Politics of Representation in North-South Relations* (Minneapolis: University of Minnesota Press, 1996); Jennifer Milliken, "The Study of Discourse in International Relations: A Critique of Research and Methods," *European Journal of International Relations* 5, no. 2 (1999): 225–54. In general, IR has had a vibrant debate about what ontological status to accord to ideas; see Albert S. Yee, "The Causal Effects of Ideas on Policies," *International Organization* 50, no. 1 (Winter 1996): 69–108; Judith Goldstein and Robert O. Keohane, eds., *Ideas and*

Foreign Policy: Beliefs, Institutions, and Political Change (Ithaca, NY: Cornell University Press, 1993).

30. Serge Moscovici, "Notes towards a Description of Social Representations," *European Journal of Social Psychology* 18, no. 3 (1988): 214, cited in Monroe, Hankin, and Van Vechten, "Psychological Foundations of Identity Politics," 437–48.

31. Yee, "Causal Effects of Ideas," 97. The mechanisms by which shifts in the intersubjective representations affect political possibilities are crucial. Once these processes are identified, we may then address the degree to which they "travel" to other cases. See Arthur L. Stinchcombe, "The Conditions of Fruitfulness of Theorizing about Mechanisms in Social Science," *Philosophy of the Social Sciences* 21, no. 3 (1991): 367–88; Charles Tilly, "Mechanisms in Political Processes," *Annual Review of Political Science* 4, no. 1 (2001): 21–41.

32. *Oxford English Dictionary*, s.v. "symbol," accessed 22 November 2011, http://oed.com/view/Entry/196197?rskey=rw5nYB&result=231708#.

33. Silone, quoted in Ajami, "Falseness of Anti-Americanism," 53.

34. Marc Lynch, "Taking Arabs Seriously," *Foreign Affairs* 82, no. 5 (2003): 207.

35. Lynch, "Taking Arabs Seriously," 208; Manar Shorbaghy, "The Egyptian Movement For Change—Kefaya: Redefining Politics in Egypt," *Public Culture* 19, no. 1 (2007): 175–96.

36. Gwenn Okruhlik, "Empowering Civility through Nationalism: Reformist Islam and Belonging in Saudi Arabia," in *Remaking Muslim Politics: Pluralism, Contestation, Democratization*, ed. Robert Hefner (Princeton, NJ: Princeton University Press, 2005), 195–96.

37. Wedeen, *Peripheral Visions*.

38. McPherson, *Yankee No!*, 10.

39. Erving Goffman, *Frame Analysis: An Essay on the Organization of Experience* (Cambridge, MA: Harvard University Press, 1974), 21.

40. Social movement theorists do not reduce social mobilization to framing processes. For fuller treatment of the range of such theories, see Doug McAdam, Sidney G. Tarrow, and Charles Tilly, *Dynamics of Contention* (Cambridge: Cambridge University Press, 2001). For an application of social movement theory to Islamist mobilization, see Quintan Wiktorowicz, ed., *Islamic Activism: A Social Movement Theory Approach* (Bloomington: Indiana University Press, 2003). For one early and particularly thoughtful application of the study of contentious politics to the study of terrorism, see David Leheney, "Symbols, Strategies, and Choices for International Relations Scholarship after September 11," *Dialog-IO* (Spring 2002): 57–70.

41. Robert D. Benford and David A. Snow, "Framing Processes and Social Movements: An Overview and Assessment," *Annual Review of Sociology* 26, no. 1 (2000): 614.

42. The quote is from Kowalewski, "Protest Uses of Symbolic Politics," 440.

43. The quote is from Willard A. Mullins, "On the Concept of Ideology in Political Science," *American Political Science Review* 66, no. 2 (June 1972): 509. He is

referring to ideology rather than symbols, but his logic mirrors that in studies downplaying the role of symbols.

44. Monroe, Hankin, and Van Vechten, "Psychological Foundations of Identity Politics," 442, argues that social identity theory (as developed by psychologists) could help to explain instances of "prolonged mobilization better than do theories stressing access to resources or self-interests."

45. Lawrence P. Markowitz, "How Master Frames Mislead: The Eclipse and Division of Nationalist Movements in Tajikistan and Uzbekistan," *Ethnic and Racial Studies* 32, no. 4 (2009): 716–38. Markowitz distinguishes frames from master frames, but his logic applies equally to this discussion. On master frames, see David A. Snow and Robert Benford, "Master Frames and Cycles of Protest," in *Frontiers in Social Movement Theory*, ed. Aldon Morris and Carol McClurg Mueller (New Haven, CT: Yale University Press, 1992), 133–223.

46. Jorge Domínguez, "Culture: Is It Key to the Troubles in U.S.-Cuban Relations?," *Diplomatic History* 25, no. 3 (Summer 2001): 514.

47. On the politically thinkable, see Schatzberg, *Political Legitimacy in Middle Africa*.

48. McAdam, Tarrow, and Tilly, *Dynamics of Contention*, 48; Bert Klandermans, *The Social Psychology of Protest* (Oxford: Blackwell, 1997), 46.

49. Kevin Gillan, "Understanding Meaning in Movements: A Hermeneutic Approach to Frames and Ideologies," *Social Movement Studies* 7, no. 3 (December 2008): 247–63. For a similar argument about the centrality of semiotic practices to politics, see Wedeen, "Conceptualizing Culture."

50. McAdam, Tarrow and Tilly, *Dynamics of Contention*.

51. McAdam, Tarrow and Tilly, *Dynamics of Contention*, 7–9.

52. Wedeen, *Ambiguities of Domination*; Wedeen, *Peripheral Visions*; Jillian Schwedler, *Faith in Moderation: Islamist Parties in Jordan and Yemen* (New York: Cambridge University Press, 2006); Edward Schatz, "The Soft Authoritarian 'Tool Kit': Agenda-Setting Power in Kazakhstan and Kyrgyzstan," *Comparative Politics* 41, no. 2 (2009): 203–22.

53. For one study that anticipated the political potential of a broad social movement, see the treatment of the Muslim Brotherhood in Egypt under Mubarak in Sheri Berman, "Islamism, Revolution, and Civil Society," *Perspectives on Politics* 1, no. 2 (2003): 257–72.

54. Whether or not social movements achieve their goals is a separate matter; see Marco G. Giugni, "Was It Worth the Effort? The Outcomes and Consequences of Social Movements," *Annual Review of Sociology* 24, no. 1 (1998): 371–93. Even social movements that fail to achieve their goals can succeed in changing the political landscape.

55. This is the logic in Benedict Anderson, *Imagined Communities: Reflections on the Origin and Spread of Nationalism* (New York: Verso, 1991).

56. Frame bridging and frame amplification are from David A. Snow et al., "Frame Alignment Processes, Micromobilization, and Movement Participation," *American*

Sociological Review 51, no. 4 (August 1986): 467. They add frame extension and frame transformation to the list.

57. Zbigniew Brzezinski, *The Grand Chessboard: American Primacy and Its Geostrategic Imperatives* (New York: Basic Books, 1998).

58. Robert Austin, personal communication, 14 August 2014

59. H. J. Mackinder, "The Geographical Pivot of History," *Geographical Journal* 23, no. 4 (April 1904): 421–37.

60. On varieties of state weakness in Eurasia, see John Heathershaw and Edward Schatz, eds., *Paradox of Power: The Logics of State Weakness in Eurasia* (Pittsburgh: University of Pittsburgh Press, 2017).

61. If one focuses solely on areas where militancy had already arisen, one might follow Rashid to the mistaken conclusion that militant jihad in Central Asia is likely. See Ahmed Rashid, "They're Only Sleeping," *New Yorker*, January 14, 2002. For a more sober evaluation of the potential for Central Asia to experience revolution, see Mark N. Katz, "Will There Be a Revolution in Central Asia?," *Communist and Post-Communist Studies* 40, no. 2 (June 2007): 129–41. On ISIL's recruitment efforts in Central Asia, see Edward J. Lemon, "Daesh and Tajikistan: The Regime's (In)Security Policy," *RUSI Journal* 160, no. 5 (2015): 68–76.

62. On such "reverberation effects" see Anna Seleny, "Tradition, Modernity, and Democracy: The Many Promises of Islam," *Perspectives on Politics* 4, no. 3 (2006): 481–94.

63. See Alexander Warkotsch, "The OSCE as an Agent of Socialisation? International Norm Dynamics and Political Change in Central Asia," *Europe-Asia Studies* 59, no. 5 (2007): 829–46.

64. On how degrees of secularism affect the trajectories of anti-Americanism, see Lisa Blaydes and Drew A. Linzer, "Elite Competition, Religiosity, and Anti-Americanism in the Islamic World," *American Political Science Review* 106, no. 2 (2012): 225–43.

65. The clear exception is the densely populated Ferghana Valley.

66. Moreover, whether "quiet" or "everyday" forms of individual behavior constitute mobilization is related to how adequate our methodologies for examining them are. On quiet mobilization, see Mark R. Beissinger, *Nationalist Mobilization and the Collapse of the Soviet State* (Cambridge: Cambridge University Press, 2002). On everyday resistance, see James C. Scott, *Weapons of the Weak: Everyday Forms of Peasant Resistance* (New Haven, CT: Yale University Press, 1985). On methodologies attuned to these phenomena, see Schatz, *Political Ethnography*. On pre-Soviet mobilization, see Chika Obiya, "The Basmachi Movement as a Mirror of Central Asian Society in the Revolutionary Period," in *Social Protests and Nation-Building in the Middle East and Central Asia*, ed. Keiko Sakai (Chiba: Institute of Developing Economies, JETRO, 2003). On Soviet-era mobilization, see Yaacov Ro'i, "Central Asian Riots and Disturbances, 1989–1990: Causes and Context," *Central Asian Survey* 10, no. 3 (1991): 21–54; Edward Schatz, "Notes on the 'Dog That Didn't Bark': Eco-Internationalism in Late Soviet Kazakhstan," *Ethnic and Racial Studies* 22, no. 1 (1999): 136–61; Tomohiko

Uyama, "Why Are Social Protest Movements Weak in Central Asia?," in Sakai, *Social Protests and Nation-Building*.

67. Beissinger, *Nationalist Mobilization*.

68. Jessica Allina-Pisano, *The Post-Soviet Potemkin Village: Politics and Property Rights in the Black Earth* (Cambridge: Cambridge University Press, 2007).

69. For one treatment, see Tony Judt, *Postwar: A History of Europe since 1945* (New York: Penguin, 2006).

70. For McAdam, there is a critical juncture in which an ideological constitution is produced by the "winning coalition" of actors. This ideological space delineates the possibilities for politics in path-dependent ways. Once this occurs, it is hard for Iran or Cuba, for example, to change their respective anti-American orientations. Doug McAdam, "Legacies of Anti-Americanism: A Sociological Perspective," in Keohane and Katzenstein, *Anti-Americanisms in World Politics*, 251–69.

71. James Mahoney and Gary Goertz, "The Possibility Principle: Choosing Negative Cases in Comparative Research," *American Political Science Review* 98, no. 4 (2004): 653–69.

72. The classic debate about case selection is between Barbara Geddes, "How the Cases You Choose Affect the Answers You Get: Selection Bias in Comparative Politics," *Political Analysis* 2, no. 1 (1990): 131–50; and Douglas Dion, "Evidence and Inference in the Comparative Case Study," *Comparative Politics* 30, no. 2 (1998): 127–45.

73. Katzenstein and Keohane, "Political Consequences of Anti-Americanism," 275.

CHAPTER 1: AMERICA'S CHANGING IMAGE

1. Barry A. Sanders, *American Avatar: The United States in the Global Imagination* (Washington, DC: Potomac Books, 2011), 56.

2. Vivien A. Schmidt, "Reconciling Ideas and Institutions through Discursive Institutionalism," in *Ideas and Politics in Social Science Research*, ed. Daniel Beland and Robert Henry Cox (New York: Oxford University Press, 2011), 60.

3. The phrase is usually ascribed to Otto von Bismarck. See also Mark Blyth, "Structures Do Not Come with an Instruction Sheet: Interests, Ideas, and Progress in Political Science," *Perspectives on Politics* 1, no. 4 (2003): 695–706.

4. On Soviet transformations, see Adrienne Edgar, "Bolshevism, Patriarchy, and the Nation: The Soviet 'Emancipation' of Muslim Women in Pan-Islamic Perspective," *Slavic Review* 65, no. 2 (Summer 2006); and Adeeb Khalid, "Backwardness and the Quest for Civilization: Early Soviet Central Asia in Comparative Perspective," *Slavic Review* 65, no. 2 (Summer 2006): 231–51.

5. On the Middle East, see Giacomo Chiozza, *Anti-Americanism and the American World Order* (Baltimore: Johns Hopkins University Press, 2009).

6. On Latin America, see Alan McPherson, *Yankee No! Anti-Americanism in U.S.–Latin American Relations* (Cambridge, MA: Harvard University Press 2003).

7. Richard K. Herrmann, *Perceptions and Behavior in Soviet Foreign Policy* (Pittsburgh: University of Pittsburgh Press, 1985), 691.

8. Herrmann, *Perceptions and Behavior*, 694.

9. Vladimir Shlapentokh, "The Changeable Soviet Image of America," *Annals of the American Academy of Political and Social Science* 497, no. 1 (1988): 166.

10. Shlapentokh, "Changeable Soviet Image," 157.

11. Alexei Yurchak, *Everything Was Forever, Until It Was No More: The Last Soviet Generation* (Princeton, NJ, and Oxford: Princeton University Press, 2005), 175–81.

12. Yurchak, *Everything Was Forever*, 165.

13. Robert J. Lifton, *The Nazi Doctors: Medical Killing and the Psychology of Genocide* (New York: Basic Books, 1986), 418.

14. Yurchak, *Everything Was Forever*, 117. The language of "performances" should not invite theatrical metaphors in which the "actual," "real," or "authentic" is counterposed to the "staged" or "fake"; see Lisa Wedeen, *Peripheral Visions: Politics, Power, and Performance in Yemen* (Chicago: University of Chicago Press, 2008). To the contrary, everyday life—in Soviet contexts as elsewhere—is full of performances that, ipso facto, are not true or false but rather "felicitous or infelicitous." Yurchak, *Everything Was Forever*, 19.

15. This is the powerful, if reductionist, logic proposed in Timur Kuran, "Now Out of Never: The Element of Surprise in the East European Revolution of 1989," *World Politics* 44, no. 1 (1991): 7–48.

16. For one take on how people cope with ambivalence, see Seki Zemir, "Artistic Creativity and the Brain," *Science* 293, no. 6 (July 2001): 51–52.

17. T. Jeremy Gunn, "Shaping an Islamic Identity: Religion, Islamism, and the State in Central Asia," *Sociology of Religion* 64, no. 3 (2003): 390.

18. See Chiozza, *Anti-Americanism and the American World Order*. On Muslim communities in the Russian empire, see Robert D. Crews, *For Prophet and Tsar* (Cambridge, MA: Harvard University Press, 2009).

19. Adeeb Khalid, *Islam after Communism: Religion and Politics in Central Asia* (Berkeley: University of California Press, 2007).

20. Edgar, "Bolshevism, Patriarchy, and the Nation"; Khalid, "Backwardness and the Quest for Civilization."

21. See Bruce Privatsky, *Muslim Turkistan: Kazak Religion and Collective Memory* (London and New York: Routledge, 2001); Maria Louw, *Everyday Islam in Post-Soviet Central Asia* (London and New York: Routledge, 2007); Johan Rasanayagam, *Islam in Post-Soviet Uzbekistan: The Morality of Experience* (New York: Cambridge University Press, 2011).

22. Sergei P. Poliakov, *Everyday Islam: Religion and Tradition in Rural Central Asia*, ed. Martha Brill Olcott, trans. Anthony Olcott (Armonk, NY: M. E. Sharpe, 1992); Bakhtiar Babadjanov and Muzaffar Kamilov, "Domulla Hindustani and the Beginning of the 'Great Schism' among Moslems of Uzbekistan," in *Islam in Politics in Russia and Central Asia (Early Eighteenth to Late Twentieth Centuries)*, ed. Stéphane A. Dudoignon and Komatso Hisao (London, New York, and Bahrain: Kegan Paul,

2002); Martha Brill Olcott, "Roots of Radical Islam in Central Asia," Carnegie Papers no. 77 (Washington, DC: Carnegie Endowment for International Peace, January 2007).

23. This strategy was designed to co-opt those Muslims interested in Islamic learning but uninterested in official religious institutions; see Khalid, *Islam after Communism*, 113. On how Tashkent became a way to showcase Soviet Islamic culture to the non-Soviet world, see Paul Stronski, *Tashkent: Forging a Soviet City, 1930–1966* (Pittsburgh: University of Pittsburgh Press, 2010).

24. See Stéphane A. Dudoignon, "From Revival to Mutation: The Religious Personnel of Islam in Tajikistan, from De-Stalinization to Independence (1955–91)," *Central Asian Survey* 30, no. 1 (2011): 53–80.

25. Khalid, *Islam after Communism*, 114.

26. For early thinking about defections and the withdrawal of troops, see Leo J. Daughtery III, "Ethnic Minorities in the Soviet Armed Forces: The Plight of Central Asians in a Russian-Dominated Military," *Journal of Slavic Military Studies* 7, no. 2 (1994): 55–197; Leo J. Daughtery III, "The Bear and the Scimitar: Soviet Central Asians and the War in Afghanistan, 1979–1989," *Journal of Slavic Military Studies* 8, no. 1 (1995): 73–96; Pinar Akcali, "Islam as a 'Common Bond' in Central Asia: Islamic Renaissance Party and the Afghan Mujahidin," *Central Asian Survey* 17, no. 2 (1998): 274, respectively.

27. Noah Tucker, a leading expert on the jihadists of Central Asia, warns us to be "careful not to back-read [the IMU's] motivations" onto earlier movements and actors (personal communication, 23 August 2013).

28. Artemy M. Kalinovsky, *A Long Goodbye: The Soviet Withdrawal from Afghanistan* (Cambridge, MA: Harvard University Press, 2011), 51.

29. Daughtery III, "Ethnic Minorities in the Soviet Armed Forces."

30. Svetlana Alexievich, *Zinky Boys: Soviet Voices form the Afghanistan War* (New York: Norton, 1992).

31. For testimonies, see Alexievich, *Zinky Boys*.

32. Olivier Roy, *Islam and Resistance in Afghanistan* (New York: Cambridge University Press, 1990), 110–12.

33. Aidrey Shalinsky, "Ethnic Reactions to the Current Regime in Afghanistan," *Central Asian Survey* 3, no. 4 (1984): 49–60.

34. Sultan M. Akimbelov, *Afganskii uzel i problemy bezopasnosti Tsentral'noi Azii* (Almaty: Kazakhstanskii institut strategicheskikh issledovanii pri Presidente Respubliki Kazakhstan 1998), 113–26.

35. Alexievich, *Zinky Boys*, 49.

36. Jeff Sahadeo, "Epidemic and Empire: Ethnicity, Class, and 'Civilization' in the 1892 Tashkent Cholera Riot," *Slavic Review* 64, no. 1 (Spring 2005): 117–39.

37. On legacies of state socialism, see Mark R. Beissinger and Stephen Kotkin, eds., *Historical Legacies of Communism in Russia and Eastern Europe* (New York: Cambridge University Press, 2014); Michael H. Bernhard and Jan Kubik, eds., *Twenty*

Years after Communism: The Politics of Memory and Commemoration (Oxford: Oxford University Press, 2014). This ambivalence would remain as raw material to be quarried later. For one parallel example of how deep-seated skepticism about US policies originating with the Spanish-American War of 1898 would reemerge socially and politically much later, see Carlos Alonso Zaldívar, "Miradas torcidas: Percepciones mutuas entre España y Estados Unidos," *Real Instituto Elcano*, September 2003. For expressions of the "vacuum" thesis, see A. G. Kosychenko et al., *Sovremennyi terrorizm: vzgliad iz Tsentral'noi Azii* (Almaty: Daik-Press 2002), 139; and Emmanuel Karagiannis, *Political Islam in Central Asia: The Challenge of Hizb ut-Tahrir* (London and New York: Routledge, 2010).

38. On liberalism and normality in the region, see Stephen E. Hansen, "The Leninist Legacy and Institutional Change," *Comparative Political Studies* 28, no. 2 (July 1995): 306–14. The nationalist movements that propelled the Soviet Union to collapse (see Beissinger, *Nationalist Mobilization*) were generally open to external (i.e., American) links and influence. This remained the practice of most post-Soviet ruling elites as well. With the exception of Uzbekistan and Turkmenistan, nationalist ideologies pushing for greater autonomy from the West would not emerge until the late 1990s and early 2000s.

39. For an example that normalizes the American experience, see N. A. Shaikenov, "Problemy Kazakhstanskoi gosudarstvennosti," *Saiasat* 10, no. 17 (October 1996): 5. On financing, see Marina Ottaway and Thomas Carothers, eds., *Funding Virtue: Civil Society Aid and Democracy Promotion* (Washington, DC: Carnegie Endowment for International Peace, 2000). On the late-coming, alternative discourse of global Islam, see Fiona Adamson, "Global Liberalism versus Political Islam: Competing Ideological Frameworks in International Politics," *International Studies Review* 7, no. 4 (2005): 547–69.

40. Ekaterina Latypova, "Fond 'Soros-Kazakhstan' provel seminar po obrazovaniiu v mnogokul'turnoi srede," *Panorama* no. 37 (September 1998).

41. For example, A. B. Parkanskii, "Biudjet saiasatynyng aimaqtyq qubylnamalary: AQSh pen Resei tajiribesi," *Saiasat* 2, no. 9 (February 1996), assumes that budget policies between the federal and state governments in the US are exemplary for unitary Kazakhstan.

42. Latypova, "Fond 'Soros-Kazakhstan.'"

43. Iaroslav Razumov, "Rukovoditeli energeticheskikh kompanii, gosstruktur i dippredstavitel'sv obsudili puti dal'neishego reformirovaniia otrasli," *Panorama*, no. 33, (28 August 1998): 8.

44. Adil Dzhalilov, "Hewlett-Packard poluchila zakaz Ministerstva obrazovaniia RK na $11 mln," *Panorama* no. 38 (2 October 1998).

45. "Novye standarty fizpodgotovki vvodit armia SShA," *Narodnoe slovo* 1787, 6 January 1998: 3.

46. "Impichment kak simvol," *Delovaia nedelia*, 31 July 1998, 8. Igor' Demidenko and Evgennia Lenskaia, "Boris Berezovskii: chelovek i legenda," *Delovaia nedelia*, 31 July 1998. Likewise, written constitutions were discussed as fundamental to the

building of a functioning polity (e.g., E. M. Abenov, "Osnovnye printsipy gosudarstvennogo ustroistva sovremennogo Kazakhstana (konstitutsii 1993 i 1995 gg.)," *Saiasat* 10, no. 17, (October 1996).

47. Zbigniew Brzezinski, "The Premature Partnership," *Foreign Affairs* 73, no. 2 (March/April 1994): 67–82, was among the first to offer skepticism about prospects for economic and political liberalism in post-Soviet space.

48. Anastasiaa Kupriianova, "Amerika nam pomozhet?," *Delo Nomer* 23 (April 1991): 5.

49. O. Kovalenko, "Po odezhde, ili chtoby vygliadit' O'Kei," *Kazakhstanskaia pravda*, 30 January 1992, 4.

50. In Kepel's view, geography matters since it allows for the construction of the "nearby enemy" and the "faraway enemy." See Gilles Kepel, *The War for Muslim Minds: Islam and the West*, trans. Pascale Ghazaleh (Cambridge and London: Belknap Press of Harvard University Press, 2004), 72.

51. Richard Giragosian, "The US Military Engagement in Central Asia and the Southern Caucasus: An Overview," *Journal of Slavic Military Studies* 17, no. 1 (2004): 45–50. For a useful summary of US relations with Central Asia, see Fiona Hill, *A Not-So-Grand Strategy: United States Policy toward Central Asia before the Events of September 2001* (Washington, DC: Brookings Institution, 2001).

52. Olga Oliker and David A. Shlapak, *U.S. Interests in Central Asia: Policy Priorities and Military Roles* (Santa Monica, CA: RAND Corporation, 2005), 8. Moreover, military-to-military ties were not a politicized issue. See Interfaks, "Ucheniia 'Tsentrazbat' provodiatsia v tseliakh obespecheniia bezopasnosti stran Tsentral'noi Azii iz-za situatsii v Afganistane," *Panorama* no. 37, (25 September 1998), for a sober, non-politicized discussion of joint exercises.

53. *Washington Post* and *New York Times* editorials and opinion pieces reflected on these matters, but discussion was typically vague and sometimes ill-informed.

54. For background on US-Russian relations after the Soviet collapse, see James M. Goldgeier and Michael McFaul, *Power and Purpose: U.S. Policy toward Russia after the Cold War* (Washington, DC: Brookings Institution Press, 2003).

55. One of the reasons for the commercial success of British comic Sasha Baron Cohen's film *Borat* about a fictional "Kazakhstan" was that most Americans knew so little about the countries ending in "-stan" that such lands became synonymous with faraway, irrelevant places. On the film, see Paula A. Michaels, "If the Subaltern Speaks in the Woods and Nobody's Listening, Does He Make a Sound?" *Slavic Review* 67, no.1 (2008), 81–83; and Edward Schatz, "Transnational Image Making and Soft Authoritarian Kazakhstan," *Slavic Review* 67, No. 1 (Spring 2008), 40–62.

56. Oliker and Shlapak, *U.S. Interests in Central Asia*, 14.

57. Alexander Cooley, *Base Politics: Democratic Change and the U.S. Military Overseas* (Ithaca, NY: Cornell University Press, 2008); Alexander Cooley, *Great Games, Local Rules: The New Great Power Contest in Central Asia* (New York: Oxford University Press, 2012); John Heathershaw and Alexander Cooley, "Offshore Central Asia: An Introduction," *Central Asian Survey* 34, no.1 (2015): 1–10.

58. I first laid out the argument in this section in Edward Schatz, "Islamism and Anti-Americanism in Central Asia," *Current History* 101, no. 657 (October 2002): 337–43.

59. Oliker and Shlapak, *U.S. Interests in Central Asia*, 10. I discuss the IMU at greater length in chapter 2.

60. Gul'zada Bafina, "Amerikanskie vooruzhennye sily atakovali Afganistan i Sudan," *Panorama* 33 (28 August 1998), 5.

61. Goldgeier and McFaul, *Power and Purpose*, 266. The limits of pan-Slavism would be on display during the Russo-Ukrainian war in 2014–15.

62. Radio Free Europe / Radio Liberty, "Central Asian Popular Support for America May Be Shaky," *Central Asia Report* 1, no. 15 (1 November 2001).

63. Peter Ford, "Why Do They Hate Us?" *Christian Science Monitor*, 27 September 2001, offers a catalog of immediate reactions globally.

64. Igor Savin, personal communication, 15 September 2001, characterizing public reactions in Shymkent after the attacks.

65. Serik Aidossov, personal communication, 14 September 2001, characterizing public reactions in Shymkent after the attacks.

66. Radio Free Europe / Radio Liberty, "Central Asian Popular Support for America."

67. This quote is from the journalist Farrukh Akhrorov (*Leninabadskaia pravda*), as covered by Igor' Rotar', "Tsentral'naia Aziia—sleduiushchaia mishen' ekstremistov," *Nezavisimaia gazeta*, 14 September 2001, and cited in Karagiannis, *Political Islam in Central Asia*, 100.

68. Radio Free Europe / Radio Liberty, "Anti-American Books among Russia's Best-Sellers," *Newsline*, 6 June 2003, lists Russia's best-selling books with titles such as *Broken Sword of Empire*, *Why America Is on the Offensive*, and *Why People Hate America*.

69. "Uzbek Paper Looks at Motives for Attacks on USA," *Times of Central Asia*, 27 September 2001.

70. It is difficult to know how widely accepted these rumors were; in any case, they were widely considered plausible. For example, the director of a semi-official think tank openly speculated that the US or Israel could have conspired in the attacks (Magbat Spanov, interview by author, 13 June 2002, Almaty, Kazakhstan). One common question in conversations about politics in post-Soviet space is "Who stands to benefit?" (Komu eto vygodno?), used to imply that an explanation for a political outcome is self-evident and reducible to the self-interest of conspirers. See Scott Radnitz and Patrick Underwood, "Is Belief in Conspiracy Theories Pathological? A Survey Experiment on the Cognitive Roots of Extreme Suspicion," *British Journal of Political Science* 47, no. 1 (2017): 113–29.

71. This sentiment is from the fascist Ukrainian National Assembly / Ukrainian National Self-Defense. See Radio Free Europe / Radio Liberty, "Ukrainian Radical Nationalists see Attacks on U.S. as 'Moral Satisfaction,'" *Newsline*, 5, no. 174 (13 September 2001).

72. Peter Svoik, "Kazakhstan i Rossiia: Byt' li v novom soiuze?" *Karavan*, 20 March 1998, 36, offers a particularly vivid account of the "cocktail of former

feudal-nomenklatura Bolshevism, the market, and democracy . . . which creates a permanent and all-encompassing crisis." On economic transitions in the region, see Richard Pomfret, *The Central Asian Economies since Independence* (Princeton, NJ: Princeton University Press, 2006). For one ethnography of this period in Kazakhstan, see Joma Nazpary, *Post-Soviet Chaos: Violence and Dispossession in Kazakhstan* (London: Pluto Press: 2001).

73. "Pravitel'stvo Soedinennykh Shtatov oprovergaet sdelannye ministrom Medvedevym zaiiavleniia," *Panorama* no. 27 (9 July 1994): 12.

74. Zhenis Kenzhes-uly, "SP 'Tengizshevroil' povysheny limity na vybrosy vrednykh veshchestv v atmosferu," *Panorama* no. 32 (21 August 1998): 9.

75. On ostensible American interests in Central Asia, see Aleksei Ikonnikov, "Vremia sobirat' kamni?" *Kontinent*, 12–27 December 2005, 19.

76. Vladimir Il'ich Lenin, *Imperialism: The Highest Stage of Capitalism* (Chippendale, NSW, Australia: Resistance Books, 1999).

77. Fatima Kelimbetova and Erbolat Nazarbaev, "Politika Kazakhstana: ot integratsii k sotrudnichestvu," *Saiasat* 10, no. 17 (October 1996): 52; Svetlana Fel'de, "CCL OIL lukavit: Vypolnenie investitsionnykh obiazatel'stv — blef," *Novoe pokolenie* (Almaty), 14 August 1998; Gul'mira Ongarbaeva and Anton Sel'nitskii, "Ugol'nye razrezy Ekibastuza stali polem bitvy," *Novoe pokolenie*, 31 July 1998.

78. Author's fieldnotes from fieldwork in 1997, 1998, 2002. See also Marat Nurgozhin, "Tengizskaia odisseia amerikanskoi akuly," *Delovaia nedelia*, 31 July 1998.

79. "Rasslabimsia!" *Narodnoe slovo* 1804, 29 January 1998: 3.

80. "Kto mirovoi lider?" *Narodnoe slovo* 2013, 26 November 1998: 3.

81. *Respublika* quote from Azat Akchokoev, "Investitsii zapada—istochnik korruptsii," *Respublika* (30 November 1999): 1. Activist's quote from Asel Berimzharova, personal communication, 23 October 2002. In a similar vein, Omelicheva writes, "Disillusionment with the Western models of democracy, mistrust of the international donors whose activities have been perceived as stuffing the pockets of corrupted elites, and resentment towards the influence of dissolute Western sub-culture have all contributed to the development of anti-Western attitudes in Kyrgyzstan." See Mariya Y. Omelicheva, *Counterterrorism Policies in Central Asia* (London and New York: Routledge, 2011), 48.

82. Serguei Alex Oushakine, *The Patriotism of Despair: Nation, War, and Loss in Russia* (Ithaca and London: Cornell University Press: 2009), 34.

83. Nancy Lubin, *Central Asians Take Stock: Reform, Corruption, and Identity*, Peaceworks no. 2 (Washington, DC: United States Institute of Peace, 1995), 3.

84. In Kazakhstan, where I conducted the bulk of my field research, this usually took the form of resentment against foreign multinational corporations—perceived to be American—for extracting the region's natural resources.

85. Lubin's early surveys showed that "that strong leadership, stability, law and order, and economic improvement are far higher priorities [for Central Asians] than the construction of any particular government system." See Lubin, *Central Asians Take Stock*, v.

86. It is difficult to assess the basis for longitudinal claims made in Nancy Lubin and Arustan Joldasov, "Snapshots from Central Asia: Is America Losing in Public Opinion?," *Problems of Post-Communism* 57, no. 3 (2010): 40–54. On the limitations of polling data, see Katherine Cramer Walsh, *Talking about Politics: Informal Groups and Social Identity in American Life* (Chicago: University of Chicago Press, 2004); and Elisabeth Noelle-Neumann, "The Spiral of Silence: A Theory of Public Opinion," *Journal of Communication* 24, no. 2 (June 1974): 43–51.

87. Thursdays were chosen to avoid "slow news days," and the period covered easily captures the onset of major changes. I devised a coding instrument that took into account challenges highlighted in a pilot exercise. Methodologically, this is a blunt instrument, but the approach nonetheless charts major changes over time with great clarity. The book's Appendix details some of the coding choices.

88. The apparently wide swings in Central Asian attitudes are an artifact of RFE/RL's less consistent coverage of the region. For an early discussion of Russia's turn from the West and the possibility of a new cold war, see Dmitri Trenin, "Russia Leaves the West," *Foreign Affairs* 85, no. 4 (July/August 2006): 87–96.

89. Edward Schatz, "The Soft Authoritarian 'Tool Kit': Agenda-Setting Power in Kazakhstan and Kyrgyzstan," *Comparative Politics* 41, no. 2 (2009): 203–22.

90. Todd Hall, "Sympathetic States: State Strategies, Norms of Emotional Behavior, and the 9/11 Attacks," *Political Science Quarterly* 127, no. 3 (2012) 369–400.

91. On the rise of anti-American views in Russia proper, see Georgi Derluguian, "Anti-Americanism on the Rise? Suggestions toward a Rational Program of Study," PONARS Eurasia, Policy Memo no. 266, October 2002, http://www.ponarseurasia.org/memo/anti-americanism-rise-suggestions-toward-rational-program-study; Theodore P. Gerber and Sarah E. Mendelson, "Young, Educated, Urban—and Anti-American: Recent Survey Data from Russia," PONARS Eurasia, Policy Memo no. 267, October 2002, http://www.ponarseurasia.org/memo/young-educated-urban-and-anti-american-recent-survey-data-russia; Sarah E. Mendelson and Theodore P. Gerber, "Us and Them: Anti-American Views of the Putin Generation," *Washington Quarterly* 31, no. 2 (2008): 131–50.

92. Mark R. Beissinger, "The Persisting Ambiguity of Empire," *Post-Soviet Affairs* 11, no. 2 (April 1995): 149–84.

93. Sally N. Cummings, "Happier Bedfellows? Russia and Central Asia under Putin," *Asian Affairs* 32, no. 2 (June 2001): 148. Changing images of the United States also animated the actions of neo-Nazi and skinhead groups in Russia, as well as those of the radical left, such as the National-Bolshevik Party under Eduard Limonov. See A. A. Arutiunov, *Terrorizm i terroristy: Sovremennaia Rossiia* (Moscow: Tsentr politicheskoi informatsii, 2003), 14–29.

94. On the nationalizing practices of Central Asian states, see Annette Bohr, "The Central Asian States as Nationalising Regimes," in *Nation-Building in the Post-Soviet Borderlands: the Politics of National Identities*, ed. Graham Smith et al. (Cambridge: Cambridge University Press, 1998), 139–66.

95. Peter Rollberg and Marlène Laruelle, "The Media Landscape in Central Asia: Introduction to the Special Issue," *Demokratizatsiya: Journal of Post-Soviet Democratization* 23, no. 3 (Summer 2015): 227–32.

96. Frederick Emrich, Yevgeniya Plakhina, and Dariya Tsyrenzhapova, *Mapping Digital Media: Kazakhstan* (Almaty: Open Society Foundation, 2013), 7, 19

97. Emrich, Plakhina and Tsyrenzhapova, *Mapping Digital Media*, 28.

98. Rounding out the top-five list were Facebook and YouTube. See Emrich, Plakhina and Tsyrenzhapova, *Mapping Digital Media*, 48.

99. V. N. Ushakov, *Politicheskii Islam v Tsentral'noi Azii* (Moscow and Bishkek: Izdatel'stvo KRSU, 2005), 88.

100. On the marketplace for such literature, see Wendell Schwab, "Establishing an Islamic Niche in Kazakhstan: Musylman Publishing House and Its Publications," *Central Asian Survey* 30, no. 2 (2011): 227–42.

101. On Protestant missionaries, see Mathijs Pelkmans, "'Culture' as a Tool and an Obstacle: Missionary Encounters in Post-Soviet Kyrgyzstan," *Journal of the Royal Anthropological Institute* 13, no. 4 (2007): 881–89; and Irene Hilgers, *Why Do Uzbeks Have to Be Muslims? Exploring Religiosity in the Ferghana Valley* (Berlin: Lit Verlag, 2009).

102. Mathijs Pelkmans, "The 'Transparency' of Christian Proselytizing in Kyrgyzstan," *Anthropological Quarterly* 82, no. 2 (2009): 424.

103. On Tengrism as an ethno-nationalist spiritual movement against globalization, see Marlène Laruelle, "Religious Revival, Nationalism and the 'Invention of Tradition': Political Tengrism in Central Asia and Tatarstan," *Central Asian Survey* 26, no. 2 (2007): 208.

CHAPTER 2: ISLAMIST TRAJECTORIES

1. This chapter uses some material from Edward Schatz, "Islamism and Anti-Americanism in Central Asia," *Current History* 101, no. 657 (October 2002): 337–43; and Edward Schatz, "Understanding Anti-Americanism in Central Asia," in *Global Perspectives on the United States: Pro-Americanism, Anti-Americanism, and the Discourses Between*, ed. Virginia R. Domínguez and Jane C. Desmond (Champaign: University of Illinois Press, 2017), 131–51.

2. Mehdi Mozaffari, "What Is Islamism? History and Definition of a Concept," *Totalitarian Movements and Political Religions* 8, no. 1 (March 2007): 17.

3. Igor Dobaev, "On the Typology of the Radical Islamic Movements," *Central Asia and the Caucasus* 3, no. 15 (2002): 96–103.

4. Ira M. Lapidus, "The Separation of State and Religion in the Development of Early Islamic Society," *International Journal of Middle East Studies* 6 (1975): 383–84.

5. Charles E. Butterworth, "Political Islam: The Origins," *Annals of the American Academy of Political and Social Science* 524 (November 1992): 33.

6. On Turkey, see M. Hakan Yavuz, *Secularism and Muslim Democracy in Turkey*, Cambridge Middle East Studies, vol. 28 (New York: Cambridge University Press,

2009). On Egypt, see Mona El-Ghobashy, "The Metamorphosis of the Egyptian Muslim Brothers," *International Journal of Middle East Studies* 37, no. 3 (2005); and Carrie Rosefsky Wickham, "The Path to Moderation: Strategy and Learning in the Formation of Egypt's Wasat Party," *Comparative Politics* 36, no. 2 (2004): 205–28.

7. For nuanced views on the prospects, practical and theological, for reconciling liberal democracy and Islam, see John L. Esposito, *Islam: The Straight Path* (Oxford: Oxford University Press, 1991); John L. Esposito, *The Islamic Threat: Myth or Reality?* (New York: Oxford University Press, 1992); John L. Esposito and John Obert Voll, *Islam and Democracy* (New York: Oxford University Press, 1996); Francois Burgat, *L'islamisme en face* (Paris: La Découverte, 1997); Francois Burgat, *The Islamic Movement in North Africa* (Austin: University of Texas Press, 1997); Mark Tessler, "Islam and Democracy in the Middle East: The Impact of Religious Orientations on Attitudes toward Democracy in Four Arab Countries," *Comparative Politics* 34 (April 2002): 337–54; Muhammad Qasim Zaman, *The Ulama in Contemporary Islam: Custodians of Change* (Princeton, NJ: Princeton University Press, 2010). One study of Kyrgyzstan finds "that Islamic belief does not drive intolerance. So, although intolerance may be widespread in Kyrgyzstan, much as it is in other post-Soviet societies, Muslims are not particularly predisposed to deny the basic political rights of their opponents." Joseph F. Fletcher and Boris Sergeyev, "Islam and Intolerance in Central Asia: The Case of Kyrgyzstan," *Europe-Asia Studies* 54, no. 2 (2002): 268. For the view that political parties need not participate in democratic institutions to moderate, see Wickham, "The Path to Moderation."

8. Central Asia has also historically witnessed a variety of quietist groups that eschew politics; see Yahya Sadowski, "Political Islam: Asking the Wrong Questions?" *Annual Review of Political Science* 9 (2006): 218–19.

9. For an exceptional recent discussion of varieties of Islam in Central Asia, see Pauline Jones, ed., *Islam, Society, and Politics in Central Asia* (Pittsburgh: University of Pittsburgh Press, 2017).

10. Robert Bruce Ware and Enver Kisriev, "The Islamic Factor in Dagestan," *Central Asian Survey* 19, no. 2 (2000): 235–52, describes how Dagestan experienced both a steep rise in Islamic piety and a steep rise in secular attitudes. In short, the religious-secular dimension became significantly polarized in that context.

11. On Islamization as early as the mid-1990s, see Office of Research and Media Reaction, United States Information Agency, "'Islamization' Is Gradual in Uzbekistan," *Opinion Analysis*, 8 March 1996.

12. For descriptive statistics of the self-reported levels of religious faith in Central Asia, see Nancy Lubin and Arustan Joldasov, "Snapshots from Central Asia: Is America Losing in Public Opinion?," *Problems of Post-Communism* 57, no. 3 (2010): 40–54.

13. Office of Research and Media Reaction, United States Information Agency, "Islam Yes, Islamic State No for Muslim Kazakhstanis," *Opinion Analysis*, 24 December 1997.

14. Such alarmism is widespread. See L. B. Maevskaia, *Ostorozhno, ekstremizm!* (Kiev: Mezhregional'naia akademiia upravleniia personalom, 2002); Vitalii

Viacheslavovich Naumkin, *Radical Islam in Central Asia: Between Pen and Rifle* (Latham, MD: Rowman & Littlefield, 2005); Garun Kurbanov, "How Dagestan Is Opposing Religious Extremism," *Central Asia and the Caucasus* 5 (September 2002): 120–27; and Garun Kurbanov, "Religion in Post-Soviet Dagestan: Sociological Aspects," *Central Asia and the Caucasus* 6 (November 2002): 130–38. Naumkin conflates three things: a belief-system (Islam), a radical political orientation (Islamism), and an embrace of violence (militancy). He covers the IMU (which uses all three), HT (which uses only the first two), and the IRPT (which uses only the first). With this rhetorical structure, he implies that HT and IRPT are essentially the same, if marginally diminished versions, as the IMU. They are not. For early, nonalarmist treatments, see Vladimir Sergiienko, "'Politicheskii islam' v tsentral'noi as: prizrachnaia ili real'naia?" *Kontinent* (19 April–2 May 2000); and Nargis Kassenova, "Religious Extremism in Central Asia: Self-Fulfilling Prophecy in the Making?," *Central Asia and the Caucasus* (September 2000): 43–49.

15. David W. Montgomery and John Heathershaw, "Islam, Secularism and Danger: A Reconsideration of the Link between Religiosity, Radicalism and Rebellion in Central Asia," *Religion, State & Society* 44, no. 3 (2016): 192–218. In Central Asia, the term *Wahhabi* is used synonymously with *militant Islamists*. See A. Ak. Lukoianov, "Igry v vakhkhabizm," in *Islam i politika*, ed. G. V. Minorca (Moscow: Institut vostokovedeniia RAN, 2001). Historically, Wahhabism was a puritanical movement born in eighteenth-century Arabia. On the difference between the popular use of the term *Wahhabi* and the theological framework of the Wahhabi movement itself, see B. Babadzhanov, A. K. Muminov, and Anke von Kügelgen, *Disputy musul'manskikh religioznykh avtoritetov v Tsentral'noi Azii v XX veke* (Almaty: Daik-Press, 2007). Only in Dagestan (Russian Federation) would Wahhabism find resonance; an estimated 3–5 percent of the population there so identified; see Enver Kisriev, "Islam's Political Role in Dagestan," *Central Asia and the Caucasus* 5 (September 2000): 65–70.

16. Adeeb Khalid, *Islam after Communism: Religion and Politics in Central Asia* (Berkeley: University of California Press, 2007).

17. See, for example, William Fierman, ed. *Soviet Central Asia: The Failed Transformation* (Boulder, CO: Westview Press, 1991).

18. On Soviet-era treatment of Islam, see especially Khalid, *Islam after Communism*; Douglas Northrop, *Veiled Empire: Gender and Power in Stalinist Central Asia* (Ithaca, NY: Cornell University Press, 2004); Shoshana Keller, *To Moscow, Not Mecca: The Soviet Campaign against Islam in Central Asia, 1917–1941* (Westport, CT: Praeger Publishers, 2001); Marianne Kamp, *The New Woman in Uzbekistan: Islam, Modernity, and Unveiling under Communism* (Seattle: University of Washington Press, 2006); Eren Murat Tasar, "Islamically Informed Soviet Patriotism in Postwar Kyrgyzstan," *Cahiers du monde russe* 52, no. 2 (2012): 387–404.

19. Sergei P. Poliakov, *Everyday Islam: Religion and Tradition in Rural Central Asia*, ed. Martha Brill Olcott, trans. Anthony Olcott (Armonk, NY: M. E. Sharpe, 1992).

20. Martha Brill Olcott and Bakhtiyar Babajanov, "The Terrorist Notebooks," *Foreign Policy* 135 (March-April 2003): 30–40; Bakhtiar Babadjanov and Muzaffar Kamilov, "Domulla Hindustani and the Beginning of the 'Great Schism' among Moslems of Uzbekistan," in *Islam in Politics in Russia and Central Asia (Early Eighteenth to Late Twentieth Centuries)*, ed. Stéphane A. Dudoignon and Komatso Hisao (London, New York, and Bahrain: Kegan Paul, 2002); Martha Brill Olcott, "Roots of Radical Islam in Central Asia," Carnegie Papers no. 77 (Washington, DC: Carnegie Endowment for International Peace, January 2007).

21. Naumkin, *Radical Islam in Central Asia*, 21.

22. Naumkin, *Radical Islam in Central Asia*, 52.

23. On preference falsification, see Timur Kuran, "Now Out of Never: The Element of Surprise in the East European Revolution of 1989," *World Politics* 44, no. 1 (1991): 7–48.

24. Informing my reasoning are Lisa Wedeen, *Ambiguities of Domination: Politics, Rhetoric, and Symbols in Contemporary Syria* (Chicago: University of Chicago Press, 1999); and Alexei Yurchak, *Everything Was Forever, Until It Was No More: The Last Soviet Generation* (Princeton, NJ, and Oxford: Princeton University Press, 2005).

25. Ahmed Rashid, "They're Only Sleeping," *New Yorker*, January 14, 2002; italics original.

26. As Khalid (*Islam after Communism*, 136) puts it, "The resurgence of piety does not lead directly to the politicization of Islam." For a contrary view, see V. N. Ushakov, *Politicheskii Islam v Tsentral'noi Azii* (Moscow and Bishkek: Izdatel'stvo KRSU, 2005), 81, 92.

27. See Olivier Roy, *The Foreign Policy of the Central Asian Islamic Renaissance Party* (New York: Council on Foreign Relations, 2000) on how the IRPT desperately sought, but ultimately botched, its transnational connections.

28. The Tajik president would drop the Russian *-ov* from his last name in 2007, becoming Rakhmon.

29. On how the Karimov regime reified a binary between "good" and "bad" Islam, see Johan Rasanayagam, *Islam in Post-Soviet Uzbekistan: The Morality of Experience* (New York: Cambridge University Press, 2011), 96–120. For the official view of the 1999 bombings, see O. Ostonov, Zh. Razzaqov, and R. Shoghulomov, *Fevral' vokealari; 1999 iil 16 fevral* (Tashkent: Uzbekiston, 1999).

30. Roy, *Foreign Policy of the Central Asian Islamic Renaissance Party*, 24.

31. Schatz, "Islamism and Anti-Americanism in Central Asia."

32. International Crisis Group, "Central Asia: Uzbekistan at Ten—Repression and Instability," *Asia Report* 21 (21 August 2001).

33. On the Uzbeks of southern Kyrgyzstan, see Morgan Y. Liu, *Under Solomon's Throne* (Pittsburgh: University of Pittsburgh Press, 2012). In retrospect, it is clear that Uzbeks in Kyrgyzstan were more included under Akaev than they would be under his successor, Kurmanbek Bakiev.

34. Radical literature and preachers began to appear in Kazakhstan in 1998, if not earlier, using links with Moscow and Dagestan. Public discourse routinely

emphasized their foreign provenance. Igor Savin, "Ethnic and Confessional Situation in Southern Kazakhstan and Major Regional Challenges," *Central Asia and the Caucasus* 3, no. 9 (2001): 131–37; and Igor Savin, "Religioznyi ekstremizm v Kazakhstane," *Biulleten': Set' etnologicheskogo monitoringa* 37 (2001): 75–77, as reprinted in *Rossiia i musul'manskii mir* 3 (2002), describe the appearance of Wahhabi groups in southern Kazakhstan, especially among ethnic Uzbeks of the Sairam *raion*.

35. Stuart Horsman, "Themes in Official Discourses on Terrorism in Central Asia," *Third World Quarterly* 26, no. 1 (2005): 199–213. Rashid, "They're Only Sleeping," depicts militant jihad in Central Asia as likely—a leap of imagination made possible through selection bias: by focusing on areas where radical sentiment had already arisen.

36. For perspectives on Islam in Kazakhstan, see Alma Sultangalieva, *Islam v Kazakhstan: istoriia, etnichnost', obschchestvo* (Almaty: Kazakhstanskii institut strategicheskikh issledovanii, 1998); and Bruce Privatsky, *Muslim Turkistan: Kazak Religion and Collective Memory* (London and New York: Routledge, 2001).

37. David A. Snow and Robert Benford, "Master Frames and Cycles of Protest," in *Frontiers in Social Movement Theory*, ed. Aldon Morris and Carol McClurg Mueller (New Haven, CT: Yale University Press, 1992), 138.

38. HTs began to appear in southern Kyrgyzstan in the mid-1990s. See A. G. Kosychenko et al., *Sovremennyi terrorizm: vzgliad iz Tsentral'noi Azii* (Almaty: Daik-Press 2002), 150. Karagiannis aspires to holistic treatment of HT's rise in Central Asia in *Political Islam in Central Asia: The Challenge of Hizb ut-Tahrir* (London and New York: Routledge, 2010).

39. Perhaps this is why some analysts view HT as an overwhelming threat. See Zeyno Baran, *Hizb ut-Tahrir: Islam's Political Insurgency* (Washington, DC: Nixon Center, 2004). Otherwise competent analysts have sometimes conflated the terrorist IMU and self-proclaimed nonviolent HT; see Alexander Kniazev, "Afghanistan: Religious Extremism and Terrorism—The Year 2000," *Central Asia and the Caucasus*, no. 5 (2000): 82.

40. The vagueness of HT injunctions broadened its potential appeal. On the mass appeal, see also Uran Botobekov, "Vnedrenie idei islamskoi partii 'Hizb at-Takhrir,'" in *Islam na postsovetskom prostranstve: vzgliad iznutri*, ed. Aleksei Malashenko and Martha Brill Olcott (Moscow: Carnegie Center, 2001).

41. Discussing HT in Southern Kazakhstan, Savin reports that financial incentives were minimal; to the contrary, there were financial burdens, which increased as one rose from the rank and file to the central organization. See Igor Savin, "'Khizb ut-Takhrir' v Iuzhnom Kazakhstane: sotsial'nyi portret iavleniia," *TsentrAziia* (28 December 2002): 4.

42. See Suha Taji-Farouki, *A Fundamental Quest: Hizb al-Tahrir and the Search for the Islamic Caliphate* (London: Grey Seal, 1996).

43. Karagiannis, *Political Islam in Central Asia*, 89.

44. Karagiannis, *Political Islam in Central Asia*, 93.

45. Karagiannis, *Political Islam in Central Asia*, 96.

46. Khalid, *Islam after Communism*, 15.

47. Sayyid Qutb, *Milestones* (CreateSpace, 2005), 29, http://www.izharudeen.com/uploads/4/1/2/2/4122615/milestones_www.izharudeen.com.pdf.

48. Igor Rotar', *Pod zelenym znamenem: Islamskie radikaly v Rossii i SNG* (Moscow: AIRO-XX, 2001), 20, also finds parallels between Soviet ideology and Islamist worldviews.

49. On the economies of Central Asia in the post-Soviet period, see Richard Pomfret, *The Central Asian Economies since Independence* (Princeton, NJ: Princeton University Press, 2006).

50. Karagiannis, *Political Islam in Central Asia*, 94. See also Bakhtiar Babadzhanov, "O deiatel'nosti 'Khizb at-Takhrir al-islami' v Uzbekistane," in *Islam na postsovetskom prostranstve: vzgliad iznutri*, ed. A. Malashenko and M. B. Olcott (Moscow: Mosk. Tsentr Karnegi, 2001), 161.

51. Karagiannis, *Political Islam in Central Asia*, 77. This was echoed in the author's interview with an activist in Southern Kyrgyzstan (22 June 2002).

52. It could be that in the context of violent interethnic strife in southern Kyrgyzstan, such rhetoric was doubly resonant, especially among minority Uzbeks who were disproportionately the victims of violence in 2010. Botobekov, "Vnedrenie idei islamskoi partii," argues that alienation and repression of the Uzbek population in Osh are the reasons for HT's popularity among Uzbeks (3, 7). He adds that HT leaflets were first found in the Kyrgyz language in 1999 (16).

This is consistent with patterns of HT's rise. In Kazakhstan, the southern and western regions—which harbor grievances based on ethnic discrimination and economic injustice—saw the steepest rise of HT membership. In Kyrgyzstan, HT was most successful in the south for similar reasons. In Tajikistan, the Soghd region in the north, largely locked out of the post–civil war spoils that accrued to other regions, witnessed a startling rise of HT activism. Author's interview with local journalist, Khujand, Tajikistan, 13 May 2006. See also International Crisis Group, "The IMU and the Hizb-ut-Tahrir: Implications of the Afghanistan Campaign," Central Asia Briefing, 30 January 2002, 12; and Saodat Olimova, "Islam and Construction of a National State in Central Asia: Islamic Movement in Tajikistan," in *Social Protests and Nation-Building in the Middle East and Central Asia*, ed. Keiko Sakai (Chiba, Japan: Institute of Developing Economies, 2003), 176. The Gorno-Badakhshan region was equally marginalized, but its concentration of Ismaili Muslims meant that HT's largely Sunni vision fell on deaf ears.

53. An exceptional Kyrgyz parliamentarian argued, "We should not condemn people for utopian ideas. We should recognize that we have communists and people who support other ideas and would like to change the constitutional order." See Uulu Bakir, "Problemy islamizatsii v Kyrgyzstane," *Vechernyi Bishkek* (3 October 2001), as cited in Erkin Kurmanov, "Hizb ut-Tahrir in Kyrgyzstan," *Central Asia and the Caucasus* 15, no. 3 (2002): 125.

54. For one treatment of violence, see Joma Nazpary, *Post-Soviet Chaos: Violence and Dispossession in Kazakhstan* (London: Pluto Press: 2001).

55. One HT activist stated in a January 2002 interview: "We will not become violent just because the kafirs [non-believers] attacked Afghanistan. They have been doing it for centuries, and this case is another example of cruelty of America and the West against Muslims. We will continue our struggle and not change our methods," International Crisis Group, "The IMU and the Hizb-ut-Tahrir," 8.

56. Khalid, *Islam after Communism*, 167, correctly argues that Central Asian regimes sought to link militant insurgency in Central Asia to global jihadist movements in ways that would "[come] in handy for the regime." The same is true of local movements: by hitching themselves to a broader frame, they take part in something of larger, even transcendent, value and purpose.

57. Naumkin, *Radical Islam in Central Asia*, 187. On reactions in Kazakhstan to the Iraq war, see T. Tungatarova, "Does the USA Really Threaten Central Asian Region?," *Central Asia's Affairs: Quarterly Analytic Review* 1, no. 5 (2004).

58. See also International Crisis Group, "Radical Islam in Central Asia: Responding to Hizb ut-Tahrir," *ICG Asia Report* 58 (30 June 2003): 6–7.

59. Khalid, *Islam after Communism*, 163.

60. For English-language examples of HT's explicitly anti-American perspectives, see Hizb ut-Tahrir, *The American Campaign to Suppress Islam* (London: Al-Khalifa, 1996); Hizb ut-Tahrir, *Dangerous Concepts to Attack Islam and Consolidate the Western Culture* (London: Al-Khalifa, 1997.) See also Botobekov, "Vnedrenie idei islamskoi partii," 6.

61. Rotar', *Pod zelenym znamenem*, 77.

62. Karagiannis, *Political Islam in Central Asia*, 11, 78, 111, 76, 78. In Tajikistan, HT was especially strong in the northern Sughd region. Olimova, "Islam and Construction of a National State," 176. The IRPT, discussed later in this chapter, had a strong regional base of support outside the north, so HT was better positioned to be influential in the north than elsewhere.

63. Savin, "'Khizb ut-Takhrir' v Iuzhnom Kazakhstane," 8. HT began to appear prominently in Kazakhstan in 2000 (Asel' Berimzharova, personal communication, 20 October 2006). For more examples of HT's anti-American rhetoric, see Khalid, *Islam after Communism*, 162; Zumrat Salmorbekova and Galina Yemelianova, "Islam and Islamism in the Ferghana Valley," in *Radical Islam in the Former Soviet Union*, ed. Galina Yemelianova (London and New York: Routledge, 2010);), 234, 238; and Ushakov, *Politicheskii Islam*, 107.

64. Igor' Rotar', "Tsentral'naia Aziia—sleduiushchaia mishen' ekstremistov," *Nezavisimaia gazeta*, 14 September 2001.

65. Karagiannis, personal communication; and quoted in Karagiannis, *Political Islam in Central Asia*, 90.

66. See Bert Klandermans and Dirk Oegema, "Potentials, Networks, Motivations, and Barriers: Steps towards Participation in Social Movements," *American Sociological Review* 52, no. 4 (August 1987): 519–31.

67. Savin, "'Khizb ut-Takhrir' v Iuzhnom Kazakhstane," 5, describes how a single inexplicable event leads to a moment of epiphany among those who become HT

members. For a similar perspective, see Quintan Wiktorowicz, *Radical Islam Rising: Muslim Extremism in the West* (Lanham, MD: Rowman & Littlefield, 2005).

68. While we cannot be present at the moment of recruitment itself, the Conclusion addresses the efficacy of framing efforts via a survey experiment.

69. Savin, "'Khizb ut-Takhrir' v Iuzhnom Kazakhstane," 7, 65. This appeal to global imaginings was perhaps made possible by the fact that HT appeared to target the educated, and especially those with degrees from prestigious educational institutions.

70. Salmorbekova and Yemelianova, "Islam and Islamism."

71. Babadzhanov, "O deiatel'nosti," 159.

72. International Crisis Group, "The IMU and the Hizb-ut-Tahrir," 7.

73. Interview with the author, 22 June 2002.

74. Interview with the author, 22 June 2002, and fieldnotes June 2002. Salmorbekova and Yemelianova, "Islam and Islamism" 238, offers a similar observation.

75. For a summary of the IRPT's rise and role, see Saodat Olimova, "Opposition in Tajikistan: Pro et Contra," in *Democracy and Pluralism in Muslim Eurasia*, ed. Yaakov Ro'i (London and New York: Frank Cass, 2004).

76. Tim Epkenhans, "The Islamic Revival Party of Tajikistan: Episodes of Islamic Activism, Postconflict Accommodation, and Political Marginalization," *Central Asian Affairs* 2, no. 4 (2015): 332.

77. Saodat Olimova and Muzaffar Olimov, "The Islamic Revival Party of Tajikistan in the Context of the Tajik Conflict and its Settlement," *Central Asia and the Caucasus* 1, no. 7 (2001): 114–15. In addition, the Party's main spiritual guide from its founding in 1990, Akbar Turajonzoda, declined to run for elected office in 1991, "citing the incompatible objectives of the religious and political offices." See Shahram Akbarzadeh, "Islamic Clerical Establishment in Central Asia," *South Asia: Journal of South Asian Studies* 2 (December 1997): 95.

78. D. V. Mikul'skii, *Ideologicheskaia kontseptsiia Islamskoi partii vozrozhdeniia* (Moscow: Mezhdunarodnyi fond sotsial'no-ekonomicheskikh i politologicheskikh issledovanii [Gorbachev-fond], 1993), 9.

79. On the politics of regions, see Pauline Jones Luong, *Institutional Change and Political Continuity in Post-Soviet Central Asia: Power, Perceptions, and Pacts* (Cambridge: Cambridge University Press, 2002); and Kathleen Collins, *Clan Politics and Regime Transition in Central Asia* (New York: Cambridge University Press, 2006).

80. Qadi Akbar Turajonzoda, "Religion: The Pillar of Society," in *Central Asia: Conflict, Resolution, and Change*, ed. Roald Z. Sagdeev and Susan Eisenhower (Chevy Chase, MD: CPSS Press, 1995), as discussed in Khalid, *Islam after Communism*, 149.

81. Mikul'skii, *Ideologicheskaia kontseptsiia*, 21.

82. Mikul'skii, *Ideologicheskaia kontseptsiia*, 10.

83. Mikul'skii, *Ideologicheskaia kontseptsiia*, 12–13.

84. Roy, *Foreign Policy of the Central Asian Islamic Renaissance Party*, 12–13.

85. As late as 2007, one local pro-Rakhmon intellectual equated the rising popularity of hijabs among Tajik women with what he, apparently following George W. Bush, called "Islamic fascism." Author's interview with Iskandar K. Asadullaev,

Institute of Philosophy of the Academy of Sciences, Republic of Tajikistan, 2 May 2007. Karagiannis, in *Political Islam in Central Asia*, writes that "after the start of the civil war, the party joined the armed opposition and became a guerilla force, implicitly fighting for the establishment of an Islamic state" (97). In fact, fighting in a civil war and fighting for an Islamic state are different things.

86. Kosychenko et al., *Sovremennyi terrorizm*, 145, correctly note that the IRPT "does not raise the question about creating an Islamic state." This orientation continued through 2015, when the party was banned. Naumkin, *Radical Islam in Central Asia*, 201–60, reiterates the IRPT role in the civil war violence. While violence was widespread in Tajikistan, it is unclear that the IRPT should be described as a unitary actor since it lacked corporate integrity during the period. Moreover, relying on Uzbek law-enforcement documents for evidence, as Naumkin, *Radical Islam in Central Asia*, 231–32, does, is problematic since Uzbek authorities routinely painted all devout Muslims with the same brush. See Khalid, *Islam after Communism*.

87. Naumkin, *Radical Islam in Central Asia*, 224, wrongly implies the contrary.

88. Olimova and Olimov, "The Islamic Revival Party," 114.

89. Naumkin, *Radical Islam in Central Asia*, 215.

90. Epkenhans, "The Islamic Revival Party of Tajikistan," 336.

91. Naumkin, *Radical Islam in Central Asia*, 239.

92. Naumkin, *Radical Islam in Central Asia*, 252

93. Anonymous participants, focus group, Khujand, Tajikistan, 29 January 2006.

94. Kiemiddin Sattori, "Tajik Press about the Youth and Islam," *Central Asia and the Caucasus* (2002): 128.

95. Sattori, "Tajik Press," 129.

96. Sattori, "Tajik Press," 129–30.

97. Sattori, "Tajik Press," 130.

98. Sattori, "Tajik Press," 130.

99. Sattori, "Tajik Press," 128–29.

100. Author's interview with Saifullo Safarov, Centre for Strategic Studies under the President, Dushanbe, Tajikistan, 8 May 2006.

101. Author's interviews and fieldnotes, Dushanbe and Khujand, May 2007.

102. See Karagiannis, *Political Islam in Central Asia*, 100; Naumkin, *Radical Islam in Central Asia*, 240. On similar efforts by the Moroccan regime to coopt the Islamic Party of Justice and Development, see Eva Wegner and Miquel Pellicer, "Islamist Moderation without Democratization: The Coming of Age of the Moroccan Party of Justice and Development?," *Democratization* 16, no. 1 (2009): 157–75.

103. Naumkin, *Radical Islam in Central Asia*, 242.

104. On Europe's accommodation of Islam, see Joel S. Fetzer and J. Christopher Soper, *Muslims and the State in Britain, France, and Germany* (New York: Cambridge University Press, 2005).

105. See Ian Buruma, "Tariq Ramadan Has an Identity Issue," *New York Times Magazine*, 4 February 2007, on the figure Tariq Ramadan whom IRPT leader Kabiri praised effusively in interviews.

106. See Yavuz, *Secularism and Muslim Democracy*.

107. Author's interview with Muhiddin Kabiri, 2 May 2007, Dushanbe, Tajikistan. The Turkish regime would begin backsliding into authoritarianism by the 2010s.

108. Author's interviews and fieldnotes, Dushanbe and Khujand, May 2007.

109. Author's interview with local journalist, Khujand, Tajikistan, 13 May 2006. See also Naumkin, *Radical Islam in Central Asia*, 248.

110. Naumkin, *Radical Islam in Central Asia*, 250, and author's interview with Kabiri; Author's interview with Sunatullo Jonboboev, 5 May 2006. For claims about the radicalization of the population of Isfara in particular, see Negmatullo Mirsaidov, "Isfara Becomes Terrorist Hub," *Tajikistan Times* 45, no. 82 (10 November 2010).

111. Epkenhans, "The Islamic Revival Party of Tajikistan," 327.

112. "Opposition Party Refuses to Print Independent Publications," *Tajikistan Times* 45, no. 82 (10 November 2010). See also Christian Neef, "An Islamist Uprising," *Spiegel Online International*, as reprinted in *Tajikistan Times* 45, no. 82 (10 November 2010).

113. Epkenhans, "The Islamic Revival Party of Tajikistan," 339.

114. Naumkin, *Radical Islam in Central Asia*, 57.

115. Naumkin, *Radical Islam in Central Asia*, 68. The very few proponents of sharia likely had scant knowledge of Islam and probably no clear sense of what sharia would involve in concrete circumstances; see Olcott and Babajanov, "The Terrorist Notebooks." Naumkin, *Radical Islam in Central Asia*, 97, characterizes Adolat's members "not only as Salafis but also as jihadists," a claim that reifies nascent links to global militants and produces a teleology in which Islamism is assumed always to be on the path to violence.

116. Ushakov proposes that radical groups gain recruits because the region's regimes repress pious Muslims. While this may be true of radical groups, Uzbeks' spirituality is not simply a function of repression. See Ushakov, *Politicheskii Islam*, 110–11. As Rasanayagam writes in *Islam in Post-Soviet Uzbekistan*, "A subdued, even fearful atmosphere surrounds religious practices.... There is, at the same time, a riot of exploration with regards to Islam and also expressed in the variety of Christian and other groups that emerged after independence and are attracting adherents. Muslims in Uzbekistan are creatively developing understandings of moral selfhood and of moral community resulting in a great diversity in interpretations of Islam and what it means to be a Muslim" (230).

117. Maria Louw, *Everyday Islam in Post-Soviet Central Asia* (London and New York: Routledge, 2007), 26.

118. Quoted in Naumkin, *Radical Islam in Central Asia*, 75.

119. Quoted in Naumkin, *Radical Islam in Central Asia*, 83.

120. Olcott and Babajanov, "The Terrorist Notebooks," 36.

121. "Uzbek Islamic Movement," as cited in Khalid, *Islam after Communism*, 157.

122. Karagiannis, *Political Islam in Central Asia*, 111.

123. Igor Rotar, "The Islamic Movement of Uzbekistan: A Resurgent IMU?," *Terrorism Monitor* (Jamestown Foundation) 1, no. 8 (18 December 2003).

124. Jamestown Monitor, "Militant Islamic Group Serves Ultimatum on Uzbekistan from Iran," *Terrorism Monitor: In-Depth Analysis of the War on Terror* 5, no. 60 (March 1999).

125. Bakhtiyar Babajanov, "Teologicheskoe obosnovanie i etapy jihada v dokumentakh islamskogo dvijeniia Uzbekistana, perevod i komentarii Babajanova B.S. i Olkotta M.B.," *Kazakhstan-Spektr* 3 (2002), cited in Naumkin, *Radical Islam in Central Asia*, 100.

126. Olcott and Babajanov, "The Terrorist Notebooks," 37.

127. Rotar', *Pod zelenym znamenem*, 20–21, writes that "many rank-and-file Tajik Islamist fighters told the author that they were for the Soviet Union and an Islamic republic."

128. For one sober analysis, see Christian Bleuer, "Instability in Tajikistan? The Islamic Movement of Uzbekistan and the Afghanistan Factor," *Central Asia Security Policy Brief* no. 7, OSCE Academy, Bishkek (2012).

129. Similar processes were at play elsewhere. On Russia's north Caucasus, see Gordon Hahn, "Anti-Americanism, Anti-Westernism, and Anti-Semitism among Russia's Muslims," *Demokratizatsiia* 16, no. 1 (Winter 2008): 49–60. Kratov, "K voprosu ob ideologii sovremennogo religiozno-politicheskogo ekstremizma (na osnovanii materialov, rasprostraniaemykh v Karachaevo-Cherkesskoi respublike," in *Terrorizm i politicheskii ekstremizm: vyzovy i poiski adekvatnykh otvetov*, ed. A. A. Sharavin and S. M. Markedonov (Moscow: Institut politicheskogo i voennogo analiza, 2002). Similarly, Ware and Kisriev, "The Islamic Factor in Dagestan," 238, note foreign influence in Islamizing Dagestan: "The growth of Wahhabism may be viewed as a product of Western influences, for it is a potent reaction against the present excesses of modernization. It springs from a deep disillusionment with the prospects for economic transition and feeds on widespread despair over the myriad forms of moral and political decay that are rapidly overwhelming Dagestani society."

130. This built upon the Soviet approach (see Khalid, *Islam after Communism*), which in turn built upon the tsarist one (see Robert D. Crews, *For Prophet and Tsar* [Cambridge, MA: Harvard University Press, 2009]).

131. On the conflict between sufi (what he calls Taraqist) and Salafi Islam, see D. V. Makarov, *Offitsial'nyi i neofitsial'nyi Islam v Dagestane* (Moscow: Tsentr strategicheskikh i politicheskikh issledovanii, 2000). Sergei Abashin, "Islamic Fundamentalism in Central Asia: Why It Appeared and What to Expect," *Central Asia and the Caucasus* (March 2002): 65, reminds us that there is no necessary opposition between Sufis and non-Sufis. To the contrary, Naqshibandi leaders at key moments pushed for stricter implementation of sharia law.

132. See Eric M. McGlinchey, "Islamic Leaders in Uzbekistan," *Asia Policy* 1, no. 1 (January 2006): 123–44. Also, on how ineffective the official religious establishment's approach to Islam was in the late 1990s and early 2000s in Uzbekistan, see Bakhtyar Babadjanov, "Islam officiel contre islam politique en Ouzbékistan aujourd'hui: la direction des musulmans et les groupes non-hanafi," *Revue d'études comparatives Est-Ouest* 31, no. 3 (2000): 151–64.

133. Criticism of Grand Mufti Absattar Derbisaliev's qualifications was widespread (e.g., Artur Artem'ev, "Esche raz k voprosu o svobode sovesti i veroterpimosti," *Saiasat* [March 2001]; Iakov Trofimov, "Gosudarstvo, obshchestvo i religiia v sovremennom Kazakhstane," *Rossiia i musul'manskii mir* 11 [2001]: 91), even as Derbisaliev offered a spirited defense of his credentials; see Sultana Akimbekova, "Islam—odna iz samykh miroliubivykh religii: interv'iu 'Kontinenta' s glavoi Dukhovnogo upravleniia musul'man Kazakhstana Absattarom-kazhy Derbisalievym," *Kontinent*, October 2001: 10–23.

134. Makarov, *Offitsial'nyi i neofitsial'nyi Islam v Dagestane*, 28.

135. See McGlinchey, "Islamic Leaders in Uzbekistan."

136. Quintan Wiktorowicz, ed., *Islamic Activism: A Social Movement Theory Approach* (Bloomington: Indiana University Press, 2003), 26–27. Anti-Semitism can link up, as well, as when the front page of a newspaper in Kyrgyzstan in 1994 depicted a Star of David "with the figure of the president of Kyrgyzstan at its centre appearing as an Israeli underling." Leonid Levitin, "Liberalization in Kyrgyzstan: 'An Island of Democracy,' in *Democracy and Pluralism in Muslim Eurasia*, ed. Yaakov Ro'i (London and New York: Frank Cass), 208. Similarly, one erstwhile figure in the IRPT believed that HT had been created by "Zionism and Freemasonry" to undermine true Islamic values. See Tim Epkenhans, "Defining Normative Islam: Some Remarks on Contemporary Islamic Thought in Tajikistan—Hofi Akbar Turajonzoda's Sharia and Society," *Central Asian Survey* 30, no.1 (March 2011): 90.

137. Mohammed Ayoob, "The Future of Political Islam: the Importance of External Variables," *International Affairs* 81, no. 5 (2005): 960.

CHAPTER 3: HUMAN RIGHTS TRAJECTORIES

1. By the early 2010s, most analysts were ready to conclude that US hegemony was at least in relative decline. See, for example, John G. Ikenberry, "The Liberal International Order and its Discontents," in *After Liberalism? The Future of Liberalism in International Relations*, ed. Rebekka Friedman, Kevork Oskanian, and Ramon Pacheco Pardo (Houndills, Basingstoke, Hampshire: Palgrave Macmillan, 2013), 91–102. For one account that treats political change in East Europe as part of the global processes that democratized Latin America, southern Europe, and East Asia, see Samuel P. Huntington, *The Third Wave: Democratization in the Late Twentieth Century* (Norman: University of Oklahoma Press, 1991).

2. On the impact of the West's "linkage" and "leverage," see Steven Levitsky and Lucan A. Way, "Linkage versus Leverage: Rethinking the International Dimension of Regime," *Comparative Politics* 38, no. 4 (2006).

3. John Anderson, *Kyrgyzstan: Central Asia's Island of Democracy?* (Australia: Harwood Academic Publishers, 1999). To be fair, Anderson hedged by providing a question mark in his book's title. The optimism is nonetheless noteworthy.

4. Eric McGlinchey, *Chaos, Violence, Dynasty: Politics and Islam in Central Asia*

(Pittsburgh: University of Pittsburgh Press, 2011), 87–88. On how Kyrgyzstan's freewheeling information environment did not translate into significant democratization pressure, see Rachel Vanderhill, "Limits on the Democratizing Influence of the Internet: Lessons from Post-Soviet States," *Demokratizatsiya: Journal of Post-Soviet Democratization* 23, no. 1 (2015): 31–56.

5. This much was evident from the early years of his tenure. See Mezhdudarodnyi fond sotsial'no-ekonomicheskikh i politologicheskikh issledovaniii, *Respublika Kyrgyzstan: kratkii analiz sotsial'no-politicheskoi situatsii* (Moscow: Gorbachev-Fond, 1993), 4.

6. For Akaev's references to Jefferson, see Kathleen Collins, *Clan Politics and Regime Transition*, 177; and Askar A. Akaev, *Pamiatnoe desiatiletie: trudnaia doroga k demokratii* (Moskva: Mezhdunarodnye otnosheniia, 2002), 160. Dmitrii E. Furman and Sanobar A. Shermatova, *Kirgizskie Tsikly: Kak Rushatsia Rezhimy* (Moscow: Territoriia budushchego 2013), 131, quotes Akaev as writing, "Our democracy descends from the mountains of Tian-Shan"; see Melis Eshimkanov and Kanybek Imanaliev, *Askar Akaev* (Bishkek: Asaba, 1993), 74. Kyrgyz pastoral nomads also descended from the mountains during seasonal migrations.

7. McGlinchey, *Chaos, Violence, Dynasty*, 82.

8. On the challenges civil society faced in Kyrgyzstan, see Charles Buxton, "In Good Times and Hard Times: Civil Society Roles in Kyrgyzstan Today," in *Civil Society and Politics in Central Asia*, ed. Charles E. Ziegler (Lexington: University Press of Kentucky, 2015). McGlinchey, *Chaos, Violence, Dynasty*, argues that this external funding generated a rentier effect in which regime elites lived large off corruption.

9. McGlinchey, *Chaos, Violence, Dynasty*, 93.

10. McGlinchey, *Chaos, Violence, Dynasty*, 94–96.

11. Rafis Abazov, "The Parliamentary Elections in Kyrgyzstan, February 2000," *Electoral Studies* 22, no. 3 (2003): 545–52.

12. OSCE Office for Democratic Institutions and Human Rights, *Kyrgyz Republic Parliamentary Elections: 20 February and 12 March 2000*, final report, (Warsaw: Organization for Security and Co-operation in Europe, 10 April 2000).

13. Christopher H. Smith, "Human Rights and Democracy in Kyrgyzstan," opening statement, Hearing before the Commission on Security and Cooperation in Europe, 107th Congress, First Session, 12 December 2001, CSCE 107-1-8. See also McGlinchey, *Chaos, Violence, Dynasty*, 185n22.

14. See Alexander Kupatadze, "Organized Crime and the State in Post-Soviet Eurasia," in *Paradox of Power: The Logics of State Weakness in Eurasia*, ed. John Heathershaw and Edward Schatz (Pittsburgh: University of Pittsburgh Press, 2017), 60–72; and Scott Radnitz, "Power, Peripheries, and Pyramids in Post-Soviet Kyrgyzstan and Georgia," in Heathershaw and Schatz, *Paradox of Power*, 44–59. One longtime opposition figure claimed that state officials often refer to state weakness vis-à-vis criminal groups to excuse their own behavior. Author's interview with Bakhyt Beshimov, Bishkek, 19 May 2006.

15. Dan Slater, "Democratic Careening," *World Politics* 65, no. 4 (2014): 730.

16. Slater, "Democratic Careening," 730.

17. By contrast, in Uzbekistan elites lacked the economic and political autonomy of their Kyrgyz counterparts and therefore failed to mobilize. See Scott Radnitz, "The Color of Money: Privatization, Economic Dispersion, and the Post-Soviet 'Revolutions,'" *Comparative Politics* 42, no. 2 (2010): 127–46. See also Kelly M. McMann, *Economic Autonomy and Democracy: Hybrid Regimes in Russia and Kyrgyzstan* (New York: Cambridge University Press, 2006).

18. See Dmitrii E. Furman and Sanobar A. Shermatova, *Kirgizskie Tsikly*.

19. Henry E. Hale, *Patronal Politics: Eurasian Regime Dynamics in Comparative Perspective* (New York: Cambridge University Press, 2015).

20. For exceptional work that links the domestic to the geostrategic in Central Asia, see Alexander Cooley, *Base Politics: Democratic Change and the U.S. Military Overseas* (Ithaca, NY: Cornell University Press, 2008); and Alexander Cooley, *Great Games, Local Rules: The New Great Power Contest in Central Asia* (New York: Oxford University Press, 2012).

21. See Levitsky and Way, "Linkage versus Leverage."

22. For perspectives that assume that when an outcome is desirable for the United States, the US must have been the main driver of the outcome, see the contributions to Gleb Pavlovskii, *Kirgizskii Perevorot: Mart-aprel' 2005* (Moscow: Izdatel'stvo "Evropa," 2005). In the Egyptian and Tunisian cases, the proliferation of civil society groups did not promote liberalization because these groups advocated support for disadvantaged groups rather than pushing for broad change; see Vickie Langhor, "Too Much Civil Society, Too Little Politics: Egypt and Liberalizing Arab Regimes," *Comparative Politics* 36, no. 2 (2004): 182. On the limits to Western influence in Afghanistan, see Jennifer Brick Murtazashvili, *Informal Order and the State in Afghanistan* (New York: Cambridge University Press, 2016), chapter 3. On Kyrgyzstan, see N. Omuraliev, "Stanovlenie grazhdanskogo obshchestva v Kyrgyzstane," in *Grazhdanskoe obshchestvo v Kyrgyzstane: Sbornik statei*, ed. E. A. Voronina (Bishkek: Mezhdunarodnyi Tsentr Interbilim, 2003). On Kazakhstan, see Ruslan Kazkenov and Charles E. Ziegler, "Civil Society in a Period of Transition: The Perspective from the State," in *Civil Society and Politics in Central Asia*, ed. Charles E. Ziegler (Lexington: University Press of Kentucky, 2015), 197–221.

23. I view the language of democracy as one important element in a causal chain. My reasoning follows the so-called INUS approach proposed by John L. Mackie, *The Cement of the Universe: A Study of Causation* (Oxford: Clarendon Press, 1974).

24. Erica Marat, *The Tulip Revolution: Kyrgyzstan One Year After* (Washington, DC: Jamestown Foundation, 2006). See also Emir Kulov, "March 2005: Parliamentary Elections as a Catalyst of Protests," *Central Asian Survey* 27, no. 3–4 (2008), 337–47.

25. See Joshua A. Tucker, "Enough! Electoral Fraud, Collective Action Problems, and Post-Communist Colored Revolutions," *Perspectives on Politics* 5, no. 3 (2007): 535–51.

26. Aidana Abdyramanova, "Amerikanskaia i kyrgyzskaia sistemy obrazovaniia glazami studenta," *Tribuna* 7, no. 3 (11–25 May 2001): 5.

27. Leila Saralieva, "Kyrgyzstan: osobennosti mestnoi zhurnalistiki," *Tribuna*, 7, no. 36 (2 October 2003): 2.

28. For example, see "Demokraticheskii Institut SShA kritikuet kyrgyzskie vlasti," *Respublika* 17, no. 389 (12 September 2000): 2. See also "Nikakoi on ne Dzhefferson: Tsentral'naia Aziia prevratilas' v tsidatel' avtoritarizma," *Respublika* 26, no. 398 (14 November 2000): 13.

29. Narodnyi Kongress Kyrgyzstana, "Obrashchenie k Kongressu Soedinennykh Shtatov Ameriki," *Respublika* 44, no. 448 (11 December 2001): 3.

30. Thanks to Chiara Fabrizio for this insight.

31. Sergei Bogdanov, "Vecherkintsy ob'iavili kholodnuiu voinu amerikantsam?" *Tribuna* 4, no. 23 (28 February–13 March 2002): 1–2.

32. This letter was co-written with Chinara Zhakypova. See Chinara Zhakypova and Tolekan Ismailova, "Vlast' i grazhdanskii sektor: obrashchenie predstavitelei grazhdanskogo sektora," open letter, 2002, http://journalist.kg/monitoring/iyun-2002-g/.

33. Kurmanbek Bakiev, "Nikto ne gotovil revoliutsiiu: ni Amerika, ni Rossiia. Eto Kyrgyzskaia narodnaia revoliutsiia, a ne perevorot," *AKI-Press*, 9 May 2005, quoted by Furman and Shermatova, *Kirgizskie Tsikly*, 131–32.

34. Author's interview with Emil Aliev, head, Ar-Namys Party, Bishkek, 19 May 2005. The assumption of course is that close relations with Russia and close relations with the West are necessarily mutually exclusive.

35. Tengiz Gudava, "Interv'iu Feliksa Kulova Radio Svoboda," *Radio Svoboda*, 8 August 2000.

36. Kurmanbek Bakiev, *Dorogu osilit idushchii* (Bishkek: Megamedia, 2003), 116; see especially 108–18 for reflections on his own past, including the Aksy events.

37. The quotes are from Bakiev, *Dorogu osilit idushchii*, 11, 12, 78.

38. The quotes are from Bakiev, *Dorogu osilit idushchii*, 15, 59, 59, 80.

39. The quotes are from Bakiev, *Dorogu osilit idushchii*, 90, 92, 92, 93.

40. Thanks to Edil Baisalov for this observation.

41. Radnitz, "The Color of Money," 135.

42. Author's interview with Emil Aliev, head of Ar-Namys Party, 19 May 2005, Bishkek, Kyrgyzstan.

43. Scott Radnitz, *Weapons of the Wealthy: Predatory Regimes and Elite-Led Protests in Central Asia* (Ithaca, NY: Cornell University Press, 2010), 204.

44. On organized crime and the state in Kyrgyzstan, see Kupatadze, "Organized Crime and the State"; and Gavin Slade, "Punishment and State-Building in Post-Soviet Georgia," in *Paradox of Power: The Logics of State Weakness in Eurasia*, ed. John Heathershaw and Edward Schatz (Pittsburgh: University of Pittsburgh Press, 2017), 88–104. On patronage in the Kyrgyzstani context, see Askana Ismailbekova, *Blood Ties and the Native Son: Poetics of Patronage in Kyrgyzstan* (Bloomington: Indiana University Press, 2017); as well as McGlinchey, *Chaos, Violence, Dynasty*.

45. The phrase comes from Steven Levitsky and Lucan A. Way, *Competitive Authoritarianism: Hybrid Regimes after the Cold War* (New York: Cambridge University Press, 2010), 69.

46. Radnitz, *Weapons of the Wealthy*, 205.

47. Radio Free Europe / Radio Liberty, "Kyrgyz President Won't Back Down, As Opposition Claims Power," 8 April 2010, https://www.rferl.org/a/Kyrgyz_Opposition_Claims_Power_Vows_To_Investigate_Bakievs_Rule/2006140.html.

48. Aleksei Vasilivetskii, *Prelomlenie: sobytiia 2010 goda v Kyrgyzstane glazami istorika i ochevidtsev* (Bishkek: Tipografiia OcOO Kirland, 2014), 163–64.

49. Vasilivetskii, *Prelomlenie*, 164–77.

50. B. Kytaibekov, "Tarykh kaitalandy," 2010, translated and reprinted in *Narodnye revoliutsii, obnovivshie epokhu: sbornik, posviashchennyi iubileiam narodnykh revoliutsii sovershivshikhsia v Kyrgyzstane 24 marta 2005 goda i 7 aprelia 2010 goda*, ed. V. Moldokasymov, A. Ibraeva, and A. Kadyrova (Bishkek: Fond "Muras," 2015), 161–62.

51. United Opposition, "Zaiavlenie shtaba po provedeniiu 29 aprelia mirnogo shestviia 'Demokraticheskie reformy dlia protsvetaniia Kyrgyzstana," *AKI-Press*, 18 April 2006, http://www.kg.akipress.org/news:27502.

52. "Oppozitsiia KR podpisala memorandum dlia vykhoda iz krizisa upravleniia gosudarstvom," *AKI-Press*, 3 November 2008, http://kg.akipress.org/news:63527?f=cp.

53. A. Allakbarov, "Tsirk zazhigaet ogni," *Slovo Kyrgyzstana*, 1 February 2002, 3.

54. During my fieldwork in Kyrgyzstan, Tajikistan, and Uzbekistan in 2005, border guards at each international frontier asked me in an accusatory tone, "Are you a journalist?" or "What are you—a journalist?" In none of my prior fieldwork had I ever been asked this question.

55. Author's interview with Alla Piatibratova, Coordinator, Osh Media Resource Center, 20 May 2009, Osh, Kyrgyzstan. On the political use of employment to mobilize in favor of the authoritarian regime, see Timothy Frye, Ora John Reuter, and David Szakonyi, "Political Machines at Work: Voter Mobilization and Electoral Subversion in the Workplace," *World Politics* 66, no. 2 (2014): 195–228. Likewise, students in Central Asia were routinely mobilized to perform pro-regime celebrations, such as that commemorating 2,700 years since the founding of Kulob, Tajikistan, President Rakhmon's home region (Author's conversations in Kulob, Tajikistan, May 2006).

56. Interview with Irysbek Omurzakov, Chief Editor of *Tribuna*, conducted by Chiara Fabrizio, 1 June 2013, Bishkek, Kyrgyzstan.

57. Interview with Natalia Ablova, Bureau of Human Rights and the Rule of Law, conducted by Chiara Fabrizio, 1 June 2013, Bishkek, Kyrgyzstan.

58. Svetlana Nesterova, "V SShA vozmozhen konstitutsionnyi krizis," *Respublika* 26, no. 398 (14 November 2000): 10.

59. John Heathershaw, *Post-Conflict Tajikistan: The Politics of Peacebuilding and the Emergence of Legitimate Order* (Routledge, 2009).

60. Tim Epkenhans, "The Islamic Revival Party of Tajikistan: Episodes of Islamic Activism, Postconflict Accommodation, and Political Marginalization," *Central

Asian Affairs 2, no. 4 (2015): 321–46. This perspective was confirmed by the author's interviews in Tajikistan with IRPT activists, May 2006.

61. Heathershaw, *Post-Conflict Tajikistan*.

62. Margaret Keck and Kathryn Sikkink, *Activists beyond Borders: Transnational Activist Networks in International Politics* (Ithaca, NY: Cornell University Press, 1998), 8–9.

63. Such depictions would prove to be woefully inadequate. For a recent discussion, see John Heathershaw and Edward Schatz, eds., *Paradox of Power: The Logics of State Weakness in Eurasia* (Pittsburgh: University of Pittsburgh Press, 2017).

64. This was the bedrock assumption of the "transitology" approach to postsocialist transformations. See Valerie Bunce, "Should Transitologists be Grounded?" *Slavic Review* 54, no. 1 (1995): 111–27.

65. Sarah Henderson, *Building Democracy in Contemporary Russia: Western Support for Grassroots Organizations* (Ithaca, NY: Cornell University Press, 2003), 152.

66. See, for example, Noah Coburn, *Bazaar Politics: Power and Pottery in an Afghan Market Town* (Stanford, CA: Stanford University Press, 2011). On how the importance of the internal organizational culture of the World Bank (rather than local realities on the ground) shaped its ongoing programs, see Catherine Weaver, *Hypocrisy Trap: The World Bank and the Poverty of Reform* (Princeton, NJ: Princeton University Press, 2008).

67. Coburn, *Bazaar Politics*, 212–13.

68. See Murtazashvili, *Informal Order and the State*, 208–9.

69. On this watchdog role, see Edward Schatz, "Access by Accident: Legitimacy Claims and Democracy Promotion in Authoritarian Central Asia," *International Political Science Review* 27, no. 3 (2006): 263–84.

70. Pauline Jones Luong and Erika Weinthal, "The NGO Paradox: Democratic Goals and Non-democratic Outcomes in Kazakhstan," *Europe-Asia Studies* 51, no. 7 (1999): 1267–84.

71. Sarah E. Mendelson and Theodore P. Gerber, "Activist Culture and Transnational Diffusion: Social Marketing and Human Rights Groups in Russia," *Post-Soviet Affairs* 23, no. 1 (2007): 50–75.

72. Jeffrey S. Kopstein and David A. Reilly, "Geographic Diffusion and the Transformation of the Postcommunist World," *World Politics* 53, no. 1 (2000): 1–37.

73. Sodiqov had been working on a research contract with the University of Exeter at the time of his detention. As his PhD supervisor, I have intimate knowledge of how this case unfolded and was ultimately resolved.

74. Author's interview with human rights lawyer, Dushanbe, Tajikistan, 4 May 2006.

75. Author's interview with Faiziniso Vokhidova, lawyer and human rights activist, Khujand, Tajikistan, 12 May 2006.

76. Author's interview with Vokhidova.

77. Cai Wilkinson, "LGBT Activism in Kyrgyzstan: What Role for Europe?," in Phillip Ayoub and David Paternotte, eds., *LGBT Activism and the Making of Europe* (London: Palgrave Macmillan, 2014), 50–72.

78. See Edward Schatz, "The Soft Authoritarian 'Tool Kit': Agenda-Setting Power in Kazakhstan and Kyrgyzstan," *Comparative Politics* 41, no. 2 (2009): 203-22.

79. Thanks to Jacques Bertrand for stimulating this line of thinking.

CHAPTER 4: LABOR, DISORGANIZED

1. On the challenges of choosing and analyzing negative cases, see James Mahoney and Gary Goertz, "The Possibility Principle: Choosing Negative Cases in Comparative Research," *American Political Science Review* 98, no. 4 (2004): 653-69.

2. On labor's incorporation into politics in Latin American cases, see Ruth Berins Collier and David Collier, *Shaping the Political Arena: Critical Junctures, the Labor Movement, and Regime Dynamics in Latin America* (Princeton, NJ: Princeton University Press, 1991).

3. On the dynamics created as the Soviet Union attempted to champion a working class that barely existed, see Gregory J. Massell, *The Surrogate Proletariat: Moslem Women and Revolutionary Strategies in Soviet Central Asia, 1919-1929* (Princeton, NJ: Princeton University Press, 1974); and Matthew J. Payne, *Stalin's Railroad: Turksib and the Building of Socialism* (Pittsburgh: University of Pittsburgh Press, 2001). The first trade unions seem to have emerged in the nineteenth century among "clerks" (prikazchiki) in the towns of Osh, Semipalatinsk, and Vernyi (now Almaty); see K. K. Chatybekova, *Istoriia profsoiuzov Kazakhstana: obrazovanie i stanovlenie (konets XIX–pervaia chetvert' XX vv.)* (Almaty: Kurmet, 2006), 112.

4. On the evolving relationship between the party-state and trade unions from 1917 through the 1970s, see Blair A. Ruble, *Soviet Trade Unions: Their Development in the 1970s* (Cambridge: Cambridge University Press, 1981).

5. Rudra Sil, "The Fluidity of Labor Relations in Post-Communist Transitions: Rethinking the Narrative of Russian Labor Quiescence," in *Political Creativity: Reconfiguring Institutional Order and Change*, ed. Gerald Berk, Dennis Galvan, and Victoria Hattam (Philadelphia: University of Pennsylvania Press, 2013), 191-92.

6. Sil, "Fluidity of Labor Relations," 192-93.

7. Compared to mobilization on nonlabor issues, labor mobilization was quite limited. See Mark R. Beissinger, *Nationalist Mobilization and the Collapse of the Soviet State* (Cambridge: Cambridge University Press, 2002).

8. David Ost, "The Peculiarities of Communism and Weak Unions in Poland," in *Working through the Past: Labor and Authoritarian Legacies in Comparative Perspective*, ed. Teri L. Caraway et al. (Ithaca, NY: Cornell University Press, 2015), 82-102.

9. Valerie Bunce, "The Political Economy of Postsocialism," *Slavic Review* 58, no. 4 (1999): 766. Bunce divides countries between former Soviet ones (minus the Baltic states) and other former state-socialist ones.

10. David Ost, "The Consequences of Postcommunism: Trade Unions in Eastern Europe's Future," *East European Politics and Societies* 23, no. 1 (2009): 14. On the exceptional case of Romania and its labor mobilization, see Mihai Varga, *Worker Protests in Post-communist Romania and Ukraine: Striking with Tied Hands* (Manchester, UK: Manchester University Press, 2014).

11. Paul Kubicek, "Organized Labor in Postcommunist States: Will the Western Sun Set on It, Too?" *Comparative Politics* 32, no. 1 (1999): 87.

12. International Labour Organization, *Central Asian Trade Union Movement: Situation Analysis Paper* (Geneva: ILO, September 2013), 39.

13. International Labour Organization, *Central Asian Trade Union Movement*, 38.

14. In Beissinger and Kotkin's definition, a legacy can only occur where there has been "a significant rupture between past and present." In cases of a significant rupture, legacies can reassert themselves through processes of fragmentation, translation, bricolage, parameter-setting, and cultural schemata. See Mark R. Beissinger and Stephen Kotkin, eds., *Historical Legacies of Communism in Russia and Eastern Europe* (New York: Cambridge University Press, 2014), 7–8.

15. On the cotton harvest and human rights violations, see Human Rights Watch, *"We Can't Refuse to Pick Cotton": Forced and Child Labor Linked to World Bank Group Investments in Uzbekistan*, report (New York: HRW, 27 June 2017).

16. I created the figure based on data provided in Leandro Medina and Friedrich Schneider, *Shadow Economies around the World: What Did We Learn over the Last 20 Years?*, IMF Working Paper no. 18/17 (Washington, DC: International Monetary Fund, 2018).

17. David Ost, "Illusory Corporatism in Eastern Europe: Neoliberal Tripartism and Postcommunist Class Identities," *Politics & Society* 28, no. 4 (2000): 503–30.

18. World Bank, "Jobs," databank, last accessed 30 August 2018, http://databank.worldbank.org/data/reports.aspx?source=jobs.

19. On the reconstitution of the Tajik state after the civil war, see Jesse Driscoll, *Warlords and Coalition Politics in Post-Soviet States* (New York: Cambridge University Press, 2015).

20. World Bank, "Jobs," databank.

21. World Bank, "World Development Indicators," databank, last accessed 6 September 2018, http://databank.worldbank.org/data/source/world-development-indicators#.

22. International Labour Organization, *Central Asian Trade Union Movement*, 38.

23. International Labour Organization, *Central Asian Trade Union Movement*, 39.

24. International Labour Organization, *Central Asian Trade Union Movement*, 37.

25. For perspectives on informality, see Regine A. Spector, *Order at the Bazaar: Power and Trade in Central Asia* (Ithaca, NY: Cornell University Press, 2017); Hasan H. Karrar, "Between Border and Bazaar: Central Asia's Informal Economy," *Journal of Contemporary Asia* (2018): 1–22; and John Heathershaw and Edward Schatz, "The Logics of State Weakness: An Introduction," in *Paradox of Power: The Logics of State Weakness in Eurasia*, ed. John Heathershaw and Edward Schatz (Pittsburgh: University of Pittsburgh Press, 2017), 3–21.

26. Asel Doolotkeldieva, "Peripheral Protests as an Opportunity: 'Brokers' in Action," in *Kyrgyzstan beyond "Democracy Island" and "Failing State,"* ed. Marlène Laruelle and Johan Engvall (Lanham, MD: Lexington Books, 2015), 59–78.

27. World Bank, "Jobs," Databank, last accessed 30 August 2018.

28. Richard Pomfret, *The Central Asian Economies in the Twenty-First Century: Paving a New Silk Road* (Princeton, NJ: Princeton University Press, 2019), 91. On how in general, privatization is a boon to opposition mobilization, see Scott Radnitz, "The Color of Money: Privatization, Economic Dispersion, and the Post-Soviet 'Revolutions,'" *Comparative Politics* 42, no. 2 (2010).

29. On the move of the capital city from Almaty to Akmola, which would be first renamed Astana and then renamed Nur-sultan, see Edward Schatz, "What Capital Cities Say about State and Nation Building," *Nationalism and Ethnic Politics* 9, no. 4 (2004): 111–40.

30. On "soft authoritarianism," see Edward Schatz, "The Soft Authoritarian 'Tool Kit': Agenda-Setting Power in Kazakhstan and Kyrgyzstan," *Comparative Politics* 41, no. 2 (2009): 203–22.

31. If an existing order reproduces itself, it does so via identifiable mechanisms of reproduction. See Kathleen Thelen, "Historical Institutionalism in Comparative Politics," *Annual Review of Political Science* 2, no. 1 (1999): 369–404.

32. "Oil Workers in Western Kazakhstan Prosecuted for 'Illegal' Hunger Strike," *Times of Central Asia*, no.1–24 (24 January 2017).

33. International Labour Organization, *Central Asian Trade Union Movement*, 19.

34. Elena Maltseva, "Cracks in the System: What the Zhanaozen Incident Says about Regime Performance in Kazakhstan," in *Paradox of Power: The Logics of State Weakness in Eurasia*, ed. John Heathershaw and Edward Schatz (Pittsburgh: University of Pittsburgh Press, 2017), 190.

35. Baker & McKenzie, "Kazakhstan Adopts New Labor Code," Legal Alert, 29 March 2016; Saule Emrich-Bakenova and Frederick Emrich, "Kazakhstan: New Labor Code Squeezes Older Workers," *Eurasianet*, 5 August 2016.

36. On the similar predicament that labor unions faced under neoliberal economic arrangements in largely democratic Latin American cases, see M. Victoria Murillo, "From Populism to Neoliberalism: Labor Unions and Market Reforms in Latin America," *World Politics* 52, no. 2 (2000). On the need for a "level playing field" for a regime to qualify as democratic, see Steven Levitsky and Lucan A. Way, "Why Democracy Needs a Level Playing Field," *Journal of Democracy* 21 no. 1 (2010): 57–68.

37. Saulesh Yessenova, "Tengiz Crude: A View from Below," in *The Economics and Politics of Oil in the Caspian Basin: The Redistribution of Oil Revenues in Azerbaijan and Central Asia*, ed. Boris Najman, Richard Pomfret, and Gäel Raballand (New York: Routledge, 2008), 180, describes Tengiz in these terms in her excellent ethnographic account. For my part, I was unsuccessful in my efforts to gain access to Tengiz during visits in 1998 and 2002. It is possible that I was insufficiently creative in my attempts to do so, but I was consistently told not to expect access to materialize.

38. Yessenova, "Tengiz Crude," 183–85.

39. Author's interview with Sergei Plotnikov, East-Kazakhstan State Technical University, 15 May 2009, Ust-Kamenogorsk.

40. Yessenova, "Tengiz Crude," 188. For a discussion of the logic of kickbacks, job buying, and rent-seeking in neighboring Kyrgyzstan, see Johan Engvall, "License

to Seek Rents: 'Corruption' as a Method of Post-Soviet Governance," in *Paradox of Power: The Logics of State Weakness in Eurasia*, ed. John Heathershaw and Edward Schatz (Pittsburgh: University of Pittsburgh Press, 2017), 73–87.

41. See, for example, Lev Guzikov, "TShO: budem 'kodirovat'!" *Aq zhaiyq* 803, 17 May 2007: 1.

42. Sergei Tereshchenko, "Kazakhmys nado sudit': Za izdevatel'stvo nad rabochimi," *TsentrAziia*, 10 May 2007.

43. International Labour Organization, *Central Asian Trade Union Movement*, 35.

44. Author's conversations with journalists, activists, and Tengiz employees, Atyrau, Kazakhstan, June 2002.

45. Author's conversations, Atyrau, June 2002.

46. Ol'ga Oreshnikova, "Golodovka poka ne ob'iavlena: Na obrashchenie rabochikh Zhezkazganskogo medeplaveil'nogo zavoda ne otreagirovali ni profsoiuz, ni deputat," *Respublika*, 8 June 2001.

47. Author's interview with Plotnikov, 15 May 2009.

48. Radio Azattyq, "Delo o zabastovke bliz Ural'ska ostalos' bez rassmotreniia," 4 August 2015.

49. Author's interview with member of the political opposition, Almaty, Kazakhstan, 8 August 2006.

50. The FPRK boasted on its website that "of the 188 Conventions of the International Labor Organization (ILO), Kazakhstan has ratified 21," last accessed 31 August 2018, http://fprk.kz/about/.

51. Human Rights Watch, *"Hellish Work": Exploitation of Tobacco Workers in Kazakhstan*, report (New York: HRW, 14 July 2010).

52. For example, see RFE/RL Kazakh Service, "Kazakh Authorities Jail Rights Activist Representing Zhanaozen Victims," 7 December 2012, https://www.rferl.org/a/kazakhstan-rights-zhanaozen-victims-lawyer-jailed/24791902.html.

53. Casey Michel, "Kazakhstan's Labor Union Crackdown Draws International Criticism," *Diplomat*, 16 June 2017, http://thediplomat.com/2017/06/kazakhstans-labor-union-crackdown-draws-international-criticism/.

54. Steve Hess, *Authoritarian Landscapes: Popular Mobilization and the Institutional Sources of Resilience in Nondemocracies* (New York: Springer Science & Business Media, 2013), 191.

55. Hess, *Authoritarian Landscapes*, 193.

56. Tat'iana Seroshtanova, "Kazakhmys khochet obespechit' syr'em Irtyshskii medzavod v techenie avgusta," Reuters, 6 August 2002, https://kase.kz/ru/news/show/103420/.

57. See the testimony in Ainur Kurmanov, "Protivostoianie v poselke Glubokom," Left.ru, 8 July 2003, http://www.left.ru/2003/16/glubokoe92.html.

58. Zauresh Battalova, "'Kazakhmysu' Ia ne veriu!" socialismkz.info, 20 October 2013, http://socialismkz.info/?p=9691.

59. This paragraph is based on the ground-level account provided in Yessenova, "Tengiz Crude," 190–93.

60. AFP, "Workers Clash at Kazakh Oilfield," Al-Jazeera News, 24 October 2006, https://www.aljazeera.com/archive/2006/10/2008410115626658653.html.

61. Konstantin Tumanov, "The Tengiz Carnage: Some Details of the Scuffle in Kazakhstan," *Fergana News*, 11 November 2006.

62. Maltseva, "Cracks in the System," 191.

63. Maltseva, "Cracks in the System," 191–92.

64. For a chronology of events, see Dossym Satpayev and Tolganay Umbetaliyeva, "The Protests in Zhanaozen and the Kazakh Oil Sector: Conflicting Interests in a Rentier State," *Journal of Eurasian Studies* 6, no. 2 (2015).

65. Worker solidarity and commitment to staying in the square was evident as this played out through the very cold months of November and December. Oil work is almost exclusively performed by men, which may have contributed to the sense of solidarity. See Philipp Frank Jäger, "Flows of Oil, Flows of People: Resource-Extraction Industry, Labour Market and Migration in Western Kazakhstan," *Central Asian Survey* 33, no. 4 (2014): 508.

66. Nurlan Kurmanov et al., "Motivation of Employees' Labor Activity in Oil and Gas Companies in Kazakhstan," *World Applied Sciences Journal* 26, no. 12 (2013): 1556–61.

67. Human Rights Watch, *We are Not the Enemy: Violations of Workers' Rights in Kazakhstan*, report (New York: HRW, 23 November 2016).

68. RFE/RL Kazakh Service, "Kazakh Oil-Industry Workers on Strike for Pay Raise," Radio Free Europe/Radio Liberty, 7 May 2018.

69. International Labour Organization, *Central Asian Trade Union Movement*, 47.

70. Spector, *Order at the Bazaar*, 81.

71. International Labour Organization, *Central Asian Trade Union Movement*, 16.

72. On grievances of the working poor outside Osh, Kyrgyzstan, see Elmira Satybalieva, "Why Class Matters in Kyrgyzstan," in Laruelle and Engvall, *Kyrgyzstan beyond "Democracy Island" and "Failing State*," 59–78.

73. Robert D. Benford and David A. Snow, "Framing Processes and Social Movements: An Overview and Assessment," *Annual Review of Sociology* 26, no. 1 (2000): 611–39.

74. Ainur Kurmanov, "Bespredel v Kentau," *Zashchita truda*, 2003, last accessed November 9, 2018, http://www.zaschita-truda.ru/besp_v_kentau.htm.

75. Satpayev and Umbetaliyeva, "Protests in Zhanaozen," 125–26.

76. Burkitbai Sh. Nasyrkhanov, comments at press conference entitled "O sotsial'no-ekonomicheskom polozhenii gorniakov na predpriiatiiakh korporatsii 'Kazakhmys,'" Almaty, Kazakhstan, 15 January 2007. Thanks to Toqjan Kizatova for supplying a written version of Nasyrkhanov's remarks.

77. Burkitbai Sh. Nasyrkhanov, "Obrashchenie k sootechestvennikam," *Zona.kz*, 2 March 2007.

78. Yevgeniy Zhovtis, "Ob urokakh Zhanaozena," text prepared for a roundtable, Almaty, Kazakhstan, 2 January 2013.

79. Radio Free Europe / Radio Liberty, "Striking Kazakh Oil Workers Quit Ruling Party," 11 August 2011, https://www.rferl.org/a/striking_kazakh_oil_workers_quit_ruling_party/24294248.html.

80. Madel Ismailov suffered a similar fate. See Vladimir Ardayev, "Kazakhstan Now Has a Political Prisoner," *Current Digest of the Post-Soviet Press* 14, no. 50 (6 May 1998): 20.

81. Ainur Kurmanov, "Zabastovka neftianikov v Kazakhstane: proobraz budushchikh vystuplenii rabochikh vsek otraslei," 24 June 2011, forum-msk.ru, https://forum-msk.org/material/fpolitic/6596215.html.

82. *TsentrAziia*, "'Da, my neprimirimaia oppozitsiia!' (vystuplenie lidera Rabochego dvizheniia Kazakhtana," 9 December 2003, http://www.centrasia.org/newsA.php?st=1063386540.

83. Kurmanov, "Zabostovka neftianikov v Kazakhstane."

84. As late as 2010, Kurmanov continued to advocate nationalization, a slogan that, he argued, "symbolizes the need to save jobs and production itself." It remained unclear how willing he was to distance his approach from the Soviet-era understanding of the term. See Ainur Kurmanov, "The Current State of the Trade Union Movement in Kazakhstan," *International Viewpoint*, 5 May 2010, http://internationalviewpoint.org/spip.php?article1862.

85. Hess, *Authoritarian Landscapes*, 194.

86. I am grateful to Pavel Shumkin for sharing with me his personal memoirs.

87. Liudmila Bubenshchikova, "V Glubokom perekhodiat k glubokoi oborone," *Zashchita truda*, 2003, last accessed 13 September 2018l http://www.zaschita-truda.ru/kazahstan_impk.htm.

88. *TsentrAziia*, "'Da, my neprimirimaia oppozitsiia!'"; emphasis in the original.

89. Amirzhan Khasenov, "Sobytiia na Tengize: izderzhki neokolonializma," *Zona.kz Kazakhstan*, 24 October 2006, http://www.zonakz.net/articles/15899.

90. Donatella della Porta et al., *Global Justice Movement: Cross-national and Transnational Perspectives* (Boulder, CO: Paradigm Publishers, 2007).

91. Della Porta et al., *Global Justice Movement*.

92. Herbert Reiter (with Massimiliano Andretta, Donatella della Porta, and Lorenzo Mosca), "The Global Justice Movement in Italy," in della Porta et al., *Global Justice Movement*, 71. Reiter covers the Italian variant of the movement, but his depiction applies much more broadly.

93. Paul Domjan and Matt Stone, "A Comparative Study of Resource Nationalism in Russia and Kazakhstan 2004–2008," *Europe-Asia Studies* 62, no. 1 (2010): 35–62.

94. For example, see Domjan and Stone, "Comparative Study of Resource Nationalisn," 51.

95. Farkhod Aminjonov, Alina Abylkasymova, Anna Aimée, Bahtiyor Eshchanov, Daniyar Moldokanov, Indra Overland, Roman Vakulchuk, "BRI in Central Asia: Overview of Chinese Projects," *Central Asia Regional Data Review* 20 (2019): 3.

CONCLUSION: SHAPING THE SLOW POLITICS OF ANTI-AMERICANISM

1. This trend was first identified in Pauline Jones Luong, "The Middle Easternization of Central Asia," *Current History* (October 2003): 333.

2. Salmorbekova and Yemelianova, "Islam and Islamism," 231.

3. On the ironic consequence of Western disengagement, see Edward Schatz, "How Western Disengagement Enabled Uzbekistan's 'Spring' and How to Keep It Going," Program on New Approaches to Research and Security (PONARS) Eurasia, Policy Memo no.531, June 2018, http://www.ponarseurasia.org/memo/how-western-disengagement-enabled-uzbekistans-spring-and-how-keep-it-going.

4. George W. Bush, cited in Adeeb Khalid, *Islam after Communism: Religion and Politics in Central Asia* (Berkeley: University of California Press, 2007), 8.

5. Barry A. Sanders, *American Avatar: The United States in the Global Imagination* (Washington, DC: Potomac Books, 2011), 187–88.

6. See, for example, Muqtedar Khan, "The US Must Adopt a Softer Approach to the Muslim World," *National Strategy Forum Review* 13, no. 2 (Winter 2003): 25–28.

7. Bruce Gregory, "Public Diplomacy: Sunrise of an Academic Field," *Annals of the American Academy of Political and Social Science* 616, no. 1 (2008): 276.

8. For a view that is highly skeptical of public diplomacy's value, see Stephen Brooks, *Anti-Americanism and the Limits of Public Diplomacy: Winning Hearts and Minds?* (New York: Routledge, 2015). Brooks's monograph is not informed by a ground-level view of any particular world region.

9. Edward Schatz and Renan Levine, "Framing, Public Diplomacy, and Anti-Americanism in Central Asia," *International Studies Quarterly* 54, 2010: 855–69.

10. Schatz and Levine, "Framing, Public Diplomacy, and Anti-Americanism," 859. To create a plausible frame, we based it on US government statements. This message of tolerance was the central theme of the US Department of State's Shared Values public relations campaign after 9/11, targeting the Muslim world; see Jami Fullerton and Alice Kendrick, *Advertising's War on Terrorism: The Story of the U.S. State Department's Shared Values Initiative* (Spokane, WA: Marquette Books, 2006).

11. James N. Druckman, "On the Limits of Framing Effects: Who Can Frame?" *Journal of Politics* 63, no. 4 (2001): 1041–66.

12. Michele G. Alexander, Shana Levin, and P. J. Henry, "Image Theory, Social Identity, and Social Dominance: Structural Characteristics and Individual Motives Underlying International Images," *Political Psychology* 26, no. 1 (February 2005): 42.

13. Both quotes are from Muhammad Qasim Zaman, "Pluralism, Democracy, and the 'Ulama," in *Remaking Muslim Politics: Pluralism, Contestation, Democratization*, ed. Robert W. Hefner (Princeton, NJ: Princeton University Press, 2004), 81.

14. For work on the psychological dimensions of foreign policymaking, see Richard K. Herrmann, *Perceptions and Behavior in Soviet Foreign Policy* (Pittsburgh:

University of Pittsburgh Press, 1985); Richard K. Herrmann and Michael P. Fischerkeller, "Beyond the Enemy Image and Spiral Model: Cognitive-Strategic Research After the Cold War," *International Organization* 49, no. 3 (1995); and Richard K. Herrmann et al., "Images in International Relations: An Experimental Test of Cognitive Schemata," *International Studies Quarterly* 41, no. 3 (1997): 403–33.

15. On this "polycentrism," see Vera Exnerova, "Introducing Transnationalism Studies to the Field of Public Diplomacy," *Journal of International Communication* 23, no. 2 (2017): 186–99. On cascades in international politics, see James N. Rosenau, *Turbulence in World Politics: A Theory of Change and Continuity* (Princeton, NJ: Princeton University Press, 2018).

16. Ware indicates that in Dagestan (Russian Federation), views of the Islamist movement Wahhabism are structured by views of Dagestan's relations with the Russian Federation. See Robert Bruce Ware, "Why Did Dagestan Reject Radical Islam?," *Radio Free Europe/Radio Liberty Newsline* 6, no. 212, part 1 (12 November 2002).

APPENDIX: REFLECTIONS ON METHODS AND METHODOLOGY

1. Edward Schatz, ed., *Political Ethnography: What Immersion Contributes to the Study of Power* (Chicago: University of Chicago Press, 2009).

2. Rudra Sil and Peter J. Katzenstein, *Beyond Paradigms: Analytic Eclecticism in the Study of World Politics* (Basingstoke, England: Palgrave Macmillan, 2010), 2.

3. Timothy Pachirat, *Every Twelve Seconds: Industrialized Slaughter and the Politics of Sight* (New Haven, CT: Yale University Press, 2011).

4. Thomas Nagel, *The View from Nowhere* (New York: Oxford University Press, 1989).

5. Michael Polanyi, *The Tacit Dimension* (New York: Anchor Books, 1967), 4.

6. Marc Bloch, *The Historian's Craft* (New York: Knopf, 1953), 63.

7. Bloch, *Historian's Craft*, 64.

8. For very different perspectives, see Layna Mosley, ed., *Interview Research in Political Science* (Ithaca, NY: Cornell University Press, 2013); and Frederic Charles Schaffer, "Ordinary Language Interviewing," in *Interpretation and Method*, ed. D. Yanow and P. Schwartz-Shea (Armonk, NY: M. E. Sharpe, 2006), 183–93.

9. Lee Ann Fujii, "Shades of Truth and Lies: Interpreting Testimonies of War and Violence," *Journal of Peace Research* 47, no. 2 (2010): 231.

10. Lee Ann Fujii, *Interviewing in Social Science Research: A Relational Approach* (New York: Routledge, 2018).

11. On these three types, see Robert D. Benford and David A. Snow, "Framing Processes and Social Movements: An Overview and Assessment," *Annual Review of Sociology* 26, no. 1 (2000): 611–39.

12. Our approach was based on Thomas L. Greenbaum, *Moderating Focus Groups: A Practical Guide for Group Facilitation* (Thousand Oaks, CA: Sage Publications, 2000).

13. Alena V. Ledeneva, *How Russia Really Works: The Informal Practices That Shaped Post-Soviet Politics and Business* (Ithaca, NY: Cornell University Press, 2006).

14. Sharon Werning Rivera, Polina M. Kozyreva, and Eduard G. Sarovskii, "Interviewing Political Elites: Lessons from Russia," *PS, Political Science & Politics* 35, no. 4 (2002): 683–88.

15. Sil and Katzenstein, *Beyond Paradigms*, 15.

BIBLIOGRAPHY

Abashin, Sergei. "Islamic Fundamentalism in Central Asia: Why It Appeared and What to Expect." *Central Asia and the Caucasus*, March 2002: 63–69.

Abazov, Rafis. "The Parliamentary Elections in Kyrgyzstan, February 2000." *Electoral Studies* 22, no. 3 (2003): 545–52.

Abdallah, Abdel Mahdi. "Causes of Anti-Americanism in the Arab World: A Socio-Political Perspective." *Middle East Review of International Affairs* 7, no. 4 (December 2003): 62–73.

Abdyramanova, Aidana. "Amerikanskaia i kyrgyzskaia sistemy obrazovaniia glazami studenta." *Tribuna* 7, no. 3(11–25 May 2001): 5.

Abenov, E. M. "Osnovnye printsipy gosudarstvennogo ustroistva sovremennogo Kazakhstana (konstitutsii 1993 i 1995 gg.)." *Saiasat* 10, no. 17 (October 1996): 12–29. Last accessed 26 July 2013. http://www.centrasia.ru/newsA.php?st=1041043980.

Adams, Charles. "Maududi and the Islamic State." In *Voices of Resurgent Islam*, edited by John L. Esposito, 3–16. New York: Oxford University Press, 1983.

Adamson, Fiona. "Global Liberalism versus Political Islam: Competing Ideological Frameworks in International Politics." *International Studies Review* 7, no. 4 (2005): 547–69.

AFP. "Workers Clash at Kazakh Oilfield." Al-Jazeera News, 24 October 2006. https://www.aljazeera.com/archive/2006/10/2008410115626658653.html.

Ajami, Fouad. "The Falseness of Anti-Americanism." *Foreign Policy*, September/October 2003: 53–61.

Akaev, Askar A. *Pamiatnoe desiatiletie: Trudnaia doroga k demokratii*. Moskva: Mezhdunarodnye otnosheniia, 2002.

Akbarzadeh, Shahram. "Islamic Clerical Establishment in Central Asia." *South Asia: Journal of South Asian Studies* 2 (December 1997): 73–102.

Akcali, Pinar. "Islam as a 'Common Bond' in Central Asia: Islamic Renaissance Party and the Afghan Mujahidin." *Central Asian Survey* 17, no. 2 (1998): 267–84.

Akchokoev, Azat. "Investitsii zapada—istochnik korruptsii." *Respublika* (30 November 1999): 1.

Akimbekova, Sultana. "Islam—odna iz samykh miroliubivykh religii: interv'iu 'Kontinenta' s glavoi Dukhovnogo upravleniia musul'man Kazakhstana Absattaromkazhy Derbisalievym." *Kontinent*, 10–23 October 2001: 18–19.

Akimbekov, Sultan M. *Afganskii uzel i problemy bezopasnosti Tsentral'noi Azii*. Almaty: Kazakhstanskii institut strategicheskikh issledovanii pri Prezidente Respubliki Kazakhstan, 1998.
Alexander, Michele G., Shana Levin, and P. J. Henry. "Image Theory, Social Identity, and Social Dominance: Structural Characteristics and Individual Motives Underlying International Images." *Political Psychology* 26, no. 1 (February 2005): 27–46.
Alexievich, Svetlana. *Zinky Boys: Soviet Voices from the Afghanistan War*. New York: Norton, 1992.
Alford, John. R., Carolyn L. Funk, and John R. Hibbing. "Are Political Orientations Genetically Transmitted?" *American Political Science Review* 99, no.2 (May 2005): 153–67.
Allakbarov, A. "Tsirk zazhigaet ogni." *Slovo Kyrgyzstana*, 1 February 2002: 3.
Allina-Pisano, Jessica. *The Post-Soviet Potemkin Village: Politics and Property Rights in the Black Earth*. New York: Cambridge University Press, 2007.
———. "Social Contracts and Authoritarian Projects in Post-Soviet Space: The Use of Administrative Resource." *Communist and Post-Communist Studies* 43, no. 4 (December 2010): 373–82.
Aminjonov, Farkhod, Alina Abylkasymova, Anna Aimée, Bahtiyor Eshchanov, Daniyar Moldokanov, Indra Overland, and Roman Vakulchuk. "BRI in Central Asia: Overview of Chinese Projects." *Central Asia Regional Data Review* 20 (2019): 1–5. http://osce-academy.net/upload/file/20_BRI_in_CA.pdf.
Anderson, Benedict. *Imagined Communities: Reflections on the Origin and Spread of Nationalism*. New York: Verso, 1991.
Anderson, John. *Kyrgyzstan: Central Asia's Island of Democracy?* Amsterdam: Harwood Academic Publishers, 1999.
Aponte-Moreno, Marco, and Lance Lattig. "Chávez: Rhetoric Made in Havana." *World Policy Journal* 29, no. 1 (Spring 2012): 33–42.
Applebaum, Anne. "In Search of Pro-Americanism." *Foreign Policy* 149 (July–August 2005): 32–41.
Ardayev, Vladimir. "Kazakhstan Now Has a Political Prisoner." *Current Digest of the Post-Soviet Press* 14, vol. 50 (6 May 1998): 20.
Aronoff, Myron J., and Jan Kubik. *Anthropology and Political Science: A Convergent Approach*. New York: Berghahn Books, 2012.
Arrow, Kenneth J. "Methodological Individualism and Social Knowledge." *American Economic Review* 84, no. 2 (May 1994): 1–9.
Artem'ev, Artur. "Esche raz k voprosu o svobode sovesti i veroterpimosti." *Saiasat*, March 2001: 44–47.
Arutiunov, A. A. *Terrorizm i terroristy: Sovremennaia Rossiia*. Moscow: Tsentr politicheskoi informatsii, 2003.
Ayoob, Mohammed. "The Future of Political Islam: The Importance of External Variables." *International Affairs* 81, no. 5 (2005): 951–61.
Babadjanov, Bakhtiar, and Muzaffar Kamilov. "Domulla Hindustani and the Beginning of the 'Great Schism' among Moslems of Uzbekistan." In *Islam in Politics in*

Russia and Central Asia (Early Eighteenth to Late Twentieth Centuries), edited by Stéphane A. Dudoignon and Komatso Hisao, 195–220. London, New York, and Bahrain: Kegan Paul, 2002.

Babadjanov, Bakhtyar. "Islam officiel contre islam politique en Ouzbékistan aujourd'hui: la direction des musulmans et les groupes non-hanafi." *Revue d'études comparatives Est-Ouest* 31, no. 3 (2000): 151–64.

Babadzhanov, B., A. K. Muminov, and Anke von Kügelgen. *Disputy musul'manskikh religioznykh avtoritetov v Tsentral'noii Azii v XX veke.* Almaty: Daik-Press, 2007.

Babadzhanov, Bakhtiar. "O deiatel'nosti 'Khizb at-Takhrir al-islami' v Uzbekistane." In *Islam na postsovetskom prostranstve: vzgliad iznutri*, edited by Alexei Malashenko and Martha B Olcott. Moscow: Mosk. Tsentr Karnegi, 2001.

Babajanov, Bakhtiyar. "Teologicheskoe obosnovanie i etapy jihada v dokumentakh islamskogo dvijeniia Uzbekistana, perevod i komentarii Babajanova B.S. i Olkotta M.B." *Kazakhstan-Spektr* 3 (2002): 15–21.

Bafina, Gul'zada. "Amerikanskie vooruzhennye sily atakovali Afganistan i Sudan." *Panorama* 33 (28 August 1998): 5.

Baker & McKenzie. "Kazakhstan Adopts New Labor Code." Legal Alert, 29 March 2016. http://www.bakermckenzie.com/-/media/files/insight/publications/2016/03/kazakhstan-adopts-new-labor-code/al_almaty_laborcode_mar16.pdf?la=en.

Bakiev, Kurmanbek. *Dorogu osilit idushchii.* Bishkek: Megamedia, 2003.

———. "Nikto ne gotovil revoliutsiiu: ni Amerika, ni Rossiia. Eto Kyrgyzskaia narodnaia revoliutsiia, a ne perevorot." *AKI-Press*, 9 May 2005.

Bakir uulu, Tursunbay. "Problemy islamizatsii v Kyrgyzstane." *Vechernyi Bishkek*, 3 October 2001.

Ball, Terrence. "Deadly Hermeneutics; or SINN and the Social Scientist." In *Idioms of Inquiry: Critique and Renewal in Political Science*, edited by Terrence Ball, 95–112. New York: State University of New York Press, 1987.

Baran, Zeyno. *Hizb ut-Tahrir: Islam's Political Insurgency.* Washington, DC: Nixon Center, 2004.

Battalova, Zauresh. "'Kazakhmysu' Ia ne veriu!" socialismkz.info, 20 October 2013. http://socialismkz.info/?p=9691.

Beinin, Joel, and Joe Stork. "On the Modernity, Historical Specificity, and International Context of Political Islam." In *Political Islam: Essays from Middle East Report*, edited by Joel Beinin and Joe Stork, 3–25. Berkeley: University of California Press, 1997.

———, eds. *Political Islam: Essays from Middle East Report.* Berkeley: University of California Press, 1997.

Beissinger, Mark R. *Nationalist Mobilization and the Collapse of the Soviet State.* Cambridge: Cambridge University Press, 2002.

———. "The Persisting Ambiguity of Empire." *Post-Soviet Affairs* 11, no. 2 (April 1995): 149–84.

Beissinger, Mark R., and Sarah Bush. "Empire by Reputation." Unpublished manuscript, Department of Politics, Princeton University.

Beissinger, Mark R., and Stephen Kotkin, eds. *Historical Legacies of Communism in Russia and Eastern Europe*. Cambridge: Cambridge University Press, 2014.

Benford, Robert D., and David A. Snow. "Framing Processes and Social Movements: An Overview and Assessment." *Annual Review of Sociology* 26, no. 1 (2000): 611–39.

Berger, Peter L., and Thomas Luckmann. *The Social Construction of Reality: A Treatise in the Sociology of Knowledge*. Garden City, NY: Doubleday, 1966.

Berman, Sheri. "Islamism, Revolution, and Civil Society." *Perspectives on Politics* 1, no. 2 (2003): 257–72.

Bernhard, Michael H., and Jan Kubik, eds. *Twenty Years after Communism: The Politics of Memory and Commemoration*. Oxford: Oxford University Press, 2014.

Blaydes, Lisa. *Elections and Distributive Politics in Mubarak's Egypt*. New York: Cambridge University Press, 2011.

Blaydes, Lisa, and Drew A. Linzer. "Elite Competition, Religiosity, and Anti-Americanism in the Islamic World." *American Political Science Review* 106, no. 2 (2012): 225–43.

Bleuer, Christian. "Instability in Tajikistan? The Islamic Movement of Uzbekistan and the Afghanistan Factor." *Central Asia Security Policy Brief* no. 7, OSCE Academy, Bishkek, February 2012. http://survey.osce-academy.net/upload/file/bleuer_policy_brief7.pdf.

Bloch, Marc. *The Historian's Craft*. New York: Knopf, 1953.

Blyth, Mark. "Ideas, Uncertainty, and Evolution." In *Ideas and Politics in Social Science Research*, edited by Daniel Beland and Robert Henry Cox, 83–101. New York: Oxford University Press, 2011.

———. "The Politics of (Mis)-Representation: Constructing (and Destructing) Europe in Discourses of Anti-Americanism." Paper presented at Comparative Politics Workshop, University of Toronto, 12 April 2007.

———. "Structures Do Not Come with an Instruction Sheet: Interests, Ideas, and Progress in Political Science." *Perspectives on Politics* 1, no. 4 (2003): 695–706.

Bogdanov, Sergei. "Vecherkintsy ob'iavili kholodnuiu voinu amerikantsam?" *Tribuna* 4, no. 23 (28 February–13 March 2002).

Bohr, Annette. "The Central Asian States as Nationalising Regimes." In *Nation-Building in the Post-Soviet Borderlands: The Politics of National Identities*, edited by Graham Smith, Vivien Law, Andrew Wilson, Annette Bohr, and Edward Allworth, 139–66. Cambridge: Cambridge University Press, 1998.

Bong, Yongshik. "Pragmatic Anti-Americanism in South Korea." *Brown Journal of World Affairs* 10, no. 2 (Winter/Spring 2004): 153–65.

Botobekov, Uran. "Vnedrenie idei islamskoi partii 'Hizb at-Takhrir.'" In *Islam na postsovetskom prostranstve: vzgliad iznutri*, edited by Aleksei Malashenko and Martha Brill Olcott. Moscow: Carnegie Center, 2001.

Brass, Paul R. *Theft of an Idol: Text and Context in the Representation of Ethnic Violence*. Princeton, NJ: Princeton University Press, 1997.

Brooks, Stephen. *Anti-Americanism and the Limits of Public Diplomacy: Winning Hearts and Minds?* New York: Routledge, 2015.

Brownlee, Jason. *Authoritarianism in an Age of Democratization*. New York: Cambridge University Press, 2007.
Brubaker, Rogers, and Frederick Cooper. "Beyond 'Identity.'" *Theory and Society* 29 (2000): 1–47.
Brzezinski, Zbigniew. *The Grand Chessboard: American Primacy and Its Geostrategic Imperatives*. New York: Basic Books, 1998.
———. "The Premature Partnership." *Foreign Affairs* 73, no. 2 (March/April 1994): 67–82.
Bubenshchikova, Liudmila. "V Glubokom perekhodiat k glubokoi oborone," *Zashchita truda* (2003). Last accessed 13 September 2018. http://www.zaschita-truda.ru/kazahstan_impk.htm.
Bunce, Valerie. "Should Transitologists Be Grounded?" *Slavic Review* 54, no. 1 (1995): 111–27.
Burgat, François. *The Islamic Movement in North Africa*. Austin: University of Texas Press, 1997.
———. *L'islamisme en face*. Paris: La Découverte, 1997.
Buruma, Ian. "Tariq Ramadan Has an Identity Issue." *New York Times Magazine*, 4 February 2007.
Butterworth, Charles E. "Political Islam: The Origins." *Annals of the American Academy of Political and Social Science* 524 (November 1992): 26–37.
Buxton, Charles. "In Good Times and Hard Times: Civil Society Roles in Kyrgyzstan Today." In *Civil Society and Politics in Central Asia*, edited by Charles E. Ziegler, 223–48. Lexington: University Press of Kentucky, 2015.
Buzan, Barry. *A Leader without Followers? The United States in World Politics after Bush*. Vol. 6. Global Policy Institute. London: Forumpress, 2009.
Campbell, David. "Global Inscription: How Foreign Policy Constitutes the United States." *Alternatives* 15, no. 3 (1990): 263–63.
Capoccia, Giovanni, and Daniel R. Kelemen. "The Study of Critical Junctures: Theory, Narrative, and Counterfactuals in Historical Institutionalism." *World Politics* 59, no. 3 (April 2007): 341–69.
Chatybekova, K. K. *Istoriia profsoiuzov Kazakhstana: obrazovanie i stanovlenie (konets XIX–pervaia chetvert' XX vv.)*. Almaty: Kurmet, 2006.
Chiozza, Giacomo. *Anti-Americanism and the American World Order*. Baltimore: The Johns Hopkins University Press, 2009.
Chomsky, Noam. *Rogue States: The Rule of Force in World Affairs*. London: Pluto Press, 2000.
Coburn, Noah. *Bazaar Politics: Power and Pottery in an Afghan Market Town*. Stanford, CA: Stanford University Press, 2011.
Cole, N. Scott. "Hugo Chávez and President Bush's Credibility Gap: The Struggle Against US Democracy Promotion." *International Political Science Review* 28, no. 4 (2007): 493–507.
Collier, Ruth Berins, and David Collier. *Shaping the Political Arena: Critical Junctures, the Labor Movement, and Regime Dynamics in Latin America*. Princeton, NJ: Princeton University Press, 1991.

Collins, Kathleen. *Clan Politics and Regime Transition in Central Asia.* New York: Cambridge University Press, 2006.

Cooley, Alexander. *Base Politics: Democratic Change and the U.S. Military Overseas.* Ithaca, NY: Cornell University Press, 2008.

———. *Great Games, Local Rules: The New Great Power Contest in Central Asia.* New York: Oxford University Press, 2012.

Cooley, Alexander, and Daniel Nexon. *Exit from Hegemony: The Unraveling of the American Global Order.* New York: Oxford University Press, 2020.

Crews, Robert D. *For Prophet and Tsar.* Cambridge, MA: Harvard University Press, 2009.

Cummings, Sally N. "Happier Bedfellows? Russia and Central Asia under Putin." *Asian Affairs* 32, no. 2 (June 2001): 142–52.

Daughtery, Leo J., III. "The Bear and the Scimitar: Soviet Central Asians and the War in Afghanistan, 1979–1989." *Journal of Slavic Military Studies* 8, no. 1 (1995): 73–96.

———. "Ethnic Minorities in the Soviet Armed Forces: The Plight of Central Asians in a Russian-Dominated Military." *Journal of Slavic Military Studies* 7, no. 2 (1994): 55–197.

Davenport, Christian. "State Repression and Political Order." *Annual Review of Political Science* 10 (2007): 1–23.

Della Porta, Donatella. *Social Movements, Political Violence, and the State: A Comparative Analysis of Italy and Germany.* Cambridge: Cambridge University Press, 1995.

Della Porta, Donatella, Massimiliano Andretta, Angel Calle, Helene Combes, Nina Eggert, Marco G. Giugni, Jennifer Hadden, Manuel Jimenez, and Raffaele Marchetti. *Global Justice Movement: Cross-national and Transnational Perspectives.* Boulder, CO: Paradigm Publishers, 2007.

Demidenko, Igor', and Evgeniia Lenskaia. "Boris Berezovskii: chelovek i legenda." *Delovaia nedelia*, 31 July 1998: 7.

"Demokraticheskii Institut SShA kritikuet kyrygzskie vlasti." *Respublika* 17, no. 389 (12 September 2000).

Derluguian, Georgi. "Anti-Americanism on the Rise? Suggestions toward a Rational Program of Study." PONARS Eurasia, Policy Memo no. 266, October 2002. http://www.ponarseurasia.org/memo/anti-americanism-rise-suggestions-toward-rational-program-study.

Dion, Douglas. "Evidence and Inference in the Comparative Case Study." *Comparative Politics* 30, no. 2 (1998): 127–45.

Dobaev, Igor. "On the Typology of the Radical Islamic Movements." *Central Asia and the Caucasus* 3, no. 15 (2002): 96–103.

Domínguez, Jorge I. "Culture: Is It the Key to the Troubles in U.S.-Cuban Relations?" *Diplomatic History* 25, no. 3 (Summer 2001): 511–16.

Domjan, Paul, and Matt Stone. "A Comparative Study of Resource Nationalism in Russia and Kazakhstan 2004–2008." *Europe-Asia Studies* 62, no. 1 (2010): 35–62.

Doolotkeldieva, Asel. "Peripheral Protests as an Opportunity: 'Brokers' in Action." In *Kyrgyzstan beyond "Democracy Island" and "Failing State,"* edited by Marlene Laruelle and Johan Engvall, 59–78. Lanham, MD: Lexington Books, 2015.

Doty, Roxanne. *Imperial Encounters: The Politics of Representation in North-South Relations*. Minneapolis: University of Minnesota Press, 1996.

Doyle, Arthur Conan. "Silver Blaze" (1892). The Complete Sherlock Holmes, v.3.1, 15 March 2014. https://sherlock-holm.es/stories/pdf/a4/1-sided/silv.pdf.

Driscoll, Jesse. *Warlords and Coalition Politics in Post-Soviet States*. New York: Cambridge University Press, 2015.

Druckman, James N. "On the Limits of Framing Effects: Who Can Frame?" *Journal of Politics* 63, no. 4 (2001): 1041–66.

Dudoignon, Stephane A. "From Revival to Mutation: The Religious Personnel of Islam in Tajikistan, from De-Stalinization to Independence (1955–91)." *Central Asian Survey* 30, no. 1 (2011): 53–80.

Durkheim, Emile. *The Division of Labor in Society*. Translated by W. D. Halls. New York: Free Press, 1984. First published 1893.

Dzhalilov, Adil'. "Hewlett-Packard poluchila zakaz Ministerstva obrazovaniia RK na $11 mln." *Panorama* no. 38, (2 October 1998): 10.

Edelman, Murray. *The Symbolic Uses of Politics*. 2nd ed. Urbana: University of Illinois Press, 1985.

Edgar, Adrienne. "Bolshevism, Patriarchy, and the Nation: The Soviet "Emancipation" of Muslim Women in Pan-Islamic Perspective." *Slavic Review* 65, no. 2 (Summer 2006): 252–72.

Edgar, Adrienne Lynn. *Tribal Nation: The Making of Soviet Turkmenistan*. Princeton, NJ: Princeton University Press, 2004.

El-Ghobashy, Mona. "The Metamorphosis of the Egyptian Muslim Brothers." *International Journal of Middle East Studies* 37, no. 3 (2005): 373–95.

Emirbayer, Mustafa, and Ann Mische. "What Is Agency?" *American Journal of Sociology* 103, no. 4 (January 1998): 962–1023.

Emrich, Frederick, Yevgeniya Plakhina, and Dariya Tsyrenzhapova. *Mapping Digital Media: Kazakhstan*. Almaty: Open Society Foundation, 2013.

Emrich-Bakenova, Saule, and Frederick Emrich. "Kazakhstan: New Labor Code Squeezes Older Workers." *Eurasianet*, 5 August 2016. https://eurasianet.org/kazakhstan-new-labor-code-squeezes-older-workers.

Engvall, Johan. "License to Seek Rents: 'Corruption' as a Method of Post-Soviet Governance." In *Paradox of Power: The Logics of State Weakness in Eurasia*, edited by John Heathershaw and Edward Schatz, 73–87. Pittsburgh: University of Pittsburgh Press, 2017.

Epkenhans, Tim. "Defining Normative Islam: Some Remarks on Contemporary Islamic Thought in Tajikistan—Hofi Akbar Turajonzoda's Sharia and Society." *Central Asian Survey* 30, no.1 (March 2011): 81–96.

———. "The Islamic Revival Party of Tajikistan: Episodes of Islamic Activism, Postconflict Accommodation, and Political Marginalization." *Central Asian Affairs* 2, no. 4 (2015): 321–46.

Eshimkanov, Melis, and Kanybek Imanaliev. *Askar Akaev*. Bishkek: Asaba, 1993.

Esposito, John L. *Islam: The Straight Path*. Oxford: Oxford University Press, 1991.

———. *The Islamic Threat: Myth or Reality?* New York: Oxford University Press, 1992.

Esposito, John L., and John Obert Voll. *Islam and Democracy.* New York: Oxford University Press, 1996.

Exnerova, Vera. "Introducing Transnationalism Studies to the Field of Public Diplomacy." *Journal of International Communication* 23, no. 2 (2017): 186–99.

Fabbrini, Serio. "The Domestic Sources of European Anti-Americanism." *Government and Opposition* 37, no. 1 (2002): 3–14.

Fel'de, Svetlana. "CCL OIL lukavit: Vypolnenie investitsionnykh obiazatel'stv — blef," *Novoe pokolenie* (Almaty), 14 August 1998: 2.

Fetzer, Joel S., and J. Christopher Soper. *Muslims and the State in Britain, France, and Germany.* Cambridge and New York: Cambridge University Press, 2005.

Fierman, William, ed. *Soviet Central Asia: The Failed Transformation.* Boulder, CO: Westview Press, 1991.

Fish, M. Steven. "Islam and Authoritarianism." *World Politics* 55, no. 1 (2002): 4–37.

Fletcher, Joseph F., and Boris Sergeyev. "Islam and Intolerance in Central Asia: The Case of Kyrgyzstan." *Europe-Asia Studies* 54, no. 2 (2002): 251–75.

Ford, Peter. "Why Do They Hate Us?" *Christian Science Monitor*, 27 September 2001. http://www.csmonitor.com/2001/0927/plsl-wogi.html.

Fowler, James H., Laura A. Baker, and Christopher T. Dawes. "Genetic Variation in Political Participation." *American Political Science Review* 102, no. 2 (May 2008): 233–48.

Fowler, James H., Peter J. Loewen, Jaime Settle, and Christopher T. Dawes. "Genes, Games, and Political Participation." In *Man Is by Nature a Political Animal: Evolution, Biology, and Politics,* edited by Peter K. Hatemi and Rose McDermott, 207–23. Chicago: University of Chicago Press, 2011.

Frye, Timothy, Ora John Reuter, and David Szakonyi. "Political Machines at Work: Voter Mobilization and Electoral Subversion in the Workplace." *World Politics* 66, no. 2 (2014): 195–228.

Fujii, Lee Ann. *Interviewing in Social Science Research: A Relational Approach.* New York: Routledge, 2018.

———. "Shades of Truth and Lies: Interpreting Testimonies of War and Violence." *Journal of Peace Research* 47, no. 2 (2010): 231–41.

Fullerton, Jami, and Alice Kendrick. *Advertising's War on Terrorism: The Story of the U.S. State Department's Shared Values Initiative.* Spokane, WA: Marquette Books, 2006.

Furman, Dmitrii E. and Sanobar A. Shermatova. *Kirgizskie Tsikly: Kak Rushatsia Rezhimy.* Moscow: Territoriia budushchego, 2013.

Gandhi, Jennifer, and Adam Przeworski. "Authoritarian Institutions and the Survival of Autocrats." *Comparative Political Studies* 40, no. 11 (2007): 1279–301.

Geddes, Barbara. "How the Cases You Choose Affect the Answers You Get: Selection Bias in Comparative Politics." *Political Analysis* 2, no. 1 (1990): 131–50.

Geertz, Clifford. "Ritual and Social Change: A Javanese Example." In *The Interpretation of Cultures*, edited by Clifford Geertz, 242–69. New York: Basic Books, 1973.
———. "Which Way to Mecca? Part II." *New York Review of Books*, 3 July 2003: 36–39.
Gellner, Ernest. *Muslim Society*. Cambridge and New York: Cambridge University Press, 1983.
Gerber, Theodore P., and Sarah E. Mendelson. "Young, Educated, Urban—and Anti-American: Recent Survey Data from Russia." PONARS Eurasia, Policy Memo no. 267, October 2002. http://www.ponarseurasia.org/memo/young-educated-urban-and-anti-american-recent-survey-data-russia.
Gerhards, Jurgen and Dieter Rucht. "Mesomobilization Contexts: Organizing and Framing in Two Protest Campaigns in West Germany." *American Journal of Sociology* 98 (1992): 555–96.
Gillan, Kevin. "Understanding Meaning in Movements: A Hermeneutic Approach to Frames and Ideologies." *Social Movement Studies* 7, no. 3 (December 2008): 247–63.
Giragosian, Richard. "The US Military Engagement in Central Asia and the Southern Caucasus: An Overview." *Journal of Slavic Military Studies* 17, no. 1 (2004): 43–77.
Giugni, Marco G. "Was it Worth the Effort? The Outcomes and Consequences of Social Movements." *Annual Review of Sociology* 24, no. 1 (1998): 371–93.
Goffman, Erving. *Frame Analysis: An Essay on the Organization of Experience*. Cambridge, MA: Harvard University Press, 1974.
Goldgeier, James M., and Michael McFaul. *Power and Purpose: U.S. Policy toward Russia after the Cold War*. Washington, DC: Brookings Institution Press, 2003.
Goldstein, Judith, and Robert O. Keohane, eds. *Ideas and Foreign Policy: Beliefs, Institutions, and Political Change*. Ithaca, NY: Cornell University Press, 1993.
Goldstone, Jack A. "Toward a Fourth Generation of Revolutionary Theory." *Annual Review of Political Science* 4 (2001): 139–87.
Goode, J. Paul. "Redefining Russia: Hybrid Regimes, Fieldwork, and Russian Politics." *Perspectives on Politics* 8, no. 4 (2010): 1055–75.
Greenbaum, Thomas L. *Moderating Focus Groups: A Practical Guide for Group Facilitation*. Thousand Oaks, CA: Sage Publications, 2000.
Gregory, Bruce. "Public Diplomacy: Sunrise of an Academic Field." *Annals of the American Academy of Political and Social Science* 616, no. 1 (2008): 274–90.
Gudava, Tengiz. "Interv'iu Feliksa Kulova Radio Svoboda." *Radio Svoboda*, 8 August 2000. https://www.svoboda.org/a/24198693.html.
Gunn, T. Jeremy. "Shaping an Islamic Identity: Religion, Islamism, and the State in Central Asia." *Sociology of Religion* 64, no. 3 (2003): 389–410.
Guzikov, Lev. "TShO: budem 'kodirovat'!" *Aq zhaiyq* 803 (17 May 2007): 1.
Hahn, Gordon. "Anti-Americanism, Anti-Westernism, and Anti-Semitism among Russia's Muslims." *Demokratizatsiia* 16, no. 1 (Winter 2008): 49–60.
Hale, Henry E. *Patronal Politics: Eurasian Regime Dynamics in Comparative Perspective*. New York: Cambridge University Press, 2015.

Hall, Todd H. "Sympathetic States: State Strategies, Norms of Emotional Behavior, and the 9/11 Attacks." *Political Science Quarterly* 127, no. 3 (2012): 369–400.

Hall, Todd H., and Andrew A.G. Ross. "Affective Politics after 9/11." *International Organization* 69, no. 4 (2015): 847–79.

Hansen, Stephen E. "The Leninist Legacy and Institutional Change." *Comparative Political Studies* 28, no. 2 (July 1995): 306–14.

Heathershaw, John. *Post-conflict Tajikistan: The Politics of Peacebuilding and the Emergence of Legitimate Order.* New York: Routledge, 2009.

Heathershaw, John, and Alexander Cooley. "Offshore Central Asia: An Introduction." *Central Asian Survey* 34, no. 1 (2015): 1–10.

Heathershaw, John, and Edward Schatz. "The Logics of State Weakness: An Introduction." In *Paradox of Power: The Logics of State Weakness in Eurasia*, edited by John Heathershaw and Edward Schatz, 3–21. Pittsburgh: University of Pittsburgh Press, 2017.

———, eds. *Paradox of Power: The Logics of State Weakness in Eurasia.* Pittsburgh: University of Pittsburgh Press, 2017.

Heekeren, Hauke R., Sean Marrett, and Leslie C. Ungerleider. "The Neural Systems That Mediate Human Perceptual Decision Making." *Nature Reviews Neuroscience* 9, no. 6 (June 2008): 467–79.

Hefner, Robert W. *Civil Islam: Muslims and Democratization in Indonesia.* Princeton, NJ: Princeton University Press, 2000.

Henderson, Sarah. *Building Democracy in Contemporary Russia: Western Support for Grassroots Organizations.* Ithaca, NY: Cornell University Press, 2003.

Herrmann, Richard K. *Perceptions and Behavior in Soviet Foreign Policy.* Pittsburgh: University of Pittsburgh Press, 1985.

Herrmann, Richard K., and Michael P. Fischerkeller. "Beyond the Enemy Image and Spiral Model: Cognitive-Strategic Research after the Cold War." *International Organization* 49, no. 3 (1995): 415–50.

Herrmann, Richard K., James F. Voss, Tonya E. Schooler, and Joseph Ciarrochi. "Images in International Relations: An Experimental Test of Cognitive Schemata." *International Studies Quarterly* 41, no. 3 (1997): 403–33.

Hess, Steve. *Authoritarian Landscapes: Popular Mobilization and the Institutional Sources of Resilience in Nondemocracies.* New York: Springer Science & Business Media, 2013.

Hilgers, Irene. *Why Do Uzbeks Have to Be Muslims? Exploring Religiosity in the Ferghana Valley.* Berlin: Lit Verlag, 2009.

Hill, Fiona. "A Not-So-Grand Strategy: United States Policy toward Central Asia before the Events of September 2001." *Brookings* (blog). Brookings Institution, February 2001. https://www.brookings.edu/articles/a-not-so-grand-strategy-u-s-policy-in-the-caucasus-and-central-asia-since-1991/.

Hirschl, Ran. *Constitutional Theocracy.* Cambridge, MA: Harvard University Press, 2010.

Hizb ut-Tahrir. *The American Campaign to Suppress Islam.* London: Al-Khalifa, 1996.

———. *Dangerous Concepts to Attack Islam and Consolidate the Western Culture.* London: Al-Khalifa, 1997.
Hopf, Ted. *The Social Construction of International Politics: Identities and Foreign Policies, Moscow, 1955 and 1999.* Ithaca, NY: Cornell University Press, 2002.
Horsman, Stuart. "Themes in Official Discourses on Terrorism in Central Asia." *Third World Quarterly* 26, no. 1 (2005): 199–213.
Howard, Shawn A. "The Afghan Connection: Islamic Extremism in Central Asia." *National Security Studies Quarterly* 6, no. 6 (2000): 25–54.
Human Rights Watch. *"Hellish Work": Exploitation of Tobacco Workers in Kazakhstan.* Report. New York: Human Rights Watch, 14 July 2010. https://www.hrw.org/report/2010/07/14/hellish-work/exploitation-migrant-tobacco-workers-kazakhstan.
———. *"We Are Not the Enemy": Violations of Workers' Rights in Kazakhstan.* Report. New York: Human Rights Watch, 23 November 2016. https://www.hrw.org/report/2016/11/23/we-are-not-enemy/violations-workers-rights-kazakhstan.
———. *"We Can't Refuse to Pick Cotton": Forced and Child Labor Linked to World Bank Group Investments in Uzbekistan.* Report. New York: Human Rights Watch, 27 June 2017. https://www.hrw.org/report/2017/06/27/we-cant-refuse-pick-cotton/forced-and-child-labor-linked-world-bank-group.
Huntington, Samuel P. *The Clash of Civilizations and the Remaking of World Order.* New York: Simon & Schuster, 1996.
———. *The Third Wave: Democratization in the Late Twentieth Century.* Norman: University of Oklahoma Press, 1991.
Hurd, Ian. "Breaking and Making Norms: American Revisionism and Crises of Legitimacy." *International Politics* 44 (2007): 194–213.
Ikenberry, G. John. "The Liberal International Order and Its Discontents." In *After Liberalism?: The Future of Liberalism in International Relations*, edited by Rebekka Friedman, Kevork Oskanian, and Ramon Pacheco Pardo, 91–102. Houndmills, Basingstoke, Hampshire: Palgrave Macmillan, 2013.
Ikonnikov, Aleksei. "Vremia sobirat' kamni?" *Kontinent*, 12–27 December 2005: 16–19.
"Impichment kak simvol demokratii." *Delovaia nedelia*, 31 July 1998: 8.
Interfaks. "Ucheniia 'Tsentrazbat' provodiatsia v tseliakh obespecheniia bezopasnosti stran Tsentral'noi Azii iz-za situatsii v Afganistane." *Panorama* no. 37 (25 September 1998): 5.
International Crisis Group. "Central Asia: Uzbekistan at Ten—Repression and Instability." *Asia Report* 21 (21 August 2001).
———. "The IMU and the Hizb-ut-Tahrir: Implications of the Afghanistan Campaign." Central Asia Briefing, 30 January 2002.
———. "Radical Islam in Central Asia: Responding to Hizb ut-Tahrir." *Asia Report* 58 (30 June 2003).
Ismailbekova, Aksana. *Blood Ties and the Native Son: Poetics of Patronage in Kyrgyzstan.* Bloomington: Indiana University Press, 2017.

Jäger, Philipp Frank. "Flows of Oil, Flows of People: Resource-Extraction Industry, Labour Market and Migration in Western Kazakhstan." *Central Asian Survey* 33, no. 4 (2014): 500–16.

Jamestown Foundation. "Militant Islamic Group Serves Ultimatum on Uzbekistan from Iran." *Terrorism Monitor: In-Depth Analysis of the War on Terror* 5, no. 60 (26 March 1999). http://www.jamestown.org/single/?tx_ttnews%5Btt_news%5D =12817&tx_ttnews%5BbackPid%5D=213&no_cache=1#.Vm3NbxorLqo.

Jervis, Robert. *The Logic of Images in International Relations*. Princeton, NJ: Princeton University Press, 1970.

Joas, Hans. *The Creativity of Action*. Chicago: University of Chicago Press, 1996.

Jones, Pauline, ed. *Islam, Society, and Politics in Central Asia*. Pittsburgh: University of Pittsburgh Press, 2017.

Jourde, Cédric. "'The President Is Coming to Visit!': Dramas and the Hijack of Democratization in the Islamic Republic of Mauritania." *Comparative Politics* 37, no. 4 (July 2005): 421–40.

Judt, Tony. *Postwar: A History of Europe since 1945*. New York: Penguin, 2006.

Kalinovsky, Artemy M. *A Long Goodbye: The Soviet Withdrawal from Afghanistan*. Cambridge, MA: Harvard University Press, 2011.

Kamp, Marianne. *The New Woman in Uzbekistan: Islam, Modernity, and Unveiling under Communism*. Seattle: University of Washington Press, 2006.

Karagiannis, Emmanuel. *Political Islam in Central Asia: The Challenge of Hizb ut-Tahrir*. London and New York: Routledge, 2010.

Karrar, Hasan H. "Between Border and Bazaar: Central Asia's Informal Economy." *Journal of Contemporary Asia* 49, no. 2 (October 2018): 1–22.

Kassenova, Nargis. "Religious Extremism in Central Asia: Self-Fulfilling Prophecy in the Making?" *Central Asia and the Caucasus*, no. 5 (September 2000): 43–49. http://www.ca-c.org/online/2000/journal_eng/eng05_2000/05.kase.shtml.

Katz, Mark N. "Will There Be a Revolution in Central Asia?" *Communist and Post-Communist Studies* 40, no. 2 (June 2007): 129–41.

Katzenstein, Peter J., and Robert O. Keohane, eds. *Anti-Americanisms in World Politics*. Ithaca, NY: Cornell University Press, 2007.

———. "The Political Consequences of Anti-Americanism." In *Anti-Americanisms in World Politics*, edited by Peter J. Katzenstein and Robert O. Keohane, 273–305. Ithaca, NY: Cornell University Press, 2007.

Kaufman, Stuart J. *Modern Hatreds: The Symbolic Politics of Ethnic War*. Ithaca, NY: Cornell University Press, 2001.

Kavalski, Emilian. "Partnership or Rivalry between the EU, China and India in Central Asia: The Normative Power of Regional Actors with Global Aspirations." *European Law Journal* 13, no. 6 (November 2007): 839–56.

Kazkenov, Ruslan, and Charles E. Ziegler. "Civil Society in a Period of Transition: The Perspective from the State." In *Civil Society and Politics in Central Asia*, edited by Charles E. Ziegler, 197–221. Lexington: University of Kentucky Press, 2015.

Keck, Margaret, and Kathryn Sikkink. *Activists beyond Borders: Transnational Activist Networks in International Politics*. Ithaca, NY: Cornell University Press, 1998.

Kedourie, Elie. *Democracy and Arab Political Culture*. London: Frank Cass, 1994.

Kelimbetova, Fatima, and Erbolat Nazarbaev. "Politika Kazakhstana: ot integratsii k sotrudnichestvu." *Saiasat* 10, no. 17 (October 1996): 46-58.

Keller, Shoshana. *To Moscow, not Mecca: The Soviet Campaign against Islam in Central Asia, 1917-1941*. Westport, CT: Praeger, 2001.

Kenzhes-uly, Zhenis. "SP 'Tengizshevroil' povysheny limity na vybrosy vrednykh veshchestv v atmosferu." *Panorama* no. 32 (21 August 1998): 9.

Kepel, Gilles. *The War for Muslim Minds: Islam and the West*. Translated by Pascale Ghazaleh. Cambridge, MA: Belknap Press of Harvard University Press, 2004.

Kern, Thomas. "Anti-Americanism in South Korea: From Structural Cleavages to Protest." *Korea Journal* (Spring 2005): 257-89.

Khalid, Adeeb. "Backwardness and the Quest for Civilization: Early Soviet Central Asia in Comparative Perspective." *Slavic Review* 65, no. 2 (Summer 2006): 231-51.

———. *Islam after Communism: Religion and Politics in Central Asia*. Berkeley: University of California Press, 2007.

Khan, Muqtedar. "The US Must Adopt a Softer Approach to the Muslim World." *National Strategy Forum Review* 13, no. 2 (Winter 2003): 25-28.

Khanna, Parag. *The Second World: How Emerging Powers Are Redefining Global Competition in the 21st Century*. New York: Random House, 2008.

———. "Waving Goodbye to Hegemony." *New York Times Magazine*, 27 January 2008.

Khasenov, Amirzhan. "Sobytiia na Tengize: izderzhki neokolonializma." *Zona.kz Kazakhstan*, 24 October 2006. http://www.zonakz.net/articles/15899.

Kim, Myongsob, Suzanne L. Parker, and Jun Young Choi. "Increasing Distrust of the USA in South Korea." *International Political Science Review* 27, no. 4 (2006): 427-45.

Kisriev, Enver. "Islam's Political Role in Dagestan." *Central Asia and the Caucasus* 5 (September 2000): 65-70.

Klandermans, Bert. *The Social Psychology of Protest*. Oxford: Blackwell, 1997.

Klandermans, Bert, and Dirk Oegema. "Potentials, Networks, Motivations, and Barriers: Steps towards Participation in Social Movements." *American Sociological Review* 52, no. 4 (August 1987): 519-31.

Kniazev, Alexander. "Afghanistan: Religious Extremism and Terrorism—The Year 2000." *Central Asia and the Caucasus*, no. 5 (2000): 76-83. http://www.ca-c.org/online/2000/journal_eng/eng05_2000/11.kniaz.shtml.

Kopstein, Jeffrey S. "Anti-Americanism and the Transatlantic Relationship." *Perspectives on Politics* 7, no. 2 (2009): 367-76.

Kopstein, Jeffrey S., and David A. Reilly. "Geographic Diffusion and the Transformation of the Postcommunist World." *World Politics* 53, no. 1 (2000): 1-37.

Kosychenko, A. G., M. S. Ashimbaev, B. K. Sultanov, A. Zh. Shomanov, N. K. Begaliev, and B. Zh. Nurmukhamedov. *Sovremennyi terrorizm: vzgliad iz Tsentral'noi Azii*. Almaty: Daik-Press, 2002.

Kovalenko, O. "Po odezhde, ili chtoby vygliadit' O'Kei." *Kazakhstanskaia pravda*, 30 January 1992: 4.

Kowalewski, David. "The Protest Uses of Symbolic Politics in the USSR." *Journal of Politics* 42, no. 2 (1980): 439–60.

Krämer, Gudrun. "Islamist Notions of Democracy." In *Political Islam: Essays from Middle East Report*, edited by Joel Beinin and Joe Stork, 71–82. Berkeley: University of California Press, 1997.

Kratov, E. V. "K voprosu ob ideologii sovremennogo religiozno-politicheskogo ekstremizma (na osnovanii materialov, rasprostraniaemykh v Karachaevo-Cherkesskoi respublike." In *Terrorizm i politicheskii ekstremizm: vyzovy i poiski adekvatnykh otvetov*, edited by A. A. Sharavin and S. M. Markedonov. Moscow: Institut politicheskogo i voennogo analiza, 2002.

"Kto mirovoi lider?" *Narodnoe slovo* 2013 (26 November 1998): 3.

Kubicek, Paul. "Organized Labor in Postcommunist States: Will the Western Sun Set on It, Too?" *Comparative Politics* 32, no. 1 (1999): 83–102.

Kubik, Jan. *The Power of Symbols against the Symbols of Power: The Rise of Solidarity and the Fall of State Socialism in Poland*. University Park: Penn State University Press, 1994.

Kulov, Emir. "March 2005: Parliamentary Elections as a Catalyst of Protests." *Central Asian Survey* 27, no. 3-4 (2008): 337–47.

Kupatadze, Alexander. "Organized Crime and the State in Post-Soviet Eurasia." In *Paradox of Power: The Logics of State Weakness in Eurasia*, edited by John Heathershaw and Edward Schatz, 60–72. Pittsburgh: University of Pittsburgh Press, 2017.

Kupriianova, Anastasiia. "Amerika nam pomozhet?" *Delo Nomer* 23 (April 1991): 5.

Kuran, Timur. "Now Out of Never: The Element of Surprise in the East European Revolution of 1989." *World Politics* 44, no. 1 (1991): 7–48.

Kurbanov, Garun. "How Dagestan Is Opposing Religious Extremism." *Central Asia and the Caucasus* 5 (September 2002): 120–27.

———. "Religion in Post-Soviet Dagestan: Sociological Aspects." *Central Asia and the Caucasus* 6 (November 2002): 130–38.

Kurmanov, Ainur. "Bespredel v Kentau," *Zashchita truda* (2003). Last accessed November 9, 2018. http://www.zaschita-truda.ru/besp_v_kentau.htm.

———. "The Current State of the Trade Union Movement in Kazakhstan," *International Viewpoint*, 5 May 2010. http://internationalviewpoint.org/spip.php?article1862.

———. "Protivostoianie v poselke Glubokom." Left.ru., 8 July 2003. http://www.left.ru/2003/16/glubokoe92.html.

———. "Zabostovka neftianikov v Kazakhstane: proobraz budushchikh vystuplenii rabochikh vsek otraslei." Forum-msk.ru., 24 June 2011. https://forum-msk.org/material/fpolitic/6596215.html.

Kurmanov, Erkin. "Hizb ut-Tahrir in Kyrgyzstan." *Central Asia and the Caucasus* 15, no. 3 (2002): 119–26. https://www.ca-c.org/journal/2002/journal_eng/cac-03/14.kuren.shtml.

Kurmanov, Nurlan, Gulmira Kabdullina, Zatira Karbetova, Madina Tuzubekova, Almagul Doshan, and Sholpan Karbetova. "Motivation of Employees' Labor Activity in Oil and Gas Companies in Kazakhstan." *World Applied Sciences Journal* 26, no. 12 (2013): 1556–61.

Kytaibekov, B. "Tarykh kaitalandy." Presskg.com, 2010. http://www.presskg.com/as/10/0415_7.htm. Translated and reprinted in *Narodnye revoliutsii, obnovivshie epokhu: sbornik, posviashchennyi iubileiam narodnykh revoliutsii sovershivshikhsia v Kyrgyzstane 24 marta 2005 goda i 7 aprelia 2010 goda*, edited by V. Moldokasymov, A. Ibraeva, and A. Kadyrova, 161–62. Bishkek: Fond "Muras," 2015.

Langohr, Vickie. "Too Much Civil Society, Too Little Politics: Egypt and Liberalizing Arab Regimes." *Comparative Politics* 36, no. 2 (2004): 181–204.

LaPalombara, Joseph. "Anti-Americanism in Europe: Corporate and National Dimensions." *American Foreign Policy Interests* 26 (2004): 317–28.

Lapidus, Ira M. "The Separation of State and Religion in the Development of Early Islamic Society." *International Journal of Middle East Studies* 6 (1975): 363–85.

Laruelle, Marlène. "Religious Revival, Nationalism and the 'Invention of Tradition': Political Tengrism in Central Asia and Tatarstan." *Central Asian Survey* 26, no. 2 (2007): 203–16.

Latypova, Ekaterina. "Fond 'Soros-Kazakhstan' provel seminar po obrazovaniiu v mnogokul'turnoi srede." *Panorama* 37 (25 September 1998): 5.

———. "Nachalos' izdanie istoricheskoi serii o kazakhakh." *Panorama* 31 (14 August 1998): 11.

Ledeneva, Alena V. *How Russia Really Works: The Informal Practices That Shaped Post-Soviet Politics and Business*. Ithaca, NY: Cornell University Press, 2006.

Leheny, David. "Symbols, Strategies, and Choices for International Relations Scholarship after September 11." *Dialog-IO* (Spring 2002): 57–70.

———. "Terrorism, Social Movements, and International Security: How Al Qaeda Affects Southeast Asia." *Japanese Journal of Political Science* 6, no. 1 (2005): 87–109.

Lemon, Edward J. "Daesh and Tajikistan: The Regime's (In)Security Policy." *RUSI Journal* 160, no. 5 (2015): 68–76.

Lenin, Vladimir Il'ich. *Imperialism: The Highest Stage of Capitalism*. Chippendale NSW, Australia: Resistance Books, 1999.

Lerner, Daniel. *The Passing of Traditional Society: Modernizing the Middle East*. Glencoe, IL: Free Press, 1958.

Levitin, Leonid. "Liberalization in Kyrgyzstan: 'An Island of Democracy.'" In *Democracy and Pluralism in Muslim Eurasia*, edited by Yaakov Ro'i, 187–214. London and New York: Frank Cass, 2004.

Levitsky, Steven, and Lucan A. Way. *Competitive Authoritarianism: Hybrid Regimes after the Cold War*. New York: Cambridge University Press, 2010.

———. "Linkage versus Leverage. Rethinking the International Dimension of Regime." *Comparative Politics* 38, no. 4 (2006): 379–400.

———. "Why Democracy Needs a Level Playing Field." *Journal of Democracy* 21, no. 1 (2010): 57–68.

Lewis, Bernard. "The Roots of Muslim Rage." *Atlantic Monthly* 266, no. 3 (1990): 47–60.

Lieberman, Robert. "The 'Israel Lobby' and American Politics." *Perspectives on Politics* 7, no. 2 (2009): 235–57.

Lifton, Robert J. *The Nazi Doctors: Medical Killing and the Psychology of Genocide.* New York: Basic Books, 1986.

Liu, Morgan Y. *Under Solomon's Throne.* Pittsburgh: University of Pittsburgh Press, 2012.

Louw, Maria E. *Everyday Islam in Post-Soviet Central Asia.* London and New York: Routledge, 2007.

Lubin, Nancy. *Central Asians Take Stock: Reform, Corruption, and Identity.* Peaceworks no. 2. Washington, DC: United States Institute of Peace, 1995.

Lubin, Nancy, and Arustan Joldasov. "Snapshots from Central Asia: Is America Losing in Public Opinion?" *Problems of Post-Communism* 57, no. 3 (May/June 2010): 40–54.

Lukoianov, A. Ak. "Igry v vakhkhabizm." In *Islam i politika*, edited by G. V. Minorca, 99–113. Moscow: Institut vostokovedeniia RAN, 2001.

Luong, Pauline Jones. *Institutional Change and Political Continuity in Post-Soviet Central Asia: Power, Perceptions, and Pacts.* Cambridge University Press, 2002.

———. "The Middle Easternization of Central Asia." *Current History* 102, no. 666 (October 2003): 333–40.

Luong, Pauline Jones, and Erika Weinthal. "The NGO Paradox: Democratic Goals and Non-democratic Outcomes in Kazakhstan." *Europe-Asia Studies* 51, no. 7 (1999): 1267–84.

Lynch, Marc. "Taking Arabs Seriously." *Foreign Affairs* 82, no. 5 (2003): 81–94.

Mackie, John L. *The Cement of the Universe. A Study of Causation.* Oxford: Clarendon Press, 1974.

Mackinder, H. J. "The Geographical Pivot of History." *Geographical Journal* 23, no.4 (April 1904): 421–37. Reprinted in *Geographical Journal* 170, no. 4 (December 2004). http://www.iwp.edu/docLib/20131016_MackinderTheGeographicalJournal.pdf.

Maevskaia, L. B. 2002. *Ostorozhno, ekstremizm!* Kiev: Mezhregional'naia akademiia upravleniia personalom, 2002.

Mahoney, James, and Gary Goertz. "The Possibility Principle: Choosing Negative Cases in Comparative Research." *American Political Science Review* 98, no. 4 (2004): 653–69.

Makarov, D. V. *Offitsial'nyi i neofitsial'nyi Islam v Dagestane.* Moscow: Tsentr strategicheskikh i politicheskikh issledovanii, 2000.

Maltseva, Elena. "Cracks in the System: What the Zhanaozen Incident Says about Regime Performance in Kazakhstan." In *Paradox of Power: The Logics of State*

Weakness in Eurasia, edited by John Heathershaw and Edward Schatz, 184–99. Pittsburgh: University of Pittsburgh Press, 2017.

Marat, Erica. *The Tulip Revolution: Kyrgyzstan One Year After.* Washington, DC: Jamestown Foundation, 2006.

Markowitz, Lawrence P. "How Master Frames Mislead: The Eclipse and Division of Nationalist Movements in Tajikistan and Uzbekistan." *Ethnic and Racial Studies* 32, no. 4 (2009): 716–38.

Martin, Joanne, Maureen Scully, and Barbara Levitt. "Injustice and the Legitimation of Revolution: Damning the Past, Excusing the Present, and Neglecting the Future." *Journal of Personal Social Psychology* 59, no. 2 (August 1990): 281–90.

Massell, Gregory J. *The Surrogate Proletariat: Moslem Women and Revolutionary Strategies in Soviet Central Asia, 1919–1929.* Princeton, NJ: Princeton University Press, 1974.

Mattern, Janice Bially. "On Being Convinced: An Emotional Epistemology of International Relations." *International Theory* 6, no. 3 (2014): 589–94.

———. "A Practice Theory of Emotion for International Relations." In *International Practices*, edited by Emmanuel Adler and Vincent Pouliot, 63–86. Cambridge: Cambridge University Press, 2011.

Maududi, Abul A'la. *Political Theory of Islam.* Lahore: Islamic Publications, 1976.

McAdam, Doug. "The Framing Function of Movement Tactics: Strategic Dramaturgy in the American Civil Rights Movement." In *Comparative Perspectives on Social Movements: Political Opportunities, Mobilizing Structures, and Cultural Framings*, edited by Doug McAdam, J. D. McCarthy and M. N. Zald, 338–57. New York: Cambridge University Press, 1996.

———. "Legacies of Anti-Americanism: A Sociological Perspective." In *Anti-Americanisms in World Politics*, edited by Peter J. Katzenstein and Robert O. Keohane, 251–69. Ithaca, NY: Cornell University Press, 2007.

McAdam, Doug, John D. McCarthy, and Mayer N. Zald, eds. *Comparative Perspectives on Social Movements: Political Opportunities, Mobilizing Structures, and Cultural Framings.* New York: Cambridge University Press, 1996.

McAdam, Doug, Sidney G. Tarrow, and Charles Tilly. *Dynamics of Contention.* Cambridge: Cambridge University Press, 2001.

McCann, James A. "Ideology in the 2006 Campaign." In *Consolidating Mexico's Democracy: The 2006 Presidential Campaign in Comparative Perspective*, edited by Jorge Domínguez, Chappell Lawson, and Alejandro Moreno, 268–84. Baltimore: Johns Hopkins University Press, 2009.

McGlinchey, Eric. *Chaos, Violence, Dynasty: Politics and Islam in Central Asia.* Pittsburgh: University of Pittsburgh Press, 2011.

———. "Islamic Leaders in Uzbekistan." *Asia Policy* 1, no. 1 (January 2006): 123–44.

McKeown, Timothy. "Case Studies and the Limits of the Quantitative Worldview." In *Rethinking Social Inquiry*, edited by Henry E. Brady and David Collier, 158–62. Lanham, MD: Rowman & Littlefield, 2004.

McMann, Kelly M. *Economic Autonomy and Democracy: Hybrid Regimes in Russia and Kyrgyzstan*. New York: Cambridge University Press, 2006.

McPherson, Alan. *Yankee No! Anti-Americanism in U.S.–Latin American Relations*. Cambridge, MA: Harvard University Press, 2003.

Mearsheimer, John J. and Stephen Walt. *The Israel Lobby and U.S. Foreign Policy*. New York: Farrar, Straus and Giroux, 2007.

Medina, Leandro, and Friedrich Schneider. *Shadow Economies around the World: What Did We Learn over the Last 20 Years?* IMF Working Paper no. 18/17. Washington, DC: International Monetary Fund, 24 January 2018. https://www.imf.org/~/media/Files/Publications/WP/2018/wp1817.ashx.

Medvedev, Michael. "Hollywood's Contribution to Anti-Americanism." *National Interest* 68 (Summer 2002): 5–14.

Mendelson, Sarah E., and Theodore P. Gerber. "Activist Culture and Transnational Diffusion: Social Marketing and Human Rights Groups in Russia." *Post-Soviet Affairs* 23, no. 1 (2007): 50–75.

———. "Us and Them: Anti-American Views of the Putin Generation." *Washington Quarterly* 31, no. 2 (2008): 131–50.

Meunier, Sophie. "The Distinctiveness of French Anti-Americanism." In *Anti-Americanisms in World Politics*, edited by Peter J. Katzenstein and Robert O. Keohane, 129–56. Ithaca, NY: Cornell University Press, 2007.

Mezhdunarodnyi fond sotsial'no-ekonomicheskikh i politologicheskikh issledovaniii. *Respublika Kyrgyzstan: kratkii analiz sotsial'no-politicheskoi situatsii*. Moscow: Gorbachev-Fond, 1993.

Michaels, Paula A. "If the Subaltern Speaks in the Woods and Nobody's Listening, Does He Make a Sound?" *Slavic Review* 67, no. 1 (2008): 81–83.

Michel, Casey. "Kazakhstan's Labor Union Crackdown Draws International Criticism." *Diplomat*, 16 June 2017. http://thediplomat.com/2017/06/kazakhstans-labor-union-crackdown-draws-international-criticism/.

Mikul'skii, D. V. *Ideologicheskaia kontseptsiia Islamskoi partii vozrozhdeniia*. Moscow: Mezhdunarodnyi fond sotsial'no-ekonomicheskikh i politologicheskikh issledovanii (Gorbachev-fond), 1993.

Miller, Patrick R. "The Emotional Citizen: Emotion as a Function of Political Sophistication." *Political Psychology* 32, no. 4 (2011): 575–600.

Milliken, Jennifer. "The Study of Discourse in International Relations: A Critique of Research and Methods." *European Journal of International Relations* 5, no. 2 (1999): 225–54.

Mirsaidov, Negmatullo. "Isfara Becomes Terrorist Hub." *Tajikistan Times* 45, no. 82 (10 November 2010): 8.

Mitchell, Timothy. "American Power and Anti-Americanism in the Middle East." In *Anti-Americanism*, edited by Andrew Ross and Kristin Ross, 87–105. New York: New York University Press, 2003.

Moldokasymov, V., A. Ibraeva, and A. Kadyrova, eds. *Narodnye revoliutsii, obnovivshie epokhu: sbornik, posviashchennyi iubileiam narodnykh revoliutsii sovershivshikhsia v Kyrgyzstane 24 marta 2005 goda i 7 aprelia 2010 goda*. Bishkek: Fond "Muras," 2015.

Monroe, Kristen Renwick, James Hankin, and Renée Bukovchik Van Vechten. "The Psychological Foundations of Identity Politics." *Annual Review of Political Science* 3 (2000): 419–47.

Montgomery, David W., and John Heathershaw. "Islam, Secularism and Danger: A Reconsideration of the Link between Religiosity, Radicalism and Rebellion in Central Asia." *Religion, State & Society* 44, no. 3 (2016): 192–218.

Morgan D. L., and M. L. Schwalbe. "Mind and Self in Society—Linking Social Structure and Social Cognition." *Social Psychological Quarterly* 53, no. 2 (1990): 148–64.

Morris, Ian. *Why the West Rules—for Now: The Patterns of History, and What They Reveal about the Future*. New York: Farrar, Straus and Giroux, 2010.

Moscovici, Serge. "Notes towards a Description of Social Representations." *European Journal of Social Psychology* 18, no. 3 (1988): 211–50.

Mozaffari, Mehdi. "What Is Islamism? History and Definition of a Concept." *Totalitarian Movements and Political Religions* 8, no. 1 (March 2007): 17–33.

Mullins, Willard A. "On the Concept of Ideology in Political Science." *American Political Science Review* 66, no. 2 (June 1972): 498–510.

Murillo, M. Victoria. "From Populism to Neoliberalism: Labor Unions and Market Reforms in Latin America." *World Politics* 52, no. 2 (2000): 135–68.

Murtazashvili, Jennifer Brick. *Informal Order and the State in Afghanistan*. New York: Cambridge University Press, 2016.

Nagel, Thomas. *The View from Nowhere*. New York: Oxford University Press, 1989.

Narodnyi Kongress Kyrgyzstana. "Obrashchenie k Kongressu Soedinennykh Shtatov Ameriki." *Respublika* 44, no. 448 (11 December 2001): 3.

Nasr, Seyyed Vali Reza. "The Rise of 'Muslim Democracy.'" *Journal of Democracy* 16, no. 2 (2005): 13–27.

Nasyrkhanov, Burkitbai Sh. Comments at press conference entitled "O sotsial'no-ekonomicheskom polozhenii gorniakov na predpriiiatiiakh korporatsii 'Kazakhmys.'" Almaty, Kazakhstan, 15 January 2007.

———. "Obrashchenie k sootechestvennikam." *Zona.kz*, 2 March 2007. https://zona kz.net/2007/03/02/обращение-к-соотечественникам.

Naumkin, Vitalii Viacheslavovich. *Radical Islam in Central Asia: Between Pen and Rifle*. Latham, MD: Rowman & Littlefield, 2005.

Nazarov, Andrei, and Mukhammad Ashurali-ugli. "Vystupaia pered zhurnalistami, uzbekskii senator podverg SShA zhestkoi kritike." Ferghana.ru, 21 February 2005. https://www.fergananews.com/articles/3482.

Nazpary, Joma. *Post-Soviet Chaos: Violence and Dispossession in Kazakhstan*. London: Pluto Press, 2001.

Neef, Christian. "An Islamist Uprising." *Der Spiegel* Online International. Reprinted in *Tajikistan Times* 45, no. 82 (10 November 2010): 11.

Nesterova, Svetlana. "V SShA vozmozhen konstitutsionnyi krizis." *Respublika* 26, no. 398 (14 November 2000): 10.

"Nikakoi on ne Dzhefferson: Tsentral'naia Aziia prevratilas' v tsidatel' avtoritarizma." *Respublika* 26, no. 398 (14 November 2000): 13.

Noelle-Neumann, Elisabeth. "The Spiral of Silence: A Theory of Public Opinion." *Journal of Communication* 24, no. 2 (June 1974): 43–51.

Nolan, Mary. "Anti-Americanism and Americanization in Germany." *Politics & Society* 33, no. 1 (March 2005): 88–122.

Norrlof, Carla. *America's Global Advantage: US Hegemony and International Cooperation*. New York: Cambridge University Press, 2010.

Northrop, Douglas. *Veiled Empire: Gender and Power in Stalinist Central Asia*. Ithaca, NY: Cornell University Press, 2004.

"Novye standarty fizpodgotovki vvodit armia SShA." *Narodnoe slovo* 1787 (6 January 1998): 3.

Nurgozhin, Marat. "Tengizskaia odisseia amerikanskoi akuly." *Delovaia nedelia*, 31 July 1998: 1.

Nye, Joseph. *Soft Power: The Means to Success in World Politics*. New York: Public Affairs, 2009.

Obiya, Chika. "The Basmachi Movement as a Mirror of Central Asian Society in the Revolutionary Period." In *Social Protests and Nation-Building in the Middle East and Central Asia*, edited by Keiko Sakai, 88–104. IDE Development Perspective Series no. 1. Chiba, Japan: Institute of Developing Economies, JETRO, 2003.

Office of Research, U.S. Department of State. "Kazakhstan Elites Supportive of Campaign Against Terrorism Early On." *Kazakhstan Opinion Alert*, 30 October 2001.

Office of Research and Media Reaction, United States Information Agency. "Islam Yes, Islamic State No for Muslim Kazakhstanis." *Opinion Analysis*, 24 December 1997.

———. "'Islamization' Is Gradual in Uzbekistan." *Opinion Analysis*, 8 March 1996.

Oh, Wei Nam. *Defusing Anti-Americanism in South Korea: The Practice of U.S. Public Diplomacy*. Case #272. Pew Case Studies in International Affairs. Washington, DC: Institute for the Study of Diplomacy, Georgetown University, 2004.

"Oil Workers in Western Kazakhstan Prosecuted for 'Illegal' Hunger Strike." *Times of Central Asia*, 24 January 2017.

Okruhlik, Gwenn. "Empowering Civility through Nationalism: Reformist Islam and Belonging in Saudi Arabia." In *Remaking Muslim Politics: Pluralism, Contestation, Democratization*, edited by Robert Hefner, 189–212. Princeton, NJ: Princeton University Press, 2005.

Olcott, Martha Brill. *Roots of Radical Islam in Central Asia*. Carnegie Papers no. 77. Washington, DC: Carnegie Endowment for International Peace, January 2007. http://carnegieendowment.org/files/cp_77_olcott_roots_final.pdf.

Olcott, Martha Brill, and Bakhtiyar Babajanov. "The Terrorist Notebooks." *Foreign Policy* 135 (March-April 2003): 30–40.

Oliker, Olga, and David A. Shlapak. *US Interests in Central Asia: Policy Priorities and Military Roles*. Santa Monica, CA: RAND Corporation, 2005.

Olimova, Saodat. "Islam and Construction of a National State in Central Asia: Islamic Movement in Tajikistan." In *Social Protests and Nation-Building in the Middle East and Central Asia*, edited by Keiko Sakai, 173–80. Chiba, Japan: Institute of Developing Economies, 2003.
———. "Opposition in Tajikistan: Pro et Contra." In *Democracy and Pluralism in Muslim Eurasia*, edited by Yaakov Ro'i, 245–63. London and New York: Frank Cass, 2004.
Olimova, Saodat, and Muzaffar Olimov. "The Islamic Revival Party of Tajikistan in the Context of the Tajik Conflict and Its Settlement." *Central Asia and the Caucasus* 1, no. 7 (2001): 113–21.
Olson, Mancur. *The Logic of Collective Action: Public Goods and the Theory of Groups*. Cambridge, MA: Harvard University Press, 1965.
Omelicheva, Mariya Y. *Counterterrorism Policies in Central Asia*. London and New York: Routledge, 2011.
Omuraliev, N. "Stanovlenie grazhdanskogo obshchestva v Kyrgyzstane." In *Grazhdanskoe obshchestva v Kyrgyzstane: Sbornik statei*, edited by E. A. Voronina, 11–29. Bishkek: Mezhdunarodnyi Tsentr Interbilim, 2003.
Ongarbaeva, Gul'mira, and Anton Sel'nitskii. "Ugol'nye razrezy Ekibastuza stali polem bitvy." *Novoe pokolenie*, 31 July 1998: 1.
"Opposition Party Refuses to Print Independent Publications." *Tajikistan Times* 45, no. 82 (10 November 2010): 3.
"Oppozitsiia KR podpisala memorandum dlia vykhoda iz krizisa upravleniia gosudarstvom." *Aki-Press*, 3 November 2008. http://kg.akipress.org/news:63527?f=cp.
Oreshnikova, Ol'ga. "Golodovka poka ne ob'iavlena: Na obrashchenie rabochikh Zhezkazganskogo medeplaveil'nogo zavoda ne otreagirovali ni profsoiuz, ni deputat." *Respublika*, 8 June 2001. Accessed 1 September 2017. http://www.kub.info/respublika.php?sid=17944.
OSCE Office for Democratic Institutions and Human Rights. *Kyrgyz Republic Parliamentary Elections: 20 February and 12 March 2000*. Final report. Warsaw: Organization for Security and Co-operation in Europe, 10 April 2000. http://www.osce.org/odihr/elections/kyrgyzstan/15803?download=true.
Ostonov, O., Zh. Razzoqov, and R. Shoghulomov. *Fevral' vokealari: 1999 iil 16 fevral'*. Tashkent: Uzbekiston, 1999.
Ottaway, Marina, and Thomas Carothers, eds. *Funding Virtue: Civil Society Aid and Democracy Promotion*. Washington, DC: Carnegie Endowment for International Peace, 2000.
Oushakine, Serguei Alex. *The Patriotism of Despair: Nation, War, and Loss in Russia*. Ithaca, NY: Cornell University Press, 2009.
Pachirat, Timothy. *Every Twelve Seconds: Industrialized Slaughter and the Politics of Sight*. New Haven, CT: Yale University Press, 2011.
Parkanskii, A. B. "Budjet saiasatynyng aimaqtyq qubylnamalary: AQSh pen Resei tajiribesi." *Saiasat* 2, no. 9 (February 1996): 62–71.

Pavlovskii, Gleb. *Kirgizskii Perevorot: Mart-aprel' 2005*. Moskva: Izdatel'stvo "Evropa," 2005.

Payne, Matthew J. *Stalin's Railroad: Turksib and the Building of Socialism*. Pittsburgh: University of Pittsburgh Press, 2001.

Paz, Reuven. "Islamists and Anti-Americanism." *Middle East Review of International Affairs* 7, no. 4 (December 2003): 53–61.

Pelkmans, Mathijs. "'Culture' as a Tool and an Obstacle: Missionary Encounters in Post-Soviet Kyrgyzstan." *Journal of the Royal Anthropological Institute* 13, no. 4 (2007): 881–99.

———. "The 'Transparency' of Christian Proselytizing in Kyrgyzstan." *Anthropological Quarterly* 82, no. 2 (2009): 423–45.

Philpott, Daniel. "The Catholic Wave." *Journal of Democracy* 15, no. 2 (2004): 32–46.

Pierson, Paul. *Politics in Time: History, Institutions, and Social Analysis*. Princeton, NJ: Princeton University Press, 2004.

Pilon, Juliana Geran. *Why America Is Such a Hard Sell: Beyond Pride and Prejudice*. Lanham, MD: Rowman & Littlefield, 2007.

Pipes, Daniel. *Militant Islam Reaches America*. New York: W. W. Norton, 2003.

Polanyi, Michael. *The Tacit Dimension*. New York: Anchor Books, 1967.

Poliakov, Sergei P. *Everyday Islam: Religion and Tradition in Rural Central Asia*. Edited by Martha Brill Olcott. Translated by Anthony Olcott. Armonk, NY: M. E. Sharpe, 1992.

Pomfret, Richard. *The Central Asian Economies in the Twenty-First Century: Paving a New Silk Road*. Princeton, NJ: Princeton University Press, 2019.

———. *The Central Asian Economies since Independence*. Princeton, NJ: Princeton University Press, 2006.

Pope Pius IX. "Quanta Cura: Condemning Recent Errors." Papal Encyclicals Online, 8 December 1864. http://www.papalencyclicals.net/Pius09/p9quanta.htm.

"Pravitel'stvo Soedinennykh Shtatov oprovergaet sdelannye ministrom Medvedevym zaiiavleniia." *Panorama* 27 (9 July 1994): 12.

Privatsky, Bruce. *Muslim Turkistan: Kazak Religion and Collective Memory*. London and New York: Routledge, 2001.

Purvis, Trevor, and Alan Hunt. "Discourse, Ideology, Discourse, Ideology, Discourse, Ideology." *British Journal of Sociology* 44, no. 3 (September 1993): 473–99.

Putnam, Hilary. *The Collapse of the Fact/Value Dichotomy and Other Essays*. Cambridge, MA: Harvard University Press, 2002.

Qutb, Sayyid. *Milestones*. CreateSpace, 2005. http://www.izharudeen.com/uploads/4/1/2/2/4122615/milestones_www.izharudeen.com.pdf.

———. *The Religion of the Future*. Delhi: Markazi Maktaba Islam, 1990.

Radio Azattyq. "Delo o zabastovke bliz Ural'ska ostalos' bez rassmotreniia." 4 August 2015. https://rus.azattyq.org/a/27169254.html.

Radio Free Europe / Radio Liberty. "Anti-American Books among Russia's Best-Sellers." *Newsline*, 6 June 2003. https://www.rferl.org/a/1142931.html.

———. "Central Asian Popular Support for America May Be Shaky." *Central Asia Report* 1, no. 15 (1 November 2001).

———. "Kyrgyz President Won't Back Down, As Opposition Claims Power." 8 April 2010. https://www.rferl.org/a/Kyrgyz_Opposition_Claims_Power_Vows_To_Investigate_Bakievs_Rule/2006140.html.

———. "Striking Kazakh Oil Workers Quit Ruling Party." 11 August 2011. https://www.rferl.org/a/striking_kazakh_oil_workers_quit_ruling_party/24294248.html.

———. "Ukrainian Radical Nationalists See Attacks on U.S. as 'Moral Satisfaction.'" *Newsline*, 13 September 2001. http://www.rferl.org/content/article/1142484.html.

Radnitz, Scott. "The Color of Money: Privatization, Economic Dispersion, and the Post-Soviet 'Revolutions.'" *Comparative Politics* 42, no. 2 (2010): 127–46.

———. "Power, Peripheries, and Pyramids in Post-Soviet Kyrgyzstan and Georgia." In *Paradox of Power: The Logics of State Weakness in Eurasia*, edited by John Heathershaw and Edward Schatz, 44–59. Pittsburgh: University of Pittsburgh Press, 2017.

———. *Weapons of the Wealthy: Predatory Regimes and Elite-Led Protests in Central Asia*. Ithaca, NY: Cornell University Press, 2010.

Radnitz, Scott, and Patrick Underwood. "Is Belief in Conspiracy Theories Pathological? A Survey Experiment on the Cognitive Roots of Extreme Suspicion." *British Journal of Political Science* 47, no. 1 (2017): 113–29.

Rasanayagam, Johan. *Islam in Post-Soviet Uzbekistan: The Morality of Experience*. New York: Cambridge University Press, 2011.

Rashid, Ahmed. *Jihad: The Rise of Militant Islam in Central Asia*. New Haven, CT: Yale University Press, 2002.

———. "They're Only Sleeping." *New Yorker*, 14 January 2002. http://www.newyorker.com/magazine/2002/01/14/theyre-only-sleeping.

Razumov, Iaroslav. "Rukovoditeli energeticheskikh kompanii, gosstruktur i dippredstavitel'sv obsudili puti dal'neishego reformirovaniia otrasli." *Panorama* 33 (28 August 1998): 8.

Reiter, Herbert, with Massimiliano Andretta, Donatella Della Porta, and Lorenzo Mosca. "The Global Justice Movement in Italy." In *Global Justice Movement: Cross-national and Transnational Perspectives*, edited by Della Porta et al., 52–78. Boulder, CO: Paradigm Publishers, 2007.

Revel, Jean François, *Anti-Americanism*. New York: Encounter Books, 2003.

RFE/RL Kazakh Service. "Kazakh Authorities Jail Rights Activist Representing Zhanaozen Victims." Radio Free Europe / Radio Liberty, 7 December 2012. https://www.rferl.org/a/kazakhstan-rights-zhanaozen-victims-lawyer-jailed/24791902.html.

———. "Kazakh Oil-Industry Workers on Strike for Pay Raise." Radio Free Europe/Radio Liberty, 7 May 2018. https://www.rferl.org/a/kazakhstan-oil-industry-workers-on-strike-for-pay-rise/29213790.html.

Rivera, Sharon Werning, Polina M. Kozyreva, and Eduard G. Sarovskii. "Interviewing Political Elites: Lessons from Russia." *PS, Political Science & Politics* 35, no. 4 (2002): 683–88.

Rodrik, Dani. *Has Globalization Gone Too Far?* Washington, DC: Institute for International Economics, 1997.

Ro'i, Yaacov. "Central Asian Riots and Disturbances, 1989–1990: Causes and Context." *Central Asian Survey* 10, no. 3 (1991): 21–54.

Rollberg, Peter, and Marlene Laruelle. "The Media Landscape in Central Asia: Introduction to the Special Issue." *Demokratizatsiya: Journal of Post-Soviet Democratization* 23, no. 3 (Summer 2015): 227–32.

Rosenau, James N. *Turbulence in World Politics: A Theory of Change and Continuity.* Princeton, NJ: Princeton University Press, 2018.

Ross, Dorothy. *The Origins of American Social Science.* Cambridge and New York: Cambridge University Press, 1992.

Rotar, Igor. "The Islamic Movement of Uzbekistan: A Resurgent IMU?" *Terrorism Monitor* (Jamestown Foundation) 1, no. 8 (18 December 2003).

Rotar', Igor'. *Pod zelenym znamenem: Islamskie radikaly v Rossii i SNG.* Moscow: AIRO-XX, 2001.

———. "Tsentral'naia Aziia—sleduiushchaia mishen' ekstremistov," *Nezavisimaia gazeta*, 14 September 2001.

Roy, Olivier. *The Foreign Policy of the Central Asian Islamic Renaissance Party.* New York: Council on Foreign Relations, 2000.

———. *Islam and Resistance in Afghanistan.* Cambridge: Cambridge University Press, 1990.

Rubin, Barry. "Welcome to the Islamist Middle East and It's Not Going to Be Moderate." *Rubin Reports*, 25 October 2011. http://rubinreports.blogspot.com/2011/10/welcome-to-islamist-middle-east-and-its.html.

Ruble, Blair A. *Soviet Trade Unions: Their Development in the 1970s.* Cambridge: Cambridge University Press, 1981.

Sadowski, Yahya. "Political Islam: Asking the Wrong Questions?" *Annual Review of Political Science* 9 (2006): 215–40.

Sagdeev, Roald, and Susan Eisenhower. *Islam and Central Asia: An Enduring Legacy or an Evolving Threat?* Washington, DC: Center for Political and Strategic Studies, 2000.

Sahadeo, Jeff. "Epidemic and Empire: Ethnicity, Class, and 'Civilization' in the 1892 Tashkent Cholera Riot." *Slavic Review* 64, no. 1 (Spring 2005): 117–39.

Salmorbekova, Zumrat, and Galina Yemelianova. "Islam and Islamism in the Ferghana Valley." In *Radical Islam in the Former Soviet Union*, edited by Galina Yemelianova, 211–43. London and New York: Routledge, 2010.

Sanders, Barry A. *American Avatar: The United States in the Global Imagination.* Washington, DC: Potomac Books, 2011.

Saralieva, Leila. "Kyrgyzstan: osobennosti mestnoi zhurnalistiki." *Tribuna* 7, no. 36 (2 October 2003).

Satpayev, Dossym, and Tolganay Umbetaliyeva. "The Protests in Zhanaozen and the Kazakh Oil Sector: Conflicting Interests in a Rentier State." *Journal of Eurasian Studies* 6, no. 2 (2015): 122-29.

Sattori, Kiemiddin. "Tajik Press about the Youth and Islam." *Central Asia and the Caucasus* (2002): 126-34.

Satybalieva, Elmira. "Why Class Matters in Kyrgyzstan." In *Kyrgyzstan beyond "Democracy Island" and "Failing State,"* edited by Marlene Laruelle and Johan Engvall, 99-122. Lanham, MD: Lexington Books, 2015.

Saussure, Ferdinand de. *Course in General Linguistics.* Translated by Wade Baskin. Edited by Charles Bally and Albert Sechehaye in collaboration with Albert Reidlinger. London: Fontana, 1974.

Savin, Igor. "Ethnic and Confessional Situation in Southern Kazakhstan and Major Regional Challenges." *Central Asia and the Caucasus* 3, no. 9 (2001): 131-37.

———. "'Khizb ut-Takhrir' v Iuzhnom Kazakhstane: sotsial'nyi portret iavleniia." *TsentrAziia*, 28 December 2002.

———. "Religioznyi ekstremizm v Kazakhstane," *Biulleten': Set' etnologicheskogo monitoringa* 37 (2001): 75-77. Reprinted in *Rossiia i musul'manskii mir* 3 (2002): 63-66.

Schaffer, Frederic Charles. "Ordinary Language Interviewing." In *Interpretation and Method*, edited by Dvora Yanow and Peregerine Schwartz-Shea, 183-93. Armonk, NY: M. E. Sharp, 2006.

Schatz, Edward. "Access by Accident: Legitimacy Claims and Democracy Promotion in Authoritarian Central Asia." *International Political Science Review* 27, no. 3 (2006): 263-84.

———. "How Western Disengagement Enabled Uzbekistan's 'Spring' and How to Keep It Going." Program on New Approaches to Research and Security (PONARS) in Eurasia, Policy Memo no. 531, June 2018. http://www.ponarseurasia.org/memo/how-western-disengagement-enabled-uzbekistans-spring-and-how-keep-it-going.

———. "Islamism and Anti-Americanism in Central Asia." *Current History* 101, no. 657 (October 2002): 337-43.

———. *Modern Clan Politics: The Power of "Blood" in Kazakhstan and Beyond.* Seattle and London: University of Washington Press, 2004.

———. "Notes on the 'Dog That Didn't Bark': Eco-Internationalism in Late Soviet Kazakhstan." *Ethnic and Racial Studies* 22, no. 1 (1999): 136-61.

———, ed. *Political Ethnography: What Immersion Contributes to the Study of Power.* Chicago and London: University of Chicago Press, 2009.

———. "Proactive Policymaking and Leninism's Long Shadow in Central Asia." In *Multi-Nation States in Asia*, edited by Jacques Bertrand and André Laliberté, 244-62. New York: Cambridge University Press, 2010.

———. "The Soft Authoritarian 'Tool Kit': Agenda-Setting Power in Kazakhstan and Kyrgyzstan." *Comparative Politics* 41, no. 2 (2009): 203-22.

———. "Transnational Image Making and Soft Authoritarian Kazakhstan." *Slavic Review* 67, no. 1 (Spring 2008): 50-62.

———. "Understanding Anti-Americanism in Central Asia." In *Global Perspectives on the United States: Pro-Americanism, Anti-Americanism, and the Discourses Between*, edited by Virginia R. Domínguez and Jane C. Desmond, 131–51. Champaign: University of Illinois Press, 2017.

———. "What Capital Cities Say about State and Nation Building." *Nationalism and Ethnic Politics* 9, no. 4 (2004): 111–40.

Schatz, Edward, and Elena Maltseva. "Assumed to Be Universal: The Leap from Data to Knowledge in the *American Political Science Review*." *Polity* 44, no. 3 (July 2012): 446–72.

Schatz, Edward, and Renan Levine. 2010. "Framing, Public Diplomacy, and Anti-Americanism in Central Asia." *International Studies Quarterly* 54 (2010): 855–69.

Schatzberg, Michael. *Political Legitimacy in Middle Africa: Father, Family, Food*. Bloomington: Indiana University Press, 2001.

Schmidt, Vivien A. "Reconciling Ideas and Institutions through Discursive Institutionalism." In *Ideas and Politics in Social Science Research*, edited by Daniel Beland and Robert Henry Cox, 47–64. New York: Oxford University Press, 2011.

Schwab, Wendell. "Establishing an Islamic Niche in Kazakhstan: Musylman Publishing House and Its Publications." *Central Asian Survey* 30, no. 2 (2011): 227–42.

Schwedler, Jillian. *Faith in Moderation: Islamist Parties in Jordan and Yemen*. Cambridge and New York: Cambridge University Press, 2006.

Scott, James C. *Weapons of the Weak: Everyday Forms of Peasant Resistance*. New Haven, CT: Yale University Press, 1985.

Sears, David O. "Symbolic Politics: A Socio-Psychological Theory." In *Explorations in Political Psychology*, edited by Shanto Iyengar and William J. McGuire, 113–49. Durham, NC: Duke University Press, 1993.

Sears, David O. "The Role of Affect in Symbolic Politics." In *Citizens and Politics: Perspectives from Political Psychology*, edited by James H. Kuklinski, 14–40. New York: Cambridge University Press, 2001.

Seleny, Anna. "Tradition, Modernity, and Democracy: The Many Promises of Islam," *Perspectives on Politics* 4, no. 3 (2006): 481–94.

Sergiienko, Vladimir. "'Politicheskii islam' v tsentral'noi zii: prizrachnaia ili real'naia?" *Kontinent*, 19 April–2 May 2000: 22–25.

Seroshtanova, Tat'iana. "Kazakhmys khochet obespechit' syr'em Irtyshskii medzavod v techenie avgusta." *Reuters*, 6 August 2002. https://kase.kz/ru/news/show/103420/.

Shaheen, Jack G. "Reel Bad Arabs: How Hollywood Vilifies a People." *Annals of the American Academy of Political and Social Science* 588, no. 1 (July 2003): 171–93.

Shaikenov, N. A. "Problemy Kazakhstanskoi gosudarstvennosti." *Saiasat* 10, no. 17 (3–11 October 1996).

Shalinsky, Aidrey. "Ethnic Reactions to the Current Regime in Afghanistan." *Central Asian Survey* 3, no. 4 (1984): 49–60.

Shapiro, Michael. "Textualizing Global Politics." In *International/Intertextual Relations: Postmodern Readings of World Politics*, edited by James Der Derian and Michael Shapiro, 11–22. Lexington, MA: Lexington Books, 1989.

Shlapentokh, Vladimir. "The Changeable Soviet Image of America." *Annals of the American Academy of Political and Social Science* 497, no. 1 (1998): 157–71.

Shorbaghy, Manar. "The Egyptian Movement For Change—Kefaya: Redefining Politics in Egypt." *Public Culture* 19, no. 1 (2007): 175–96.

Shumkin, Pavel. Unpublished personal memoirs. Karaganda, Kazakhstan, n.d.

Sil, Rudra. "The Fluidity of Labor Relations in Post-Communist Transitions: Rethinking the Narrative of Russian Labor Quiescence." In *Political Creativity: Reconfiguring Institutional Order and Change*, edited by Gerald Berk, Dennis Galvan, and Victoria Hattam, 188–208. Philadelphia: University of Pennsylvania Press, 2013.

Sil, Rudra, and Peter J. Katzenstein. *Beyond Paradigms: Analytic Eclecticism in the Study of World Politics*. Basingstoke, UK: Palgrave Macmillan, 2010.

Simon, Herbert A. "A Behavioral Model of Rational Choice." *Quarterly Journal of Economics* 69 (1955): 99–118.

Singerman, Diane. "The Networked World of Islamist Social Movements." In *Islamic Activism: A Social Movement Theory Approach*, edited by Quintan Wiktorowicz, 143–63. Bloomington: Indiana University Press, 2004.

Slade, Gavin. "Punishment and State-Building in Post-Soviet Georgia." In *Paradox of Power: The Logics of State Weakness in Eurasia*, edited by John Heathershaw and Edward Schatz, 88–104. Pittsburgh: University of Pittsburgh Press, 2017.

Slater, Dan. "Democratic Careening." *World Politics* 65, no. 4 (2013): 729–63.

———. *Ordering Power: Contentious Politics and Authoritarian Leviathans in Southeast Asia*. New York: Cambridge University Press, 2010.

Smith, Christopher H. "Human Rights and Democracy in Kyrgyzstan." Opening statement, Hearing before the Commission on Security and Cooperation in Europe. 107th Congress, First Session. 12 December 2001. CSCE 107-1-8.

Snow, David A. and Robert Benford. "Master Frames and Cycles of Protest." In *Frontiers in Social Movement Theory*, edited by Aldon Morris and Carol McClurg Mueller, 133–223. New Haven, CT: Yale University Press, 1992.

Snow, David A., E. Burke Rochford, Jr., Steven K. Worden, and Robert D. Benford. "Frame Alignment Processes, Micromobilization, and Movement Participation." *American Sociological Review* 51, no. 4 (August 1986): 464–81.

Snyder, Robert. "Explaining the Iranian Revolution's Hostility toward the United States." *Journal of South Asian and Middle Eastern Studies* 17, no. 3 (Spring 1994): 19–31.

Spector, Regine A. *Order at the Bazaar: Power and Trade in Central Asia*. Ithaca, NY: Cornell University Press, 2017.

Stinchcombe, Arthur, L. "The Conditions of Fruitfulness of Theorizing about Mechanisms in Social Science." *Philosophy of the Social Sciences* 21, no. 3 (1991): 367–88.

Stronski, Paul. *Tashkent: Forging a Soviet City, 1930–1966.* Pittsburgh: University of Pittsburgh Press, 2010.
Sultangalieva, Alma. *Islam v Kazakhstane: istoriia, etnichnost', obschchestvo.* Almaty: Kazakhstanskii institut strategicheskikh issledovanii, 1998.
Svoik, Petr. "Kazakhstan i Rossiia: Byt' li v novom soiuze?" *Karavan,* 20 March 1998: 36–37.
Svolik, Milan W. *The Politics of Authoritarian Rule.* New York: Cambridge University Press, 2012.
Taji-Farouki, Suha. *A Fundamental Quest: Hizb al-Tahrir and the Search for the Islamic Caliphate.* London: Grey Seal, 1996.
Tarrow, Sydney. "Framing Collective Action." In *Power in Movement: Social Movements, Collective Action and Politics,* edited by Sydney Tarrow, 118–35. New York: Cambridge University Press, 1994.
———. *Power in Movement: Social Movements and Contentious Politics.* 2nd ed. New York: Cambridge University Press, 1998.
Tasar, Eren Murat. "Islamically Informed Soviet Patriotism in Postwar Kyrgyzstan." *Cahiers du monde russe* 52, no. 2 (2012): 387–404.
Taylor, Charles. "Interpretation and the Sciences of Man." *Review of Metaphysics* 25, no. 1 (September 1971): 3–15.
Tazhutov, Akhas. "Vozmozhen li islamskii renessans v Tsentral'noi Azii." *Megapolis,* 25 April 2002; 9.
Tchoroev, Tyntchtykbek. "Kyrgyz Political Circles Split On Manas Decision." Radio Free Europe / Radio Liberty, 9 February 2009. http://www.rferl.org/content/Kyrgyz_Political_Circles_Split_On_Manas_Decision/1467176.html.
Telhami, Shibley. "Why Do They Hate Us So Much?" Paper presented at Political Islam: Challenges for U.S. Policy, Aspen Institute, Washington, DC, 27 June–3 July 2003.
Tereshchenko, Sergei. "Kazakhmys nado sudit': Za izdevatel'stvo nad rabochimi." *TsentrAziia,* 10 May 2007. https://centrasia.org/newsA.php?st=1178744760.
Tessler, Mark. "Islam and Democracy in the Middle East: The Impact of Religious Orientations on Attitudes toward Democracy in Four Arab Countries." *Comparative Politics* 34 (April 2002): 337–54.
Thelen, Kathleen. "Historical Institutionalism in Comparative Politics." *Annual Review of Political Science* 2, no. 1 (1999): 369–404.
Tilly, Charles. "Mechanisms in Political Processes." *Annual Review of Political Science* 4, no. 1 (2001): 21–41.
Trenin, Dmitri. "Russia Leaves the West." *Foreign Affairs* 85, no. 4 (July/August 2006): 87–96.
Trofimov, Iakov. "Gosudarstvo, obshchestvo i religiia v sovremennom Kazakhstane." *Rossiia i musul'manskii mir* 11 (2001): 86–95.
TsentrAziia. "'Da, my neprimirimaia oppozitsiia!' (vystuplenie lidera Rabochego dvizheniia Kazakhstana)." *TsentrAziia,* 9 December 2003. http://www.centrasia.org/newsA.php?st=1063386540.

Tucker, Joshua A. "Enough! Electoral Fraud, Collective Action Problems, and Postcommunist Colored Revolutions." *Perspectives on Politics* 5, no. 3 (2007): 535–51.

Tumanov, Konstantin. "The Tengiz Carnage: Some Details of the Scuffle in Kazakhstan." *Fergana News*, 11 November 2006. http://enews.fergananews.com/articles/1692.

Tungatarova, T. "Does the USA Really Threaten Central Asian Region?" *Central Asia's Affairs: Quarterly Analytic Review* 1, no. 5 (2004): 8–11.

Turajonzoda, A. *Sharia va jomea*. Dushanbe: Nodir, 2006.

Turajonzoda, Qadi Akbar. "Religion: The Pillar of Society." In *Central Asia: Conflict, Resolution, and Change*, edited by Roald Z. Sagdeev and Susan Eisenhower. Chevy Chase, MD: CPSS Press, 1995.

United Opposition. "Zaiavlenie shtaba po provedeniiu 29 aprelia mirnogo shestviia 'Demokraticheskie reformy dlia protsvetaniia Kyrgyzstana." *AKI-Press*, 18 April 2006. http://www.kg.akipress.org/news:27502.

Ushakov, V. N. *Politicheskii Islam v Tsentral'noi Azii*. Moscow and Bishkek: Izdatel'stvo KRSU, 2005.

Uyama, Tomohiko. "Why Are Social Protest Movements Weak in Central Asia?" In *Social Protests and Nation-Building in the Middle East and Central Asia*, edited by Keiko Sakai, 47–56. IDE Development Perspective Series No. 1. Chiba: Institute of Developing Economies, JETRO, 2003.

"Uzbek Islamic Movement: Government Must Go or Be Removed by Force." Voice of the Islamic Republic of Iran, BBC Worldwide Monitoring, 19 March 1999.

"Uzbek Paper Looks at Motives for Attacks on USA." *Times of Central Asia*, 27 September 2001.

"V Atyrau prishli vakhkhabity." *Novoe pokolenie*, 30 October 1998: 1.

Vanderhill, Rachel. "Limits on the Democratizing Influence of the Internet: Lessons from Post-Soviet States." *Demokratizatsiya: Journal of Post-Soviet Democratization* 23, no. 1 (2015): 31–56.

Vasilivetskii, Aleksei. *Prelomlenie: sobytiia 2010 goda v Kyrgyzstane glazami istorika i ochevidtsev*. Bishkek: Tipografiia OcOO Kirland, 2014.

Villalón, Leonardo. *Islamic Society and State Power in Senegal: Disciples and Citizens in Fatick*. New York: Cambridge University Press, 1995.

Walsh, Katherine Cramer. "Scholars as Citizens: Studying Public Opinion through Ethnography." In *Political Ethnography: What Immersion Contributes to the Study of Power*, edited by Edward Schatz, 165–82. Chicago: University of Chicago Press, 2009.

———. *Talking about Politics: Informal Groups and Social Identity in American Life*. Chicago and London: University of Chicago Press, 2004.

Ware, Robert Bruce. "Why Did Dagestan Reject Radical Islam?" Radio Free Europe/Radio Liberty. *Newsline* 6, no. 212, part 1 (12 November 2002).

Ware, Robert Bruce, and Enver Kisriev. "The Islamic Factor in Dagestan." *Central Asian Survey* 19, no. 2 (2000): 235–52.

Warkotsch, Alexander. "The OSCE as an Agent of Socialisation? International Norm Dynamics and Political Change in Central Asia." *Europe-Asia Studies* 59, no. 5 (2007): 829–46.

Weaver, Catherine. *Hypocrisy Trap: The World Bank and the Poverty of Reform.* Princeton, NJ: Princeton University Press, 2008.

Wedeen, Lisa. *Ambiguities of Domination: Politics, Rhetoric, and Symbols in Contemporary Syria.* Chicago: University of Chicago Press, 1999.

———. "Conceptualizing Culture: Possibilities for Political Science." *American Political Science Review* 96, no.4 (2002): 713–28.

———. *Peripheral Visions: Politics, Power, and Performance in Yemen.* Chicago: University of Chicago Press, 2008.

Wegner, Eva, and Miquel Pellicer. "Islamist Moderation without Democratization: The Coming of Age of the Moroccan Party of Justice and Development?" *Democratization* 16, no. 1 (2009): 157–75.

Wickham, Carrie Rosefsky. "The Path to Moderation: Strategy and Learning in the Formation of Egypt's Wasat Party." *Comparative Politics* 36, no. 2 (2004): 205–28.

Wiktorowicz, Quintan, ed. *Islamic Activism: A Social Movement Theory Approach.* Bloomington and Indianapolis: Indiana University Press, 2003.

———. "The New Global Threat: Transnational Salamis and Jihad." *Middle East Policy* 8, no. 4 (December 2001): 18–38.

———. *Radical Islam Rising: Muslim Extremism in the West.* Lanham, MD: Rowman & Littlefield, 2005.

Wilkinson, Cai. "LGBT Activism in Kyrgyzstan: What Role for Europe?" In *LGBT Activism and the Making of Europe*, edited by Phillip Ayoub and David Paternotte, 50–72. London: Palgrave Macmillan, 2014.

World Bank. "Jobs." Databank. Last accessed 30 August 2018. http://databank.worldbank.org/data/reports.aspx?source=jobs.

———. "World Development Indicators." Databank. Last accessed 6 September 2018. http://databank.worldbank.org/data/source/world-development-indicators#.

Yanow, Dvora, and Peregrine Schwartz-Shea, eds. *Interpretation and Method: Empirical Research Methods and the Interpretive Turn.* New York: Routledge, 2015.

Yashar, Deborah J. "Review Article: Globalization and Collective Action." *Comparative Politics*, April 2002: 355–75.

Yavuz, M. Hakan. *Secularism and Muslim Democracy in Turkey.* Cambridge Middle East Studies, vol. 28. Cambridge: Cambridge University Press, 2009.

Yee, Albert S. "The Causal Effects of Ideas on Policies." *International Organization* 50, no. 1 (Winter 1996): 69–108.

Yemelianova, Galina, ed. *Radical Islam in the Former Soviet Union.* London and New York: Routledge, 2010.

Yessenova, Saulesh. "Tengiz Crude: A View from Below." In *The Economics and Politics of Oil in the Caspian Basin: The Redistribution of Oil Revenues in Azerbaijan and Central Asia*, edited by Boris Najman, Richard Pomfret, and Gäel Raballand, 176–98. New York: Routledge, 2008.

Yurchak, Alexei. *Everything Was Forever, Until It Was No More: The Last Soviet Generation*. Princeton, NJ, and Oxford: Princeton University Press, 2005.

Zakaria, Fareed. *The Post-American World*. New York: W. W. Norton, 2008.

Zaldívar, Carlos Alonso. "Miradas torcidas. Percepciones mutuas entre España y Estados Unidos." *Real Instituto Elcano* 4 (September 2003). http://www.realinstituto elcano.org/documents/imprimir/60imp.asp.

Zaller, John R. *The Nature and Origins of Mass Opinion*. New York: Cambridge University Press, 1992.

Zaman, Muhammad Qasim. "Pluralism, Democracy, and the 'Ulama." In *Remaking Muslim Politics: Pluralism, Contestation, Democratization*, edited by Robert W. Hefner, 64–86. Princeton, NJ: Princeton University Press, 2004.

———. *The Ulama in Contemporary Islam: Custodians of Change*. Princeton, NJ: Princeton University Press, 2010.

Zeelenberg, Marcel, Rob M. A. Nelissen, Seger M. Breugelmans, and Rik Pieters. "On Emotion Specificity in Decision Making: Why Feeling Is for Doing." *Judgment and Decision Making* 3, no. 1 (January 2008): 18–27.

Zemir, Seki. "Artistic Creativity and the Brain." *Science* 293, no. 6 (July 2001): 51–52.

Zhakypova, Chinara, and Tolekan Ismailova. "Vlast' i grazhdanskii sektor: obrashschenie predstavitelei grazhdanskogo sektora." Open letter, 2002. http://journalist.kg/monitoring/iyun-2002-g/ [last accessed: February 29, 2016].

Zhou, Yihuang. *China's Diplomacy*. Beijing: China Intercontinental Press, 2004.

Zhovtis, Yevgeniy. "Ob urokakh Zhanaozena." Text prepared for a roundtable, 2 January 2013. https://zhanaozen1216.wordpress.com/2013/01/02/02-01-2013-евгений-жовтис-об-уроках-жанаозена-evg/.

INDEX

Abu Ghraib prison, 85
Adolat, 60–61, 162
Afghanistan, 7, 9, 13, 45, 52, 55, 60, 80; Uzbeks in, 25–26; Tajiks in, 25. *See also* Soviet-Afghan War
Ahmadinejad, Mahmoud, 3
Akaev, Askar, 32, 46, 67, 68–76, 85
Ak Jol Party, 76
Aksy events, 74, 77
Aliev, Emil, 167n34,42
America. *See* United States; symbolic America; anti-Americanism; pro-Americanism
analytic eclecticism, 125–27, 134–35
anti-Americanism, 6, 9; defined, viii, 3–5, 116; impact of, viii, ix, 2–3, 116; resources for, 9. *See also* sedimentation; symbolic America
anti-globalism, 39, 46
anti-Semitism, 46, 129
anti-Westernism, ix, 46, 151n81, 163n129
Arab uprisings, 4
Ar-Namys Party, 76
atheism, 43–44, 49, 54. *See also* secularism; Soviet Union
Austin, J. L., 23
authoritarianism, viii, 4, 6, 32, 36, 43, 93, 110; in Kazakhstan, 104–5; in Kyrgyzstan, 68–76, 80, 83, 85–86; secular, 115; social movements under, 11–17, 49, 50, 53, 64; soft, 93, 95, 98, 99, 102

Bakiev, Kurmanbek, vii, 67, 70, 73–78, 85
Bakiev, Maksim, 77
Baku-Ceyhan pipeline, 38

Belt and Road Initiative (BRI), 111
Beshimov, Bakhyt, 69
Black Lives Matter movement, 11
broad-cast movements, 16–17, 59, 86, 113–14
Bush, George W., 2, 30, 66, 72, 75, 117–19, 134; on perceptions of the United States, 117–19. *See also* Bush effect
Bush effect, 119–21; defined, 12–13. *See also* frame-bridging

caliphate, 12, 42, 48–51
Canada, x, 3, 84
capitalism, 21, 31, 32, 50, 103, 107–10; crony, 95
case selection, x, 1–3, 10, 14, 18, 135–36. *See also* negative case
Castro, Fidel, 2, 11
categories, marked vs. unmarked, 16–17, 39
Central Asia: distinctiveness of, 26; economic and labor conditions in, 91–95; global importance of, 13–14, 20; labor in, 89
Chávez, Hugo, 2–3
China, 13, 37, 101, 106, 110–11, 116, 123
Clinton, Bill, 69
color revolutions, 70
conspiracy theories, 30–31, 71, 83, 129
Cooperative Threat Reduction, 28
corruption, 32, 65, 76–78, 102, 104, 106
credibility of messenger, 112, 119–22

Dagestan, 65
democracy, 4, 9, 11, 54–55, 59, 106, 109, 114; disappointment with, 33, 78; in

democracy (*continued*)
  Kyrgyzstan, 68–78, 85; liberal, 17, 58, 85; promotion of, *see under* United States
democratization, 11, 14, 107
Dostum, Rashid, 26
doubling, 22–23

Egypt, 9–10
election monitoring, 69
environmental activism, 12, 31, 110, 123
ethnic relations, 26, 46, 100–101, 115, 133
ethnographic methods, 32, 125–30, 136
Europe, role in Central Asia, 14, 37, 58, 106
expert fatigue, 33, 110

financial crisis of 2008–2009, 98
focus groups, 56, 66–67, 118–20, 126, 130–33, 136
frames, 8, 10–18, 47, 60–62, 65, 67, 73, 103, 107, 113, 118–22; diagnostic, 103, 130; motivational, 103, 106, 130; prognostic, 103–5, 130. *See also* framing; master frames
frame amplification, 13, 60
frame bridging, 13
framing, 9–18, 46, 65, 78, 86, 88, 99, 103–13, 116, 130; effects, 119–20, 133; experiment, 119; types, 103. *See also* frame bridging; public diplomacy
France, 3
Fujii, Lee Ann, 129

Georgia, 36–38, 67, 70
Germany, 3
global justice movement, 109
Glubokoe, Kazakhstan, 100, 108
Guantanamo prison, 85

Hanafism, 43–44, 54, 64. *See also* Islam
Hanbalism, 42. *See also* Islam
Hatfield, Zachary, vii
high politics, 3–4
Hizb ut-Tahrir, 13, 17, 41, 58, 84, 113–14, 129; framing strategies of, 50–53; organization of, 47; origins of, 42, 47–48; popular appeal of, 48–50

human rights activism, 17–18, 32, 58, 65, 67–69, 73–78, 79–80, 83, 85–87, 115. *See also* professionalized advocates; street protests

images. *See* symbols
informal economy, 91–95, 105
interethnic relations, 100
International Labour Organization, 90, 93
interview methods, 129–30
Iran, 13, 37, 55–57, 62, 66, 112; revolution of 1979, 2. *See also* Ahmadinejad, Mahmoud
Iraq, 66
Iraq War, 16, 50, 57, 67, 72–73, 85, 114
Islam: diversity within, 41; global resurgence of, 43; piety, 15, 40–45, 55; practices, 24, 46, 52; quietism in, 24, 40; state responses to, 24, 64; theological debates within, 41, 44, 64–65; "underground," 24, 44
Islamic Movement of Uzbekistan, 13, 17, 25, 29, 41–42, 113; framing strategies of, 60, 62, 64; organization of, 61; origins of, 45, 60; popular appeal of, 62, 63; terrorist acts, 63
Islamic Renaissance Party of Tajikistan, 17; declared a terrorist organization, 53; electoral results, 45, 55; framing strategies, 42, 58, 60, 113–14; origins of, 53–54; popular appeal of, 55
Islamism, 17–18, 40, 65; defined, 41–42; emergence in Central Asia, 43, 46. *See also* Hizb ut-Tahrir; Islamic Movement of Uzbekistan; Islamic Renaissance Party of Tajikistan
Ismailova, Tolekan, 73
Israel, 30, 48, 51, 61–62

journalism, 72, 76–78, 101, 128

Kabiri, Muhiddin, 58–59
Karaganda, Kazakhstan, 96, 99, 104, 107
Karimov, Islam, 30, 42, 45–46, 51, 60–62, 64, 68, 115

Karshi-Khanabad, vii
Katzenstein, Peter, 2–4, 125, 135
Kazakhstan: economic conditions in, 32, 92, 94–95, 98; media in, 31, 36, 38; nuclear testing in, 31; nuclear weapons removed from, 28; oil sector in, 97, 100; public opinion in, 28, 30, 33, 64; social media in, 38
Kefaya, 9
Keohane, Robert, 2–4
Kosovo, 13, 16, 29, 37
Kulov, Feliks, 69, 73
Kumtor mine, 102
Kurmanov, Ainur, 104–5
Kyrgyzstan: economic conditions in, 91–95; foreign aid, 68; media in, 36, 72. *See also* Manas Air Base

labor: codes, 94, 97, 99; incorporation, 89; movements, 91, 97; relations, 94, 98–102, 105; unions, independent, 98; unions, state-sponsored, 90; unrest, 90, 101–2
Latin America, 2–3, 9, 20, 89, 145, 164n1, 170n2, 172n36
legal system, 83–84, 99
lend-lease program, 21
Leninabad, Tajikistan, 30
leverage, 71, 99
LGBTQ activism, 84
liberalism: economic, 15, 28, 90, 104, 109–10; political, 15–18, 27, 36, 42–43, 54–57, 68, 79–81, 85–86, 110. *See also* Kyrgyzstan; United States: hegemony
likbez, 105–6
linkage, 68, 71

Manas Air Base, vii, viii. *See also* Kyrgyzstan
Marx, Karl, 49, 89
master frames, 46, 50–51, 108–10, 116
McPherson, Alan, 3, 9
messenger credibility. *See* credibility of messenger
Mexico, 2. *See also* Latin America
Middle East, 13, 20, 24, 37, 48, 65. *See also* Arab uprisings; *individual countries*

migration, 119; labor, 9, 58, 99. *See also* remittances
missionaries, religious, 39
Moscovici, Serge, 7
muftiates, 64–65
multipolarity, 4, 123

Namangani, Juma, 45, 60–63
narrow-cast movements, 13, 16–17, 59, 86, 113. *See also* frame amplification
nationalism: economic, 31, 109; in Central Asia, 10, 37, 39, 44, 51
Nazarbaev, Nursultan, 46, 65, 85, 95, 105–7
negative case, 18, 89
neoliberalism. *See* liberalism: economic
neuroscience, 135
nomadic heritage, 46, 68, 74
non-governmental organizations (NGOs), 82, 128
nonviolence, 48, 50
North Atlantic Treaty Organization (NATO), vii, 3, 16, 29, 37, 56, 63
Nur Otan Party, 105
Nye, Joseph, ix. *See also* soft power

Obama, Barack, vii
oil sector, 31, 127
Organization for Security and Cooperation in Europe (OSCE), 69, 84
Otunbaeva, Roza, 75

Palestine, 55
pan-Slavism, 30
Poland, 90
positionality, x, 126–30
power, 123
priming, 119
pro-Americanism, 5, 9, 13, 25, 37
professionalized advocates, 81–86, 113. *See also* human rights activism
Protestantism. *See* missionaries
psychology, political, 5, 120, 123
public diplomacy, xi, 112, 117–22
public opinion: in Central Asia, 33–34, 37, 81; impact of, 3; theories of, 5–6
Putin, Vladimir, 110

Qutb, Sayyid, 49

Rabbani, Burhanuddin, 26
Rakhmon(ov), Imomali, 45. *See also* Rakhmon regime
Rakhmon regime, 57, 80
rationality, ix, 5, 81
realism, 116
remittances, 93–94
research methodology, 135–36
research methods, 33–34, 126–34
Russia: as intermediary, 27, 38; media in, 29–30, 35–38, 115; role in Central Asia, 13, 24, 37–38, 45, 58, 73, 99, 110–11, 116, 123

Salafism, 43–44, 64–65
Saudi Arabia, 3, 9, 45
secularism, 14, 24, 42–43, 45, 57, 64, 115. *See also* Islam
sedimentation, 6, 8–11, 16–20, 39, 85, 88, 112, 114–16, 123, 136
September 11 attacks, 29–30, 37, 50, 67
Serbia, 67, 70
shadow economy, 92. *See also* informal economy
slow politics, viii, 122
social media, 4
social mobilization. *See* social movements
social movements: framing strategies of, 10–11; impact of, 12; in Central Asia, 13–15; political opportunities for, viii, 11–12, 113; resources for, 6, 15, 20. *See also* authoritarianism: social movements under; broad-cast movements; narrow-cast movements
social representations. *See* symbols
Sodiqov, Alexander, 83
soft power, ix, 116
Soviet-Afghan War, 25–26, 44–45
Soviet Union: collapse of, 15, 24, 27, 37, 67, 82, 88, 90; Islam in, 24; jazz in, 22; legacies of, 20–24, 27; propaganda, 20–22; radio in, 22
speech acts, 23
spiritual administrations of Muslims. *See* muftiates

state weakness, 13
street protests, 67, 70
strikes, 96, 99–102, 105–8. *See also* labor: unrest
Sufism, 64
Sydykova, Zamira, 69
symbolic America: changing material from, 40; cultural products and, 31; defined, 4, 6–8; IRPT and, 53–54; liberalism and, 19; power of, viii, 29, 77–79; shaping, 116–17; shifts in, 13, 15–17, 33, 37, 39, 59–65, 67–68, 74; Soviet construction of, 20–23, 26; street protests and, 70–72. *See also* United States
symbolic politics, 4–6, 64, 88, 113, 122–24
symbols, 1, 5–11, 14–17, 19, 124; defined, 6–7; impact, 14; in motion, 10

Tajikistan: civil war, 26, 45, 54–55, 57–60, 80, 93, 113; economy in, 92–94; media in, 36; state weakness in, 13. *See also* Islamic Renaissance Party of Tajikistan
Tengiz oilfield, 31, 97, 100–101, 108. *See also* Kazakhstan
Tengrism, 39
terrorism: in Central Asia, 13; in Kazakhstan, 46; rhetoric of, 30. *See also* Islamic Movement of Uzbekistan; Islamic Renaissance Party of Tajikistan: declared a terrorist organization; September 11 attacks
trade unions. *See* labor unions
transitology, 82
transnational advocacy networks (TANs). *See* professionalized advocates
Trump, Donald, vii, 3, 85, 114
Tunisia, 67
Turajonzoda, Akbar, 65
Turkey, 3, 58, 86, 109
Turkmenistan, 15, 25, 68, 123; attitudes towards the United States, 36; economic conditions in, 92–94; Islam in, 46, 64; research opportunities in, 126–28; union membership in, 91

Ukraine, 36, 67, 70
unipolarity. *See* United States: hegemony

United States: as imperial power, 21, 48, 121; democracy promotion, involvement in, 29, 32, 71; foreign policy toward central Asia, ix, 114, 116, 117, 121; hegemony, 15, 29, 110, 123; Soviet depictions of, 20–24; war in Afghanistan, 29, 56, 63, 66. *See also* symbolic America

United Tajik Opposition, 55

Uzbekistan: authoritarianism in, 68; economic conditions in, 92–94; fieldwork in, 127; Islam in, 45–46, 64; media in, 32–33, 36; military bases in, vii, 29, 52; repression in, 15, 64; unions in, 91. *See also* Islamic Movement of Uzbekistan

Venezuela. *See* Chávez, Hugo. *See also* Latin America

Wahhabism, 43–44

Yeltsin, Boris, 33
Yoldash, Tajir, 45

Zhanabaeva, Sakhib, 106, 108
Zhanaozen massacre, 96, 99–105, 109
Zhovtis, Yevgeniy, 105

The authorized representative in the EU for product safety and compliance is:
Mare Nostrum Group
B.V Doelen 72
4831 GR Breda
The Netherlands

www.ingramcontent.com/pod-product-compliance
Lightning Source LLC
Chambersburg PA
CBHW031812220426
43662CB00007B/613